Westwood,

Norwood, July 17. 90

My Dear Arthur Layzell

I was a little while ago at a meeting for prayer where a large number of ministers were gathered together. The subject of prayer was "our children". It soon brought the tears to my eyes to hear those good fathers pleading with God for their sons & daughters. As they went on entreating the Lord to save their families, my heart seemed ready to burst with strong desire that it might be even so. Then I thought, I will write to those sons & daughters, & remind them of their parents' prayer.

Dear Arthur, you are highly privileged in having parents who pray for you. Your name is known in the courts of heaven. Your case has been laid before the throne of God. Do you not pray for yourself? If you do not do so, why not? If other people value your soul, can it be right for you to neglect it? All the entreaties & wrestlings of Y. father will not save you if you never seek the Lord yourself. You know this.

You do not intend to cause grief to dear mother & father: but you do. So long as you are not saved, they can never rest. However obedient, & sweet, & kind you may be, they will never feel happy about you until you believe in the Lord

Jesus Christ, & so find everlasting salvation.

Think of this. Remember how much you have already sinned, & none can wash you but Jesus. When you grow up you may become very sinful, & none can change yr nature & make you Holy but the Lord Jesus, through his Spirit.

You need what father & mother seek for you, & you need it NOW. Why not seek it at once? I heard a father pray, "Lord, save our children, and save them young." It is never too soon to be safe; never too soon to be happy; never too soon to be holy. Jesus loves to receive the very young ones.

You cannot save yourself, but the great Lord Jesus can save you. Ask him to do it. "He that asketh receiveth." Then trust in Jesus to save you. He can do it, for he died & rose again that whosoever believeth in Him might not perish, but have everlasting life. Come & tell Jesus you have sinned; seek forgiveness; trust in Him for it, & be sure that you are saved.

Then imitate our Lord. Be at home what Jesus was at Nazareth. Yours will be a happy home, & yr dear father & mother will feel that the dearest wish of their hearts has been granted them.

I pray you to think of heaven & hell; for in one of those places you will live for ever. Meet me in heaven! Meet me at once at the mercy-seat. Run up stairs & pray to the great Father, through Jesus Christ.

Yours very lovingly, C.H. Spurgeon

LIVING UNDER GOD

LIVING
UN

1854

dc Talk's

TOBY MAC AND MICHAEL TAIT

DER
GOD

BETHANY HOUSE
MINNEAPOLIS, MINNESOTA

Living Under God
Copyright © 2005
Toby Mac and Michael Tait

Manuscript prepared by Rick Killian, Killian Creative, Boulder, Colorado.
www.killiancreative.com

Cover design by Lookout Design Group, Inc.

Unless otherwise identified, Scripture quotations are from the HOLY BIBLE, NEW INTERNATIONAL VERSION®. Copyright © 1973, 1978, 1984 by International Bible Society. Used by permission of Zondervan Publishing House. All rights reserved.

Scripture quotations identified KJV are from the King James Version of the Bible.

Scripture quotations identified AMP are from the Amplified Bible. Old Testament copyright © 1965, 1987 by the Zondervan Corporation. The Amplified New Testament copyright © 1958, 1987 by the Lockman Foundation. Used by permission.

Scripture quotations identified NKJV are from the New King James Version of the Bible. Copyright © 1979, 1980, 1982 by Thomas Nelson, Inc. Used by permission. All rights reserved.

Scripture quotations identified NCV are from *The Holy Bible, New Century Version.* Copyright © 1987, 1988, 1991 by Word Publishing, Dallas, Texas 75039. Used by permission.

Scripture quotations identified The Message are from *The Message.* Copyright © 1993, 1994, 1995 by Eugene H. Peterson. Used by permission of NavPress Publishing Group.

Scripture quotations identified NLT are from the *Holy Bible,* New Living Translation, copyright © 1996. Used by permission of Tyndale House Publishers, Inc., Wheaton, Illinois 60189. All rights reserved.

Scripture quotations identified NASB are taken from the NEW AMERICAN STANDARD BIBLE®, © Copyright The Lockman Foundation 1960, 1962, 1963, 1968, 1971, 1972, 1973, 1975, 1977, 1995. Used by permission. (www.Lockman.org)

Scripture quotations identified CEV are from the *Contemporary English Version.* Copyright © American Bible Society 1995. Used by permission.

Scripture quotations marked GNT are from the *Good News Translation*—Second Edition. Copyright © 1992 by American Bible Society. Used by permission.

Photo on page 202 courtesy of Smithsonian Institution, National Anthropological Archives. Negative #43.201-A, photographer F. Jay Haynes.

Published by Bethany House Publishers
11400 Hampshire Avenue South
Bloomington, Minnesota 55438

Bethany House Publishers is a division of
Baker Publishing Group, Grand Rapids, Michigan.

Printed in the United States of America

Library of Congress Cataloging-in-Publication Data

Mac, Toby.
    Living under God : discovering your part in God's plan / Toby Mac and Michael Tait.
       p. cm.
Summary: "Building from the stories in Under God, each of the readings opens with Scripture and presents a theme illustrated in the lives and events of our country's past"—Provided by publisher.
    Includes indexes.
    ISBN 0-7642-0142-5 (pbk.)
    1. Christian life—United States. 2. United States—Church history. I. Tait, Michael.
II. Title.
    BV4501.3.M19   2005
    277.3—dc22   2005021014

Contents

Introduction

You, my brothers, were called to be free. But do not
use your freedom to indulge the sinful nature;
rather, serve one another in love.

GALATIANS 5:13

The history of America has been one of the greatest experiments in
freedom the world has ever seen. The Pilgrims landed searching for
religious freedom. The American Revolution was fought to cut our ties
with European tyranny and create a unified republic of states based on
democracy—the voices of our people—and faith in God. Over the years to
follow, the voices that went against the common practice refused to be
silenced as they expressed their desires that slavery should be ended,
women should share in the rights of government, Native Americans
should be treated with the same dignity as any foreign government, or
any of a number of other issues that called all of us to stand up for the
liberty upon which we based our Declaration of Independence and our
Constitution. The ideals of America still ring strong for all of the world
to hear in all of the founding documents and articles of government left
behind as guiding lights to our time, and America's first two centuries
of history are marked by the continued fight to make those principles
of liberty true for all.

Yet at the same time, there is no question that it has been a fight.
While the American colonies fought hard for our independence and
freedom, it would be over two hundred years before even the most basic
rights of that government were extended to all within our borders.

If there is any great song of what America is, it is sung best by the
voices of our history. We have always been a place where justice will not
be completely silenced. Ours is a history of great men and women of all
races, denominations, and backgrounds who have spoken out about free-

dom as no others have ever found the words, because for many of them their sense of freedom came from knowing true freedom through faith in Jesus. Their calls to liberty were not laced with the eloquence of clever men, but built upon lives lived studying the words of God in the Bible. No human being can truly know freedom who doesn't first know Jesus as Lord and Savior.

And, in a word, that is what this book is about: freedom. In pulling these stories together, we did our best to find the voices that best expressed that song of freedom in both word and deed. They are all just human beings, and some of them had failures of their own, but our desire was not to express their weaknesses, but their triumphs. It was their highest moments we remember them for, and by which we as a nation were forever changed.

Our second desire was to show just how deeply rooted their songs were in the truths of the Bible. To show that, we have also included Bible stories and passages that parallel their stories, as well as a short section discussing what can be learned from each. It is our hope that as you read each chapter, the qualities of these stories will sink into your heart and make you a catalyst for freedom for all, just as the men and women you read about in these pages were in their times. Read it as you would a devotional, one story a day. Read it with a study group to discuss these ideals and how you can live them in your lives and community. Or merely sit and read it to soak in the rich history of America and be changed by getting to know more about the world-changers of our past.

America stands today as one of the greatest nations in history. We still stand before all other nations as a leader and a voice of influence—but what will we have to say in the next generation? Will we be a nation that continues to be a source of wisdom, invention, and democratic self-rule for the rest of the world? What will be the legacy of our generation of Americans?

As George Santayana once said, "Those who cannot remember the past are condemned to repeat it." As a generation that wants to stand for God in our nation and keep it great by continuing to follow and depend upon Him, we need to look and learn from both the good and bad of our nation's past so that we can take it properly and honestly into the future. Today, America's only hope is that this generation will live under God as no other has before us.

It is to this generation that we dedicate this book. May you learn from the historical figures, events, ideals, and aspirations recorded here. It is up to our generation if we are going to become the one nation on earth that truly stands "under God, indivisible, with liberty and justice for all."

Guided by God to Freedom

Let us keep in step with the Spirit.

GALATIANS 5:25

THE PILGRIMS' LANDING (NOVEMBER 1620)

"Land ho!" The cry rang out.

Land? Had the *Mayflower* reached land at last? For seven weeks at sea, through storm after storm, the Pilgrims had waited for this moment. They had reached the New World!

Everyone rushed up to the main deck. Such an overflow of thanksgiving followed as men, women, and children all poured out the gratitude of their hearts toward God, their Protector and Provider. The giving of thanks continued for so long that Captain Christopher Jones finally had to order the Pilgrims back down to the tween-decks so the sailors could maneuver the ship.

The Pilgrims had to content themselves with posting a few watchmen to look out the hatch and report to the others what they saw. As they grew closer, the watchmen saw a land that was already in the first stages of winter. The delays in leaving England had cost them almost two months of mild autumn weather. It would soon be bitterly cold. And how wild it looked. The long sandy beach was covered with dune grass and scrub pine—and not a single trace of humanity.

Where were they? How far had the storms blown them off course?

Finally news came back that they were at a place fishermen called Cape Cod. Amazingly enough, they were only a few hundred miles north of their original destination at the mouth of the Hudson River, the northern-most point of what was then the Virginia colony. Within a week they would arrive at their new home. There was more rejoicing!

They started south but soon encountered dangerous shoals, riptides, and roaring breakers as they tried to pass around the point of the cape. Had they come this far to see the *Mayflower* broken on the rocks? The farther they went, the more treacherous it became. The Pilgrims began to fervently pray for the safety of their ship.

The leader of the group, Elder William Brewster, called John Carver, William Bradford, and Edward Winslow aside. "Sirs, I am sensing there is more here than meets the eye. What is the Lord saying to you?"

Carver paused a moment and then answered, "The farther we go, the greater the sense of dread I feel. I wonder if God really wants us to go south to Virginia as originally planned."

They looked to Bradford. "When I looked out at the coast near Cape Cod, I felt a strange warming in my heart. I thought it was because I was so grateful to see land again. But now, I too am beginning to see that it was something more."

Brewster added thoughtfully, "In the Scripture, Paul and Silas wanted to preach in Asia, but God hindered them. He prevented them from doing what they had planned and sent them to Macedonia instead. Perhaps we were blown off course because God has something better in mind for us."

Winslow nodded. "What if God had us blown to Cape Cod because He wants us to settle at Cape Cod?"

Just then Captain Jones approached the three leaders. "The wind is very strong this time of year, and when we try to sail south around the cape, it blows mightily against us. It's too dangerous to sail this close to shore. Our only choice is to head back out to sea and wait a day to see if the wind will change."

Brewster spoke up. "Captain, before you head back to sea, permit us an hour to speak with the others."

At length, after much prayer and further discussion, the Pilgrims unanimously decided on their course of action. Brewster instructed Captain Jones to turn back toward Cape Cod. On November 11, they dropped anchor in a natural harbor on the inside of the cape.

What a joyful celebration they had. Bradford wrote in his journal, "They fell upon their knees and blessed the God of heaven, who had brought them over the vast and furious ocean, and delivered them from all the perils and miseries thereof, again to set their feet on the firm and stable earth, their proper element. And no marvel if they were thus joyful . . ."

GOD CALLS ABRAHAM (*Genesis 12:1–9*)

When Abraham was seventy-five years old, God came to him and told him:

> Leave your country, your people and your father's household and go to the land I will show you. I will make you into a great nation and I will bless you; I will make your name great, and you will be a blessing. I will bless those who bless you, and whoever curses you I will curse; and all peoples on earth will be blessed through you.

At His word, Abraham pulled up his stakes and headed west from Ur.* He took his family, servants, and animals with him.

When they arrived in Canaan, at the site of the great tree of Moreh at Shechem, Abraham surveyed the land before him and saw that it was fertile and full of promise. God appeared to him here and said: "To your offspring I will give this land."

To commemorate the event, Abraham built an altar of remembrance to the Lord there in Shechem, so that the generations that followed would remember the promise God had made to them.

{ LIVING IT! }

God has called all of us to be people of destiny—people with God-given purposes meant to accomplish great things—praying, planning, and working so that God's "will be done on earth as it is in heaven" (Matthew 6:10). As they sought God through the Scriptures and prayer, the Pilgrims discovered they needed to find a place where they could worship God freely if they were to fulfill their destiny. Abraham was called out of the land of Ur to the land God had prepared for him and his descendents. God has meticulous plans for each of us—an incredible destiny—that He wants us to enter into in the same way.

Finding our God-given destiny is different for everyone. While some seem to literally have a vision when they are young of what God wants them to do for the rest of their lives (somewhat like what Abraham had when God spoke to him), most of us discover our destiny one day at a time, with only enough light from God to take the next few steps while all else seems a dark mystery (somewhat like what the Pilgrims experi-

---

*The site of Ur is known today as Tall al Muqayyar, Iraq.

enced as they headed for the new world). For many of us, we only see God's hand in our lives by looking behind and seeing where He saved us, or led us into something good. Yet the key to it all is our dedication in seeking Him each day and being open to His leading every moment. God cannot lead any of us into His destiny for us if we are not eagerly following Him step by step.

Do you have a regular time each week of really seeking God and listening for His voice? If not, when would be the best time for you to have one? Is it something you should do daily? How can you make it part of your regular habits?

Think for a moment of times when you have really felt God was speaking to you in the past and how He did it. Often God will maintain the same patterns of communicating with us throughout our lives—how does He speak to you? Do you hear Him most often on retreats or solitary times? Do you hear Him best as you journal about Scriptures or thoughts you have had? When you are writing, drawing, composing, or creating something? Or is it in times of praise and worship? Or are there other ways He has gotten His message to you?

While God often communicates to us through our hearts when we pull away and take time to be quiet and listen, He also needs to speak to us in the midst of our busy lives. Do you leave time in your day to just stop and listen to see what He might be trying to say to you? Are you ruled by the outside circumstances around you or by His strength and rock solidness inside of you?

Government by God

*The moral principles and precepts contained in the
Scripture ought to form the basis of all our civil
constitutions and laws. All the miseries and evil men
suffer from vice, crime, ambition, injustice,
oppression, slavery, and war, proceed from their
despising or neglecting the precepts
contained in the Bible.*

NOAH WEBSTER

THE MAYFLOWER COMPACT (NOVEMBER 11, 1620)

Because the *Mayflower* was blown so far off course, there was a further delay before the passengers could go ashore. Since this was unfamiliar territory, they needed to send men to explore the coast and
decide on the best place to build their new settlement.

There was also another problem. Since the Pilgrims would be settling
outside the boundaries of the Virginia colony, Virginia's charter would
not govern them. In fact, they would have no charter at all. Brewster
called the leaders together to discuss it. "Brothers, we must pray and ask
the Lord what we should do about the government."

Winslow was puzzled. "What government? There is no government
here! No kings, no bishops, no sheriffs—"

"Exactly," Brewster replied. "No laws—and no one to enforce them if
there were. And we know how corrupt human beings are. I am not worried about our Pilgrim families. But the "strangers" outnumber us. I
heard one boast about what he planned to do once he got to shore. With
nothing to limit their behavior, we could soon have serious problems."

"I see what you mean," Bradford replied. "If we don't establish a
civil government with a firm Christian base before leaving the ship, we
will soon have mutiny and anarchy. We must pray!"

The leaders raised their voices in one accord and began to seek the
Lord for wisdom.

Before long Bradford spoke up. "Brothers, I know why God wanted us to return to this bay. He didn't want us to settle in Virginia because he doesn't want us to be governed by Virginia's charter. He wants to do a new thing—He wants all men to see what He can do with a people who totally rely on Him for everything—including their government."

Brewster caught Bradford's excitement. "Just like Jesus said: 'Ye are the light of the world. A city that is set on an hill cannot be hid'" (Matthew 5:14 KJV).

"Yes!" Bradford said.

"Listen—God has prepared us for this!" Brewster exclaimed. "Remember when we were still in Holland, how Pastor Robinson studied the Bible to discover God's pattern for church government?"

Bradford smiled. "How could we ever forget? I can hear him now: 'The self-governing Christians of the New Testament churches are the perfect model for church government. The Lord Jesus is King of His Church and holds all power in heaven and earth. Christ the Lord gives each Christian the power of self-government. Christians then elect representatives, or elders, from among themselves to serve them and be examples to them.'"

"So we take what we've learned about church government and use it to write a covenant for civil government," Bradford added. "The scriptural model is the same."

The Pilgrims knew the value of becoming one body, of submitting to one another in love. Pastor Robinson had warned them that the very survival of their little settlement would depend upon the depth of their covenant relationship with one another.

In signing the Mayflower Compact, the members of the Plymouth Colony chose to relinquish their individual independence, and as a covenanted people, "to enact . . . just and equal laws . . . from time to time . . . for the general good of the colony. Unto which we promise all due submission and obedience." The Mayflower Compact became one of the pillars of American constitutional government. It marked the first time in recorded history that free and equal men had voluntarily covenanted together to create their own new civil government.

PAUL TEACHES ABOUT GOVERNMENT
(*Romans 13:1–10* NLT)

There were a lot of questions in the early church as to what responsibilities they had to the Roman government. How were they to behave toward a system of laws that basically persecuted them and demanded their allegiance? Paul's response was simple—follow God's law first, and then they would not violate any of men's laws. Paul said it this way:

> Obey the government, for God is the one who put it there. All governments have been placed in power by God. So those who refuse to obey the laws of the land are refusing to obey God, and punishment will follow. For the authorities do not frighten people who are doing right, but they frighten those who do wrong. So do what they say, and you will get along well. The authorities are sent by God to help you. But if you are doing something wrong, of course you should be afraid, for you will be punished. The authorities are established by God for that very purpose, to punish those who do wrong. So you must obey the government for two reasons: to keep from being punished and to keep a clear conscience.
>
> Pay your taxes, too, for these same reasons. For government workers need to be paid so they can keep on doing the work God intended them to do. Give to everyone what you owe them: Pay your taxes and import duties, and give respect and honor to all to whom it is due.
>
> Pay all your debts, except the debt of love for others. You can never finish paying that! If you love your neighbor, you will fulfill all the requirements of God's law. For the commandments against adultery and murder and stealing and coveting—and any other commandment—are all summed up in this one commandment: "Love your neighbor as yourself." Love does no wrong to anyone, so love satisfies all of God's requirements.

{ LIVING IT! }

God set up a system of checks and balances in how we are to govern our lives: He has given us His Word in the Bible and His Holy Spirit in our hearts. These two will never contradict each other. While some make mistakes because they are following a whim from within, they can correct themselves by seeing what the Bible really has to say on the subject. While others get into strange interpretations of Scripture, they can be corrected by checking their hearts and seeing if what they are teaching lines up with the law of love or not. In this way, through God's Spirit and His Word, we can know His will in all matters.

Through the Mayflower Compact, the Pilgrims sought to develop a system of government that would leave each person free to follow the

Word of God and the Spirit of God for themselves; however, what about those who didn't know God or did not submit to His will? For this the Pilgrims needed the right to create laws and enforce them for the common good. God's law would be first, their laws would be beneath them to govern those who would not properly govern themselves, and all the laws they made would be based upon the Scriptures.

How do you govern yourself? Do you have an internal system of standards that direct your actions, or do you just act until someone outside of you corrects you? Are you a "by the rule book" person or a person directed by God's love in all things?

How does God's Word relate to struggles in our government today? Jesus gave us only two commandments to follow upon which He said that all the laws and the prophets hang: (1) to love God with all our heart and soul and mind, and (2) to love our neighbors as ourselves (see Matthew 22:36–40). How should we apply these rules in our daily dealings with those who don't know God and those who openly defy Him and deny He exists?

Greed v. God

No servant can serve two masters. Either he will hate the one and love the other, or he will be devoted to the one and despise the other. You cannot serve both God and Money.

LUKE 16:13

JAMESTOWN (1606)

In stark contrast to the Pilgrims' constant reliance upon God's guidance was the settlement of Jamestown, Virginia, which was established some fourteen years before the Pilgrims landed and to which they were originally headed.

With the tragedy of the lost colony of Roanoke (which had disappeared without a trace when a supply ship returned to it in 1590) less than a generation behind them, British enthusiasm for New World adventures was still significantly dampened. But the promise of wealth was enough for some, and the Virginia Company was formed. When the partners had difficulty finding investors to fund a new expedition, some of them presented it as an evangelistic outreach to the Indians. Soon clergy were endorsing the endeavor—and investors were lining up. Even the Company's charter stated its purpose as "propagating [the] Christian religion to such people as yet live in darkness and miserable ignorance of the true knowledge and worship of God."

What was so nobly pledged in word, however, was only halfheartedly carried out in deed. Among the 144 men enlisted for the first expedition, only one, Robert Hunt, was a minister. And upon arrival, despite Hunt's efforts, there was little interest in seeking God's will for the colony.

A pattern of taking the "easy way" began with the very location of Jamestown. They had landed on a small, low-lying peninsula that was heavily wooded, had no fresh water, and was surrounded by fetid swamps. But rather than find a more suitable spot, the men chose to settle where they were.

During their first year, they survived only on the corn they could buy, beg, or steal from the Indians. The following spring, a gift of corn presented an easy excuse to delay the planting of their own crops. Deaths among the colonists, from a multitude of diseases and ailments, soared and seemed obviously attributable to their horrible location, but the settlers decided that moving and starting over seemed infinitely more difficult than simply rebuilding. They even maintained their codes of conduct forbidding a gentleman from any sort of manual labor, even when faced with his own death. Chopping wood for warmth, digging a well for fresh water—it was all beneath them. Many died rather than be dishonored.

Word began to return to England about the terrible state of the settlement, but rather than admit the truth and request help, the Company tried to whitewash the truth. Sermons lauding the work being done were published and more investors were duped by the release of John Smith's *True Relations*. Others were not so easily fooled, however, and in the wake of mounting criticism, the Company turned on the last surviving member of the original ruling Council. John Smith was removed from leadership, the Council was dissolved, and a governor, Thomas Gates, was appointed by the king—bringing with him an enlarged charter for the colony.

Their goal was still to return the investment of all their partners in England. Their first plan was to mine the region's deep veins of gold—which turned out to be iron pyrite, or fool's gold. Later, the colony turned its eye to the fortune that could be made harvesting tobacco. Large tracts of land were parceled out to the non-indentured men, and the crop soon became a harvest of cash. And in choosing this path, Virginia also chose a darker path, because by 1619 the first African slaves arrived. No single family could tend such large fields; thus slavery became a tenable solution. So it would come to pass that almost 250 years later—with the outbreak of the Civil War—the country would be torn apart by the bitter fruit sown in places like Jamestown.

"WHERE IS YOUR TREASURE?" (*Matthew 6:19–25, 33* THE MESSAGE)

In the Sermon on the Mount, Jesus said the following about money:

> Don't hoard treasure down here where it gets eaten by moths and

corroded by rust or—worse!—stolen by burglars. Stockpile treasure in heaven, where it's safe from moth and rust and burglars. It's obvious, isn't it? The place where your treasure is, is the place you will most want to be, and end up being.

Your eyes are windows into your body. If you open your eyes wide in wonder and belief, your body fills up with light. If you live squinty-eyed in greed and distrust, your body is a dank cellar. If you pull the blinds on your windows, what a dark life you will have!

You can't worship two gods at once. Loving one god, you'll end up hating the other. Adoration of one feeds contempt for the other. You can't worship God and Money both.

If you decide for God, living a life of God-worship, it follows that you don't fuss about what's on the table at mealtimes or whether the clothes in your closet are in fashion. . . .

Steep your life in God-reality, God-initiative, God-provisions. Don't worry about missing out. You'll find all your everyday human concerns will be met.

{ LIVING IT! }

Jesus taught that we would serve either God or Money. Later, Paul taught that "the love of money is the root of all kinds of evil" (1 Timothy 6:10). What is your priority? What are you passionate about? What do you think about—serving God or amassing a whole bunch of stuff here on earth that will never see the light of heaven?

The Jamestown colony lived totally for profit and laziness, and in their wake they left a legacy of corruption and slavery that would last more than two and a half centuries. The Pilgrims, for the most part, lived for God, industriousness, and freedom and left a heritage that would lead to the abolition of slavery and the will to fight to hold our nation together.

Money is not evil. It is the love of money that leads to all kinds of evil. We all need money to live, and money allows us to do things to help change our world. What the Bible says instead is "Whom are you serving?" What do you desire? Are you serving money all the time, thinking about the next thing you will buy so you can build your own kingdom that the world desires? Or are you living for God by using your money wisely and serving others to help build God's kingdom here on earth?

Do you have a regular plan for managing the money you receive and making it serve God and your future, or do you tend to spend all your money almost as fast as you receive it? Do you give regularly to your church, missions, and those in need? Have you thought about how you can store treasures in heaven?

Maybe you don't have a lot of money to give, but you do have something even more valuable to invest: your time and your talents. How are you using them to build up your treasure in heaven?

Make a list of what you feel your priorities are in your life, and then take a week and track your activities. What did you do every half hour you were awake during the week? Now add all those half hours up. What did you spend the most time doing? How does your list of what you did compare with your list of priorities? What are you going to do with this information?

"A Special Instrument Sent of God"

We know that God causes all things to work together
for good to those who love God, to those who are
called according to His purpose.

ROMANS 8:28 NASB

TISQUANTUM—"SQUANTO" (c. 1590–1622)

Squanto looked at the Scripture again. "You intended to harm me, but God intended it for good to accomplish what is now being done, the saving of many lives" (Genesis 50:20). It was as if his whole life's story were wrapped up in these words of Joseph to the brothers who had sold him into slavery.

Then he looked again into the eyes of John Bradford, the leader of the Pilgrims of Plymouth colony, who had just told him the story of Joseph and held the Bible open for him to see Joseph's words. Bradford smiled at the understanding he read in Squanto's face. Years of pain and meaninglessness fell away in that instant, and Squanto began to see how God could take the evil things people had done and bring good out of it.

As a younger man, Squanto had twice been kidnapped and taken as a slave for others. In 1604, when he was about fourteen, he and four others were taken from their tribes to England to learn English and come back as guides to future explorers. He had spent nine years in England before returning to America and his people again, but that was only to be kidnapped again and taken to Spain to be sold as a slave there. This time Squanto escaped, made his way back to England, and eventually boarded a ship captained by Thomas Dermer to return to New England in 1620. Onboard the ship was another Native American returning home named Samoset who became a friend of Squanto.

After fifteen years in captivity, Squanto had hoped for nothing less than a glorious homecoming, but it was not to be. When he arrived in his home village, it was deserted, except for the remains of those who had died there. All he found of them were bones and skulls. In his absence, a disease had rampaged through his people, and his family and friends, the mighty Patuxet band of the Wampanoag tribe, were no more.

As Joseph must have felt when he was unjustly thrown into prison, everything that gave substance or purpose to Squanto's life drained from him. In despair, he asked for shelter with Massasoit, the chief of a neighboring tribe, who understood his circumstances and took pity on him. For the next six months he merely existed.

However, one day, Samoset, who had returned to New England with Squanto on Captain Dermer's ship, came to Squanto's dwelling to speak with him. English settlers had landed near the coast and were colonizing the tribal lands of Squanto's people. They were kind and peaceful people, but it seemed they had little hope of surviving as they had little food and even less knowledge of farming in the region or in that climate.

Within days Samoset, Squanto, Chief Massasoit, and all sixty of Massasoit's warriors went to visit the colony at Plymouth. Squanto helped interpret for the chief and establish a peace treaty between the two groups. When Massasoit and his warriors returned to their village, Squanto stayed. He would once again see his homeland populated and prosperous. He showed the settlers how to survive in the wild: how to plant corn and pumpkins, how to catch eels and fish, how to stalk deer, how to find herbs for food and medicine. Before long Squanto asked Jesus, the Savior of the Pilgrims, to be his Savior too.

Now as Mr. Bradford explained this Scripture again, Squanto saw Jesus had always been with him, even before he had known about Him. If he had never been kidnapped and taken to England, he never would have learned English. If he hadn't been kidnapped a second time, he would have died of the plague that decimated his tribe. If he hadn't sailed with Captain Dermer, he never would have met Samoset. If Samoset hadn't discovered the settlement when he did, the Pilgrims would have missed the time for planting corn. How would they have survived another winter?

Bradford pointed to the Scripture again. "Squanto, you have been a special instrument sent of God for good beyond expectation." At this Squanto closed his eyes and thanked the God of heaven that his life had not been without significance.

{ LIVING IT! }

Despite the most horrible of circumstances and unfair treatment, both Joseph and Squanto were used by God to save people. Through his slavery, imprisonment, and eventual revelation to Pharaoh of God's plan to save Egypt, Joseph saved the nation of Israel and most of the Middle East from a famine that would otherwise have decimated the area. Because of all Squanto suffered, he helped save the Pilgrims from certain starvation, sickness, and the end of their colony established to freely worship God as they felt the Bible told them to. Years before the famine in the Middle East or the Pilgrims had even considered sailing for Plymouth, God's plan for their salvation was put into action.

Today we often look at the circumstance of our lives and think our futures are predetermined—but always for the worst. It would have been easy for either Joseph or Squanto to do the same. Joseph spent thirteen years as a slave and in prison. Squanto spent fifteen years as a slave and a refugee only to return to find his entire world destroyed. Either could have given up on life at anytime during those years—and if they had, what would have become of the people they later saved?

The Bible tells us over and over that God has a plan and a purpose for our lives, but far too many people give up before they even realize a small fraction of it. Determine today that you will stay in pursuit of the One who has great things planned for your life, even though circumstances may seem against you at every turn.

Think for a moment of the things you dream about doing in your life. Even if you can't possibly imagine how these things will ever come to pass, do you think these dreams are from God? Joseph succeeded because he plugged himself into the Dream-giver rather than dwelling on the ridiculousness of the dream or attempting to make the dream happen on his own. How can you stay plugged in to the One that has put dreams in your heart?

Think for another moment about what the ultimate purpose of your dreams are. Are you dreaming more of things that would help others or serve yourself? Take some time today to pray over your dreams and see what God tells you about them.

Even if you don't get a clear picture of what God wants you to do for your future, what are you doing to stay available to be used by Him? Are you lending your hands to volunteer or to help others? How? Are you a positive force to make the organizations you belong to better? Again, how are you doing that?

Good Work

The Lord God took the man and put him in the
Garden of Eden to work it and take care of it.

GENESIS 2:15

THE PLYMOUTH COLONY (1623)

Susanna Winslow, walking down the dirt road that served as the
main street of Plymouth, Massachusetts, was lost in thought. "Lord, I'm
still amazed that we made it through that winter. How could we have
lived on five kernels of corn a day? Yet not one of us died. You, Lord,
are a great miracle-worker!"

Even though it was still spring, Susanna was concerned that the
coming winter of 1624 would be a repeat of that time of hunger. With
the additional settlers who had come, she knew they would need at least
twice the harvest. She had noticed that the new settlers, sent as replace-
ments by the trading company, were not hard workers like the Pilgrims.
In fact, many had been shipped off to the colony fresh from the debtors'
prisons of England. Most of the time, the newcomers sat and grumbled—
they wanted more privileges, more food, and less work. Their complain-
ing was taking its toll on the morale of the entire colony, so much so
that even the hard-working Pilgrims seemed less energetic.

"Lord, please help us. I know you have the answer!" Susanna continued to pray the whole morning as she removed weeds from among
the corn plants.

Fortunately, Governor Bradford was convinced that the answer to
every problem facing mankind was to be found in the Word of God.
"The Bible is a book about government," he would often say. "When
we don't know what to do, we should look in its pages." That morning
as he read the Bible, he was looking for answers. And he was not disappointed—there in the Scriptures was the perfect solution! Governor Bradford read this verse: " 'If any man would not work, neither should he

eat'—the Second Epistle of Paul the Apostle to the Thessalonians, chapter three, verse ten."

Governor Bradford assigned the single men in the colony to live with Pilgrim families. Then he temporarily divided the common cornfield into small tracts, giving a tract to each family. Corn grown on each family's tract would be for that family's private use.

At first the sluggards tested the Pilgrims—would they really let them go hungry if they didn't work? They soon found that the Pilgrim families were resolved to obey the Word of God and refused to let them eat if they did not work. After experiencing several days of hunger, even the laziest among them began to pull his own weight. Bradford later wrote in his journal, "Any general want or suffering hath not been among them since this day."

PAUL (*1 Corinthians 9:24–27* NCV)

In his first letter to the Corinthians, Paul spoke of the challenge of living the Christian life as if it were a race to be run. He said,

> You know that in a race all the runners run, but only one gets the prize. So run to win! All those who compete in the games use self-control so they can win a crown. That crown is an earthly thing that lasts only a short time, but our crown will never be destroyed. So I do not run without a goal. I fight like a boxer who is hitting something—not just the air. I treat my body hard and make it my slave so that I myself will not be disqualified after I have preached to others.

{ LIVING IT! }

How do we tend to "run our races"—"live our lives"—on the earth today? Do we do them in such a way so as to win the prize of a job well done held out for us, or do we do "just enough to get by," hoping to scrape through with a passing grade or minimum wage so we can spend the rest of our time "having fun?"

The Plymouth colony, and Paul in his journeys, found that the real joy in life was not being entertained, but in accomplishing the tasks set before them in the best manner possible. When everyone in the colony pulled together to work hard, everyone benefited—when a few were lazy and complained, everyone suffered.

Throughout his journeys, Paul was so excited about spreading the kingdom of God that lack of cash never deterred him. Rather than turning back, he would work as a tentmaker to buy his ticket to his next port of call or supply food for himself and his companions. Certainly he could have gotten much farther ahead in life had he stayed in one place and built up his business, but his real business was the joy of spreading the gospel, not what he could get or how comfortably he could live.

The book of Ecclesiastes tells us that good, challenging work is a blessing from God. There is great joy in a job well done. When that job is in partnership with God's purpose for your life, that joy is even greater.

If God has called you to be a musician, do you practice with all your heart? Or if He has called you to some field of missions or job where you can earn a good wage and support ministries, do you do these things to His glory? Do you find joy in doing things well and pleasing God, or are you looking just to get by?

Are there things that keep you from doing your best? What are they? Are they things you should limit or even eliminate from your life to get you closer to accomplishing what is in your heart?

Are you keeping a proper balance in pursuing your work and accomplishments? Do you realize the purpose of education is to gain wisdom and knowledge and understanding? What will it mean to get great grades or a good job, but never have any time to spend with God or your friends or family? Are you developing habits for success in all areas of your life (spirit, soul, and body; family, work, and play), or are you going to be lopsided and sacrifice some things for the sake of others?

The Holy Experiment

Governments, like clocks, go from the motion men give
them; and as governments are made and moved by
men, so by them they are ruined too.... Let men
be good, and the government cannot be bad;
if it will be ill, they will cure it.

WILLIAM PENN

WILLIAM PENN (1644–1718)

For those in England, the colonies represented one thing: promise.
To the entrepreneurial, it beckoned with the siren call of great wealth; to
the destitute and desperate, America seemed to welcome them with a
chance for a new beginning. The persecuted saw freedom. The wealthy
saw dominion.

William Penn, thirty-seven years old, saw the rarest of opportunities
to attempt something amazing. Owed a familial debt by the Crown,
Penn received a charter from King Charles for an expanse of land
between the established colonies of New York and Maryland. In this
"sylvan" spread of oak, maple, birch, and elm, Penn foreswore to carry
out "a holy experiment"—establishing a model state built on the principles of godliness, tolerance, and liberty. Pennsylvania was conceived
with nearly unattainable expectations—unattainable, that is, without
divine favor.

The morning of September 3, 1682, broke with all the subtlety of a
blacksmith's forge. To the east the sun rose, molten and fierce, as Penn
stood starboard on his passage across the Atlantic. He was finally going
to see the land for which he'd received a charter more than a year ago.
Salt spray stung his face, and though the cool wind should have been
bracing, he yawned despite himself. He'd stayed up late that evening
penning a response to a friend who inquired to his motives with the colony. The words still remained with him:

For my country, I eyed the Lord in the obtaining of it, and more was I drawn inward to look to him and to owe it to his hand and power, than to any other way. I have so obtained it, and desire that I may not be unworthy of his love, but do that which may answer his kind providence, and serve his truth and people; that an example may be set up to the nations; there may be room there, though not here, for such an holy experiment.

He could only imagine his friend's reply. "A Quaker serving as governor of an entire colony? What folly!" Penn chuckled to himself. It was an absurdity.

The Act of Uniformity, passed by Parliament in 1662, established Anglicanism as the religion of the land and made a gathering of more than five people of any faith illegal and subject to disbanding by force. The Quakers chose to continue meeting and were often fined or even imprisoned for their lawlessness. But where the Quakers—or Friends— often bore their punishments in humble acceptance, Penn would not be silenced. His words, his writings such as *The Sandy Foundation Shaken*, and his unceasing efforts to worship as God led landed him, time and again, in prison—time he used merely to further hone his religious and political sensibilities in works like *No Cross, No Crown*, a text replete with calls to honest, unfettered faith.

"And if they couldn't silence me in the Tower [of London], they thought best to place the wide Atlantic between us," Penn noted dryly, his sleepiness finally sloughing off. Terns and gulls cawed about the mast far above, and for a few minutes he watched transfixed as a pod of porpoises dove and danced with playful grace, racing the ship as she rushed to the New World.

The 1682 trip was the first of two voyages he'd make to the colony he governed, the second taken in 1699. Even then he was well at work on the *Frames of Government*, the founding document that would rest at the heart of Pennsylvania's developing constitution and serve as a template for the expression of all the colonists and Founding Fathers' purest dreams.

DAVID DANCES BEFORE THE LORD (2 *Samuel* 6:14–15)

When Saul and his sons were killed in a battle with the Philistines, David became king of Israel. One of his first acts as king was to honor God and return the ark of the covenant to Jerusalem so that God's presence and guidance would always be at the heart of his government.

Yet not only would David base his rule on God's ways, but he would also celebrate God as first in all things. Because of this, the day the ark entered Jerusalem, David took off his kingly robes and danced in praise and worship to God before it—in his underwear! His position, his dignity, his authority, his wealth, and all that he had as king would serve God and be subject to Him.

For this David received one of the most endearing titles of the Bible: He was described as a man after God's own heart (see 1 Samuel 13:14).

{ LIVING IT! }

Penn would never spend as much time in America as he wanted, only four years in the two trips, but in his time he accomplished much. He purchased land for his estate legally from the Leni-Lenape Indians and signed a treaty of friendship with the Delaware Indians. On his return, he freed all his slaves at his estate, allowing them to remain as tenants on the land. And his *Frames of Government* offered a strong beginning for the freedoms—freedom of speech and religion, the right to self-government—that would continue to be valued so highly in the coming push toward independence. His plan was that the colony would honor God from beginning to end, and his capital city, Philadelphia—"the city of brotherly love"—would serve as the United States first capital.

In a similar way, David established the nation of Israel on a covenant with God. In fact, no other two nations on earth have looked to God's Word and His leadership more than Israel and the United States. While Israel was "God's Chosen People," the United States has almost always considered itself "a Christian nation."

Today our nation needs dreamers like Penn and King David to again imagine the possibilities of being "one nation under God." We need to take off our robes of self-righteousness and again dance before God in praise and worship to let Him know that our generation will honor Him first. We need to negotiate in good faith with other people groups as Penn did with the Native Americans and live lives that show that our true allegiance is to God's principles, not our own profit alone. God is still looking for people who will stand for Him so that He can stand for them:

For the eyes of the Lord move to and fro throughout the earth

that He may strongly support those whose heart is completely His.
(2 Chronicles 16:9a NASB)

What is your commitment level to praising and worshiping God? Are you willing to "make a fool of yourself" as David did? Or do you feel you need to be seen as "cool" before others rather than being "on fire for God"?

Do you dedicate any of your new endeavors—whether it be a new job, a new relationship, a new car, or whatever—to God first? Is your first allegiance to building God's kingdom or building your own empire?

Are your dreams so big that you can only accomplish them with God's help? If not, dream a little bigger!

Protected Beyond All Human Expectation

"For I know the plans I have for you," declares the Lord, "plans to prosper you and not to harm you, plans to give you hope and a future."

JEREMIAH 29:11

GEORGE WASHINGTON (1732–1799)

The twenty-three-year-old lieutenant colonel surveyed the battle-field stoically. He had ridden all day between divisions, delivering messages from the command centers to the men at the front lines, which was the main job of the officers. As the only men on horseback, they were the main targets of the French and Indian marksmen on the other side of the battlefield. For nearly two hours of this day's fighting the young lieutenant colonel had been in the thick of the front lines, bullets blazing on all sides, but he was much too engaged in communicating orders to notice that—against all odds—he was still alive. Despite the fact that he was weak from being ill nearly all of the month before, he sat tall in his saddle pondering his next command.

The day was going badly. Though they had hoped to push to Fort Duquesne and capture it from the French and Indian troops manning it, the army had never gotten any closer than eleven miles of the fort. It was time to rally the troops one last time: this time not to charge, but to deliver them from the fight. The young Lieutenant Colonel George Washington rode one more time through the shrapnel and smoke of the cannon fire and the seductive charm of whistling bullets to the front lines to lead retreat of the British and American troops.

When the final casualties were tallied, 714 of the 1,300 American and British soldiers who fought side by side that day had fallen, injured or killed in the fighting; of the eighty-six officers, not all of whom had been on horseback, sixty-three were casualties. Among them was the commanding British General Edward Braddock, who had been killed. But young Lieutenant Colonel Washington never knew or even contemplated any of this as he led the men and wounded from harm's way to safety, while French troops and their Indian allies cheered in victory. Nevertheless, riding boldly atop his steed, young Washington gave his men the confidence they needed to muster their strength one last time to get themselves and their wounded comrades to shelter and medical care.

Later that evening as the last of the wounded were carried to the medical tents for attention, Washington stood surveying the defeated men and idly fingering the material of his coat in contemplation. Suddenly his fingers found an odd tear in the cloth that caught his attention. A hole—a bullet hole!

On further inspection, he found three others in the coat—four altogether—and remembered that twice the horses under him that day had been shot, requiring him to change mounts. Despite these things, he escaped unhurt! He also later found out that, of all the officers on horseback, he alone had escaped without being wounded—and in all the years and battles to follow in his career, George Washington never would be wounded.

PAUL AT SEA (*Acts 27:6–44* NKJV)

Paul had tried to warn the centurion acting as his guard on the way to Rome, but he wouldn't listen. It was the wrong time of the year to be traveling and the seas were sure to give them more trouble than they could handle.

And just as God had warned Paul, only days after setting out from Fair Havens, Crete, the winds kicked up and took control of the ship. The following day they were caught in a storm and had to jettison the cargo in order to stay afloat. For the next two weeks they would be driven at the storm's mercy. All aboard had given themselves up for lost, except for Paul. Just a few days into the storm, he told the others:

> Men, you should have listened to me, and not have sailed from Crete and incurred this disaster and loss. And now I urge you to take heart, for there will be no loss of life among you, but only of the ship. For there stood by me this night an angel of the God to whom I belong and whom I serve, saying, "Do not be afraid, Paul; you must

be brought before Caesar; and indeed God has granted you all those who sail with you." Therefore take heart, men, for I believe God that it will be just as it was told me. However, we must run aground on a certain island.

On the fourteenth night of the storm, the crew took a sounding and found the water was getting shallower, so they dropped anchor for fear of getting driven onto a rocky coastline they could not see in the dark. Paul encouraged them to eat to gain at least some strength in the hope of swimming to shore if necessary. A few of the crew members tried to escape on their own, but Paul warned the centurion that if they left, other lives would be lost, so the centurion stopped them.

When morning came, they spotted a beach, let up anchor, and drove the ship toward it. Striking a reef, the ship stuck tight and everyone made for shore—those who could swim went first, and the rest followed on whatever could help them float to safety.

As the angel had promised Paul, not one of the ship's company—276 passengers—was lost. All made it ashore and to safety on the island of Malta.

{ L I V I N G I T ! }

Regardless of what circumstances look like around us—whether it is a war, a storm, or any other circumstance—there is no better place to be than in the center of God's will for our lives. It was the devotion and dedication of Paul and of Washington that had placed them in harm's way, yet God's divine protection was over them both because each was on his way to doing what God had called him to do: Paul to testify of Jesus Christ before Caesar, and Washington to lead the colonial army to freedom from the British and to be the first president of the United States of America.

Like Washington and Paul, as Christians we need to trust in God's plan for our lives and seek to be in the eye of the storm at the center of His will, because it is the only place of protection. Running for apparent "safety" from duty and calling will not protect us. Instead, we should run to the safest place on earth, "under the shadow of the Almighty" (Psalm 91:1 KJV), in the center of His perfect will for our lives.

As a young man, Washington started out as a leader; from his youth, Paul was interested in being a spiritual leader. What are the things that you enjoy doing most? Psalm 37:4 tells us that God gives us the desires of our hearts, meaning that the things that we feel most competent at are often how God leads us into His will. What are the things that God seems to be leading you into? How might you use these desires and skills to serve Him? Take time to pray about these things and dedicate yourself to using these abilities to serve Him as He directs you to.

Philippians 4:6–7 tells us: "Do not be anxious about anything, but in everything, by prayer and petition, with thanksgiving, present your requests to God. And the peace of God, which transcends all understanding, will guard your hearts and your minds in Christ Jesus." This seems to show us two ways to follow God: (1) If you are "anxious about anything" then pray about it. (2) If you have God's peace, you know He has taken care of it. Do you have any fears or anxieties about what is happening now or where you are going in the future? Take a moment now to pray over them and leave them at the feet of Jesus so He can replace them with His peace—and don't stop praying about them until that peace comes.

april 18, 2020

Read this chapter during the
stay at home edict issued by Gov
& President Trump during Coronavirus
Pandemic. We are in a war against
something can't see. But we not
anxious about anything praying
& trusting that God will git
us through this. We are
protected by God.

RLW

Finding His Voice

Don't be upset when they haul you before the civil
authorities. Without knowing it, they've done you—
and me—a favor, given you a platform for preaching
the kingdom news! And don't worry about what
you'll say or how you'll say it. The right words
will be there; the Spirit of your Father
will supply the words.

MATTHEW 10:18–20 THE MESSAGE

PATRICK HENRY (1736–1799)

At age twenty-three Patrick Henry studied law and passed the state examinations to be a lawyer, but he was still unknown—and poor. Finally he landed a case no one else wanted. Virginia had passed a law limiting the salaries of clergymen—to discourage "professional churchmen" who were just in it for the money. But the king of England declared Virginia's law "null and void." The professional churchmen then sued the tax collectors for back pay—which meant that the landowners would have to pay more taxes.

Patrick stood before the court, shabby, timid, and awkward, speaking slowly, almost stopping at times. His clients, the landowners, hung their heads; the judge, Patrick's own father, covered his face with his hand.

Then, in a flash, the "feeling" hit. Patrick stood tall; his words rang out, clear and strong. "This case is not about clergymen who don't care for their congregations. It is about the rights of a people to govern themselves." With patriotic fervor Patrick thundered, "When a king overturns such beneficial laws, he degenerates into a tyrant and forfeits all right to his subjects' obedience." For several minutes he spoke on freedom and government and America. He held his listeners spellbound—tears streamed down many faces. When he stopped, the jury went out to deliberate, only to return in five minutes to award to the greedy churchmen damages . . . of only one penny! The crowd cheered and carried Patrick out on their shoulders.

That evening Patrick tried to explain to his wife what had happened to him. "It was as when Samson battled a thousand Philistines with the jawbone of a donkey. Or when Peter spoke on Pentecost, or Stephen spoke to the Jewish council. I was more than myself, more than just Patrick Henry. God's power came upon me." That night in their devotions, the family gave God heartfelt thanks. And Patrick dedicated himself anew to follow after God's will, both for himself and for his country. Patrick Henry had discovered his purpose, his destiny.

PETER (*Acts 1:8–14; 2:1–15*)

As he knelt in prayer in the Upper Room in Jerusalem with the others, waiting as Jesus had instructed them for something they couldn't even imagine, Peter's prayers were not like those of the others. Where their prayers were full of hope for the "power" Jesus told them would come in a few days, Peter's prayers were full of regret. He could think of nothing but his failures: sinking into the waves when Jesus called him to walk on the water because he took his eyes off his Lord in the midst of the storm; being rebuked as Satan himself when he spoke up against Jesus' execution on the cross; and lastly, not two months earlier, when he denied knowing Jesus three times as he waited in the hall of the high priest's home trying to hear word of Jesus' trial and what would happen to Him.

Yet neither could he get from his mind some of the last words Jesus had spoken to him as they sat on the beach eating together after His resurrection:

> "Simon, son of John, do you love Me more than these?" . . .
> "Tend My lambs."
> "Simon, son of John, do you love Me?" . . . "Shepherd My sheep."
> "Simon, son of John, do you love Me?" . . . "Tend My sheep."
> (John 21:15–17 NASB)

These words rolled over and over again in Peter's mind. How would he, as impetuous and foolish as he was, ever be expected to be responsible for his Lord's flocks? What had Jesus meant? And what had he meant by "you will receive power when the Holy Spirit has come upon you"? Peter would not have long to wait to find out.   ·

Only ten days after Jesus ascended to heaven, the Day of Pentecost literally fell. Peter had never experienced anything like it while he walked with Jesus, even though he had seen people healed and delivered at the touch of his own hands when Jesus had sent them out. This, however, was something different, something inside of him bursting to get out, something taking him beyond anything he had experienced before.

Suddenly the regret evaporated. As those around him in the Upper Room burst forth in praises and prayers in over a dozen languages, he followed them into the streets jumping, dancing, singing, and praising God with them. It was so overwhelming!

Then he heard the scoffers. "These people are drunk! Look at the fools!" Immediately Peter recognized the situation. He stood in the midst of the very type of religious men who had crucified Jesus! They were in danger! They must get out of there! What was he to do to save them all? Had that been what Jesus meant when He had asked Peter to take care of His sheep?

Yet it was something else that rose up instantly inside of him to squash that fear. It was not time to retreat, but to advance! Peter found a place from which his voice would carry throughout the square, and instead of cowering he cried out, "Men of Judea and all you who live in Jerusalem, let this be known to you and give heed to my words. . . ."

Peter spoke with a zeal and eloquence as he never had before, and by the end of the day, three thousand new believers had joined the ranks of the 120 who had been praying in the upper room. Never again would Peter deny his Lord or forsake an opportunity to proclaim His gospel.

{ LIVING IT! }

For both Patrick Henry and the apostle Peter, there was a passion and eloquence within them, fanned by the Holy Spirit, that they only learned of when they first sought to defend what they believed most in the inner depths of their hearts. Despite their previous failures and shortcomings, when they rose up to speak for Truth, they found their true voices and their life's callings.

Are there things that you feel passionate about when you start to speak of them? What are they? Do you feel like you are just repeating what you have heard others say, or is there something more about these things when you speak of them? Think about these things and study them more carefully to see what God has for you in them. It may be, as Patrick Henry and Peter discovered, in these passions are the keys to what God wants you to do with your life.

If you were asked to defend your faith, what would you say? Ask one of your church leaders if you could stage a mock trial one night and call people randomly from the audience to defend what they believe in. Take a stab at it yourself. How do you feel that God helped you in the experience? Are there things you need to learn more about before you try something like this again?

PUBLISHED WHEATLEY, NEGRO SERVANT to M.r JOHN WHEATLEY, of Boston.

Published according to Act of Parliament, Sept.r 1. 1773 by Arch.d Bell,

Bookseller N.o 8 near the Saracens Head Aldgate.

{ *Phillis Wheatley* }

True Freedom

*Servants, respectfully obey your earthly masters but
always with an eye to obeying the real master,
Christ. Don't just do what you have to do to get by,
but work heartily, as Christ's servants doing what
God wants you to do. And work with a smile on your
face, always keeping in mind that no matter
who happens to be giving the orders,
you're really serving God.*

EPHESIANS 6:5–7 THE MESSAGE

PHILLIS WHEATLEY (1753–1784)

"On Being Brought From Africa to America"

'Twas mercy brought me from my Pagan land
Taught my benighted soul to understand
That there's a God, that there's a Savior too:
Once I redemption neither sought nor knew.
Some view our sable race with scornful eye,
"Their colour is a diabolic die."
Remember, Christians, Negroes, black as Cain,
May be refin'd, and join th' angelic train.

Phillis Wheatley was born free in Senegal, kidnapped at the age of seven, and brought to Boston, where she was sold as a slave to a kind couple named John and Susannah Wheatley. The Wheatley family, including two older children, Mary and Nathaniel, was delighted with Phillis. She quickly won their hearts with her gentle temperament, affectionate nature, and pleasant ways. Phillis was never given menial tasks to do as originally planned. Instead she was treated with great kindness, as though she were a daughter of the family, and given the family name.

Susannah and Mary soon discovered Phillis was both quick to learn and perceptive. They taught her to read the Bible and to write. Within sixteen months Phillis mastered English and was able to read even the most difficult parts of the Bible with ease, and by age thirteen she wrote her first poetic verses. At sixteen she wrote her most famous elegy, a poem titled "On the Death of Mr. George Whitefield," the English evangelist so instrumental in the Great Awakening. The poem won Phillis international attention and was published in both England and America. Several other of her poems fostered great support and patriotism as the United States struggled to free itself from England.

Phillis, though still technically a slave, also proved that the greatness God had put into human souls crossed racial boundaries without prejudice. Though looked down upon and doubted by many because of her color and official place in society, Phillis saw herself blessed because, had she never left Africa, she would never have gotten to know Jesus as her Lord and Savior. She also challenged her generation's preconceived ideas of racial limitations by touching others with her charm, creativity, intelligence, kindness, and the love of God that she let shine through her everywhere she went.

JOSEPH (*Genesis 37, 39–41*)

At the age of seventeen, Joseph's pride and his father's favoritism toward him so angered Joseph's brothers that they plotted to kill him. And if the oldest of the brothers, Reuben, had not spoken up for Joseph, they would have. Instead, they sold him to a passing group of Ishmaelites, and Joseph went from favored son to forlorn slave.

Yet because of this, for the first time in Joseph's life, he learned to rely completely on God rather than on his father's graces or his own abilities. Though he was still smart and successful in the house of Potiphar, Pharaoh's captain of the guard, injustice struck again, and Joseph went from Potiphar's head slave to hated prisoner. It wasn't fair, it wasn't right, it wasn't just, but Joseph was imprisoned because of someone else's jealousy.

Joseph had the choice then to either blame God and the universe for his circumstances or cling closer to God for deliverance. Joseph thus chose to pursue God all the more, cultivate the gifts God had given him, and find joy in the solitude of his prison cell rather than despair. Again, he rose to a place of trust and responsibility, but what did it mean to be the ruler of slaves, or the chief of prisoners? Through it all, he was still a servant and an inmate.

One day, however, all that changed. Roughly thirteen years after he found himself at the end of a rope following a caravan of camels down to Egypt, Joseph was called before Pharaoh, where his spiritual gifts and wisdom moved him from lowly convict to second in the nation in one day. Could such have happened if Joseph had chosen to accept defeat rather than pursuing the God of ultimate victory?

{ L I V I N G   I T ! }

The world will tell us that we are the wrong color, the wrong ethnicity, too stupid, too uneducated, too this or not enough of that, whatever it can to keep us down, put us in our place, keep us out of the way, or prevent us from being what God has called us to be. And too often we listen to them. We look at our position in society or our workplace and see them as limitations to keep us from where we should be rather than training grounds to prepare us for where God wants us to go.

In Phillis Wheatley's society, African-American slaves were considered inferior and simple-minded, yet by the grace of God Phillis wrote poetry that touched the hearts of world leaders and shattered the false stereotypes that society put upon her. For Joseph to be sold into slavery must have seemed a surefire way to keep his God-given dreams of being a leader to the people of Israel from ever happening. Instead, it was the means to making it happen and saving not only Israel in a time of famine but also the rest of the Middle East and Northern Africa.

God has big plans for you as well. Will you let your circumstances keep you from achieving them, or will they be the springboard to the greater things He is calling you to? Certainly it won't be easy, but how many people who had easy lives ever made it into the history books?

It has often been pointed out that the Chinese character for "crisis" is made up of two other characters: "danger" and "opportunity." The same could be true for any set of obstacles we face that try to keep us from our God-given dreams—we can either accept them as blockades and excuses for failure or overcome them to learn and get one step closer to where God wants us to be. A lot of this is often determined by the attitudes with which we face them. Are there attitudes you need to adjust in your life to be more like a Phillis or a Joseph, even if you don't face anything half as difficult as they did? What are you going to do about them?

Looking on the other side of the coin, are you talented, gifted, and a recognized leader in your world like Joseph was in his home? These can often be bigger hindrances to fulfilling God's plans for our lives than external obstacles because we start to trust in our own strengths and leave God's at the wayside. Is there a way you can show God you trust in Him more than in yourself on a day-to-day basis? If so, how do you keep yourself a servant to Him in all that you do?

Freedom

The Conviction to
Stand for What
Is Right

*We have this day restored the Sovereign, to whom
alone men ought to be obedient. He reigns in heaven
and . . . from the rising to the setting sun,
may His Kingdom come.*

SAMUEL ADAMS, IN A SPEECH TO THE CONTINENTAL

CONGRESS, JULY 4, 1776

SAMUEL ADAMS (1722–1803)

It is a mistake to think that the decision of the American colonies to
seek their independence was either quick or easy. "Rebelliousness" was
not a valued characteristic in those times as it too often is today; but
rebellion would come, not because of a defiant nature, but through a
strong sense of right and wrong, as well as the continued pull of liberty
on the consciences of the majority of the colonists.

The first major act to drive a wedge between the colonies and Great
Britain came in 1765—some dozen years before the Declaration of Independence. The British Parliament imposed a tax on the printed paper
used by Americans, including legal documents, licenses, newspapers, and
other publications—it was even placed on playing cards. This Stamp Act
was viewed as an attempt by England to raise money in the colonies
without the approval of colonial legislatures. Though the actual costs of
the Stamp Act were relatively small, this tax seemed an attempt to open
the door for far more troublesome taxation later. Men such as Samuel
Adams publicly opposed the law and encouraged citizens to do the same.
For his part, Adams instigated the Stamp Act riots to intimidate poten-
tial tax agents and help force the repeal of the tax.

A few years later when Parliament placed a tax on imported products such as glass, lead, paints, paper, and tea, Adams protested again and soon had all Americans boycotting the new tax. An angry British government retaliated by sending soldiers to Boston to collect the money. Tauntings between the British and Americans were frequent, and on one riotous afternoon in March 1770, British soldiers opened fire on a crowd in Boston, killing five colonists. Samuel Adams helped dub the event the Boston Massacre (though it was far from one), and again American sentiment was raised against the edicts and actions of George III.

In 1773 Adams helped instigate another of the most famous demonstrations against the British when the Sons of Liberty, a secret patriot society, encouraged the group to board British ships and dump hundreds of chests of tea into the harbor as a protest against the tax on tea—the event later became known as the Boston Tea Party.

Yet Adams was not driven by a rebellious nature but by a devotion to what was right as reflected in his devotion to Christ. William Allen, a biographer of Adams and other Founding Fathers, wrote this of Adams' faith:

> Mr. Adams . . . early approached the table of the Lord Jesus, and the purity of his life witnessed the sincerity of his profession. On the Christian Sabbath he constantly went to the temple, and the morning and evening devotions in his family proved, that his religion attended him in his seasons of retirement from the world. The last production of his pen was in favor of Christian truth. He died in the faith of the gospel.

PAUL STANDS BEFORE GOVERNORS AND EMPERORS (*Acts 13:4–13*)

Of all of the apostles, Paul stood before governors and public officials more than any other. His first recorded encounter was on the island of Cypress in Paphos, where Paul and Barnabas stood before the proconsul, Sergius Paulus, after they were accused by the sorcerer and false prophet Bar-Jesus. In case you don't think this was nerve-racking, consider that it was here that John Mark deserted them, a fact that later caused a rift between Paul and Barnabas.

The book of Acts tells us that Paul would go on to stand before officials in Philippi, Thessalonica, Ephesus, Jerusalem, Caesarea, and eventually Rome, among likely others not mentioned in Luke's writings.

Paul stood before proconsuls, consuls, kings, and even Caesar, testifying boldly of Jesus Christ to every one.

Later in his life, after his missionary journeys and as he awaited trial in Rome, he wrote this of "standing firm" to the Ephesians:

> Therefore put on the full armor of God, so that when the day of evil comes, you may be able to stand your ground, and after you have done everything, to stand. (Ephesians 6:13)

{ L I V I N G   I T ! }

Paul's point here is that standing before anyone or anything is not something to be done in your own abilities and strengths, but to be done clothed in God's abilities and strengths. There is something interesting about the armor of God: If you put the helmet's faceplate down, it is impossible for anyone to differentiate the person inside of it from the owner of the armor—Jesus. When we stand in His armor, in a spiritual sense we look just like Him.

For Samuel Adams and others like him in colonial America, the decision to stand against British exploitation and for American independence was one that emerged from similar strengths. Men "clothed in Christ" saw that there was a need to stand so that America could become a land of freedom—a land through which God could expand His kingdom on the earth and see His will done. As we have stayed sensitive to His voice and honored Him above all else, America has been such a nation; however, in the times we have turned on Him for our own selfish causes, we have fallen short.

America needs a new generation today that is willing to put on His armor again and—"after we have done everything"—to stand again for Him, liberty, and unity among all Americans regardless of race, creed, color, or gender. God's truths are the same for all—He just needs people willing to stand up for those truths as did Paul and Samuel Adams.

Look at Ephesians chapter 6. How do you put on God's armor? What is the significance of each part? How will this armor help you stand up for Jesus?

As strange as it may sound, God is looking for revolutionaries who are not rebellious—He is looking for people who are willing to set our upside-down world back upside-right. Rebelliousness is often based in selfishness and anarchy—it attracts those who are against the present norm without really being for anything better. Such "revolutionaries" often have no vision for anything after the rebellion is over because they were only in it to destroy the status quo, not to build a better future—or simply to be in charge and noticed, not to truly lead for the benefit of others. God's revolutionaries, however, don't look for opportunities to dominate others, but chances to serve. They are revolutionary because they stand for something better. Are you such a revolutionary, or are you looking for attention by being against whatever is going on now? Pray over your "revolutionary attitudes" and ask God to help you know which ones to keep and which ones to discard.

Conviction

A World of Experience

Today I have given you the choice between life and death, between blessings and curses. I call on heaven and earth to witness the choice you make. Oh, that you would choose life, that you and your descendants might live!

DEUTERONOMY 30:19 NLT

Stewardship

OLAUDAH EQUIANO (1745–1797)

To the ten-year-old boy from a small village in the interior of Nigeria, the sights, smells, and sounds of the harbor were overwhelming. Olaudah Equiano had never even heard of such a place—with water that went as far as you could see and a slave ship riding at anchor.

Years later, writing in his autobiography, he recalled his feelings: "These sights filled me with astonishment, which was soon converted into terror, when I was carried on board the ship." Suddenly surrounded by European sailors, their unfamiliar features added to his fears. He remembered them as "ugly, horrible-looking men, with pale, reddish faces and long, loose hair."

Although Equiano was baptized as a youth and heard the fiery preaching of George Whitefield in Savannah, Georgia, in 1765, Christianity did not deeply influence his life until he faced death during a nearly disastrous Arctic expedition in 1773. After profound soul searching, he committed his life to Jesus Christ in 1774. In 1775 he traveled to Nicaragua as a Christian missionary, accompanying Dr. Irving, who wanted to establish a plantation on the Mosquito Coast and take the gospel to the Indian population there.

As a youth Equiano had been blessed with the opportunity to learn to read and write at a time when very few slaves were so allowed. As a sailor he had the time to continue to read and to improve his writing skills. As a Christian he saw how God could use his communication skills and his personal experience to give the world a glimpse of how horrific the life of a slave was.

In January 1777 Equiano traveled to England, where he became involved in the antislavery movement and spoke in a large number of public meetings, describing the cruelty of the slave trade. About this time, Equiano began writing his autobiography, *The Interesting Narrative of the Life of Olaudah Equiano, or Gustavus Vassa, the African*, which was published in 1789.

His autobiography gives a dramatic account of his life from his childhood in Africa to his passage on the slave ship to his life as a slave and then a free man. It provides unique insight into the nightmarish experiences of an African slave.

His book was famous in its time, running into seventeen editions in Great Britain and the United States and translated into Dutch and German. Equiano spent the next few years traveling throughout England promoting the book and making speeches against slavery. The book gives a glimpse into the horrors he faced as a ten-year-old being taken from his native land to be a slave among a type of people he had never seen before:

> I looked round the ship, and saw a large copper pot of boiling water, and a multitude of black people of every description chained together, every one of their countenances expressing dejection and sorrow. I no longer doubted of my fate; and, quite overpowered with horror and anguish, I fell motionless on the deck and fainted.
>
> When I recovered a little, I saw the black people who had brought me on, who were receiving their pay. They tried in vain to cheer me.
>
> I asked them, "Are we going to be eaten by these ugly white men?"
>
> They told me I was not. Soon after this, the blacks who brought me on board got off the ship and left me abandoned to despair.
>
> I was soon put down under the decks, and there I received such a greeting in my nostrils as I had never experienced in my life. With the loathsomeness of the stench, and crying together, I became so sick and low that I was not able to eat, nor had I the least desire to taste anything. I now wished for the last friend, death, to relieve me. Soon, to my grief, two of the white men offered me food. When I refused to eat, one of them held me fast by the hands, laid me across a beam, and tied my feet, while the other flogged me severely. I had never seen among my people such instances of brutal cruelty.
>
> The closeness of the place, and the heat of the climate, added to the number in the ship, which was so crowded that each had scarcely

room to turn himself. This produced much perspiration.

The air soon became unfit to breathe, from a variety of loathsome smells, and brought on a sickness among the slaves, of which many died. The wretched situation was made worse by our chains and the filth of the necessary tubs. The shrieks of the women, and the groans of the dying, rendered the whole a scene of horror almost inconceivable.

Although Equiano did not live to see the abolition of slavery in America, his narrative made the public aware of the horrors of the trade and the problems a freed slave faced. The book became a bestseller in both England and America and fueled the antislavery movement on both sides of the ocean.

CALEB (*Numbers 13 & 14; Joshua 15:13–20*)

Caleb was born a slave in Egypt and was forty years old when Moses delivered the Hebrews from Pharaoh's whip. He must have learned much of cruelty and forced labor, of hard work, little food, and bitterness. Yet he must also have learned a great deal about his God, Jehovah, and what it meant to call out to Him for deliverance. The day Moses walked into the lives of these slaves must have been a monumental one for Caleb—for the first time in his life, after years of praying, he saw the response and care of his God.

And then the miracles! The ten plagues on the Egyptians, the Red Sea parting, and the army of Pharaoh destroyed before his eyes without a single Hebrew raising a sword or suffering a wound.

The day came when they stood at the edge of the Promised Land. It must have been a horrible one for Caleb. He knew God was ready to give the land to them, but being a slave for so long had blinded the eyes of every other person with him except Joshua and Moses. They were afraid. They saw giants and problems, not possibilities and the power of God. He pleaded with them that day, but they were more willing to kill him than listen to reason. It was only a few days later that he, with all the others, would turn his back on the Promised Land to wander until all who had doubted God were gone and a new generation was in place.

For forty years they wandered in circles, but God was always with them. A pillar of smoke by day and a pillar of fire by night led them. God fed them with manna and quail. He gave them water from a rock. He delivered them from their enemies. God was with them more visibly than He would be with any other generation on the earth. Though Caleb aged, his faith grew.

When the Hebrews returned to the Promised Land, Caleb was eighty years old. But he was as strong and fit as the last time he had walked into the land of Canaan to spy out the land. This time the people were with him and Joshua, and they entered the land and conquered Jericho.

Our children's Bible storybooks are filled with different versions of the story of David and Goliath—of how a young boy killed a giant with His faith in God and a single stone. But we hear virtually nothing of Caleb and the three sons of Anak: Sheshai, Ahiman, Talmai—of how an eighty-year-old man came into the land that God had given him and drove out these three giants by his faith and trust in the power of God, and how he took the land around Hebron as a possession for his family.

From his lifetime and the many things he experienced, he chose to learn faith and hope, not despair and defeat.

{ LIVING IT! }

Both Olaudah Equiano and Caleb lived lives full of incredible experiences. They both saw the depths of what humans can sink to as master and slave, as well as the heights a person can reach if they will only trust in God. As Caleb, and probably Olaudah as well, experienced, it is one thing to be delivered from slavery, but it is quite another to free oneself from the despair and hopelessness that can accompany it. It takes an active will to choose faith in the face of what seems like hopelessness and follow God when all others around you are following defeat.

Both of these men chose to use what they had experienced to benefit others. They didn't sugarcoat the past to make it more acceptable, but told the hard facts of what they had experienced to others so they could see the reality of it and use it to fuel their desire to right wrongs. Olaudah told of his experiences as a slave and a child—innocence captured and squelched by men with consciences seared by the love of money. Caleb told his descendents of a people brought from the lash to the edge of a land flowing with milk and honey, but who refused to believe and trust in God enough to enter into what He had promised He would give them.

Have you experienced bad things in your lifetime? They can seem overwhelming. But how can you use these things that were meant to harm and discourage you as fuel to help others and trust more in God?

What talents and experiences do you have that can help others? Olaudah could write and Caleb could lead, and they both used their wealth of experience and these talents to turn bad to good. How can you do the same thing?

How do you feel about the world you live in? Do you feel circumstances dictate how you live more than your own decisions do? How do you take back control over something like that? The Bible says the choices of how we live are our own, not someone else's. How can you start making choices that will change the way you feel about yourself or what the future will hold?

Joined Together by God's Purposes

If God be for us, who can be against us? The enemy
[the British Army] has reproached us for calling on
His name and professing our trust in Him. They have
made a mock of our solemn fasts and every appearance
of serious Christianity in the land. . . . May our land
be purged from all its sins! Then the Lord will be our
refuge and our strength, a very present help in
trouble, and we will have no reason to be afraid,
though thousands of enemies set themselves
against us round about.

REVEREND SAMUEL LANAGDON, PRESIDENT OF

HARVARD COLLEGE, IN AN ADDRESS TO THE

PROVINCIAL CONGRESS OF MASSACHUSETTS, MAY 31, 1775

THE FIRST CONTINENTAL CONGRESS
(SEPTEMBER 7, 1774)

The Founding Fathers were not ashamed to admit that they were
openly relying on God. At the first meeting of the Continental Congress, it was suggested that they open with prayer. The motion was
opposed at first; because they were from such varied religious backgrounds—Episcopalians, Quakers, Anabaptists, Presbyterians, and Con-
gregationalists—some thought they would not be able to agree on a specific pastor.

Then Samuel Adams stood to address the assembly: "I am no bigot. I
could hear a prayer from a gentleman of piety and virtue, who was at
the same time a friend to his country. I am a stranger in Philadelphia,
but I have heard that Mr. Jacob Duché, an Episcopal clergyman, well

fits that description. I move that Mr. Duché be asked to read prayers to the Congress tomorrow morning."

The motion was seconded and passed.

Mr. Duché appeared the next morning in his pastoral robes and vestments. Before his arrival, however, a dreadful rumor had arrived through Israel Putnam of Connecticut that Boston, the colonies' most patriotic city, had been bombarded by the British and its inhabitants murdered by British soldiers. John Adams wrote, "The effect of the news we have both upon the Congress and the inhabitants of this city was very great—great indeed! Every gentleman seems to consider the bombardment of Boston as the bombardment of the capital of his own province." The bells of Philadelphia were muffled and tolled in token of this great sorrow.

Using the *Collect*, a book of prayers and daily Scripture readings, Mr. Duché read several formal prayers before coming to the Scripture for the day, Psalm 35.

> Plead my cause, O Lord, with them that strive with me: fight against them that fight against me. Take hold of shield and buckler, and stand up for mine help. Draw out also the spear, and stop the way against them that persecute me: say unto my soul, I am thy salvation. Let them be confounded and put to shame that seek after my soul: let them be turned back and brought to confusion that devise my hurt. Let them be as chaff before the wind: and let the angel of the Lord chase them. Let their way be dark and slippery: and let the angel of the Lord persecute them. . . . And my soul shall be joyful in the Lord: it shall rejoice in his salvation. All my bones shall say, Lord, who is like unto thee, which deliverest the poor from him that is too strong for him. (Psalm 35:1–6, 9–10a KJV)

John Adams later wrote, "I never saw a greater effect upon an audience. It seemed as if Heaven had ordained that Psalm to be read on that morning."

But that was not the end of the prayer meeting. Mr. Duché surprised everyone present by striking out in extemporaneous prayer, which was most unusual for that era.

> Be Thou present O God of Wisdom, and direct the counsel of this Honorable Assembly; enable them to settle all things on the best and surest foundations; that the scene of blood may be speedily closed; that Order, Harmony and Peace may be effectually restored, and that Truth and Justice, Religion and Piety, prevail and flourish among the

people. Preserve the health of their bodies, and the vigor of their minds, shower down on them, and the millions they here represent, such temporal blessings as Thou seeth expedient for them in this world, and crown them with everlasting Glory in the world to come. All this we ask in the Name and through the merits of Jesus Christ, Thy Son and our Savior. Amen.

John Adams said it "filled the bosom of every man present. I must confess I never heard a better prayer . . . such fervour, such ardor, such earnestness and pathos, and in language so elegant and sublime—for America, for the Congress, for the Province of Massachusetts Bay, and especially the town of Boston. It has had an excellent effect upon everybody here."

When the extended prayer was over, something else amazing happened. Another messenger came from Boston—this time with the news that the first report had been a mistake. There had been no bombardment and murdering in Boston. Imagine the joy the delegates felt! Their praises filled the hall again: "Great is the Lord!"

THE EARLY CHURCH PRAYS (*Acts 4:24–31* CEV)

When Peter and John were warned by the Jewish leaders in Jerusalem not to ever speak again in the name of Jesus, they replied that they could not obey men over God. When they returned to the other believers, they offered the following prayer to God that they would stand strong in the face of opposition:

Master, you created heaven and earth, the sea, and everything in them. And by the Holy Spirit you spoke to our ancestor David. He was your servant, and you told him to say:
"Why are all the Gentiles so furious?
Why do people make foolish plans?
The kings of earth prepare for war,
and the rulers join together
against the Lord and his Messiah."
Here in Jerusalem, Herod and Pontius Pilate got together with the Gentiles and the people of Israel. Then they turned against your holy Servant Jesus, your chosen Messiah. They did what you in your power and wisdom had already decided would happen.
Lord, listen to their threats! We are your servants. So make us brave enough to speak your message. Show your mighty power, as we heal people and work miracles and wonders in the name of your holy Servant Jesus.

After they had prayed, the building shook and they were all filled afresh with the Holy Spirit and confidence in Jesus' name.

{ LIVING IT! }

By His Word the Lord brought fresh confidence to the delegates at the first Continental Congress, and they sensed that they were on the right path. By His presence, He brought the same confidence to the early believers in Jerusalem. In the dark hours that were ahead in their fights for freedom and truth, both groups would need that assurance. Those present in Congress would never forget the day or the fact that, though they were of many different religious persuasions, they could come together before God, in the name of Jesus Christ His Son, and stand together in what they felt God had destined them to do—separate from the tyranny of King George III of Great Britain and build together a nation where they all had the freedom to worship and follow God as He compelled them.

★   ★   ★

Are there Scriptures or times of prayer that have touched your life as these touched the lives of the Founding Fathers and early believers? What Scriptures are they? What do you remember of such prayers? Write them down in your journal as best you can and then ask God if there is more He wants to communicate to you about them. Take the time to listen, write, and meditate upon them.

Whom are you "joined together with" to accomplish God's plans for your life? Whom are you accountable to? God has no Lone Rangers, but has called all of us to fit together in His body to accomplish His purposes. Where do you fit into that body? Whom are you knitted together with to touch your community, schools, or state?

The Battle Belongs to the Lord

*For we do not wrestle against flesh and blood, but
against principalities, against powers, against the
rulers of the darkness of this age, against spiritual
hosts of wickedness in the heavenly places.*

EPHESIANS 6:12 NKJV

THE BATTLES OF CONCORD AND LEXINGTON
(APRIL 19, 1775)

On April 15, 1775, British General Thomas Gage received orders to
destroy the patriots' ammunition stores in Concord, Massachusetts—it
would be the first act of Great Britain to take away the abilities of the
American colonies to defend themselves. Providentially, Dr. Joseph
Warren heard of the general's plans and on the eve of the attack, April
18, he made plans with Paul Revere and William Dawes to warn the surrounding villages to muster a defense of the city. That night the famous
"one if by land, two if by sea" signal came back to indicate the British
would attack by sea, and Revere and Dawes rode forth to sound the
alarm.

The Battle of Lexington took place at dawn the next day. The farmers' brief battle with the British was over quickly, with basically one
round of firing by both sides, and then a hasty American retreat to the
woods nearby. Eight Americans were killed and ten wounded. The brief
volley of shots would later be dubbed "the shot heard round the world."
It was the first skirmish of what would become the American Revolution.

But the fighting for the day was not over, and the battle in Lexington bought time for the patriots at Concord to hide their guns and
ammunition and gather the minutemen to bolster their defense. The

Concord farmers defended themselves well. They forced the British into retreat while the Americans shot at them from behind the cover of stone walls, hedges, and trees. It was the first time the British army suffered casualties in struggles with the Americans. By the time their reinforcements came, the British were exhausted and nearly out of bullets. In the end the British troops lost 273 men on that day; the Americans lost 93. The victory of the first day of fighting in the American Revolution clearly and gloriously belonged to the Americans.

The people in Lexington and Concord believed that the providential hand of God had moved for them—in the discovery of the British plot, in the warnings delivered, in the timing of the battles, in God's protection. What they probably did not know was that the entire colony of Connecticut was praying for them. Governor Jonathan Trumball had proclaimed that very day, April 19, 1775, as a day of prayer and fasting for all the colonies. His proclamation asked that God "would restore, preserve, and secure the Liberties of this and all the other British American colonies and make the Land a mountain of Holiness and Habitation of Righteousness forever."

JUDAH CALLS UPON THE LORD FOR VICTORY
(*2 Chronicles 20:1–25* NASB)

News was brought to King Jehoshaphat that a great army of three peoples was gathering to invade Judah. Jehoshaphat, being a godly king, knew that trusting in the strength of his army alone would not be enough. So instead of first gathering his troops to defend his people, he called for a day of fasting and prayer throughout the entire land.

Jehoshaphat stood before all the those gathered in the courts of the temple and prayed:

> O Lord, the God of our fathers, are You not God in the heavens? And are You not ruler over all the kingdoms of the nations? Power and might are in Your hand so that no one can stand against You. Did You not, O our God, drive out the inhabitants of this land before Your people Israel and give it to the descendants of Abraham Your friend forever? They have lived in it, and have built You a sanctuary there for Your name, saying, "Should evil come upon us, the sword, or judgment, or pestilence, or famine, we will stand before this house and before You (for Your name is in this house) and cry to You in our distress, and You will hear and deliver us." Now behold, the sons of Ammon and Moab and Mount Seir, whom You did not let Israel

invade when they came out of the land of Egypt (they turned aside from them and did not destroy them), see how they are rewarding us by coming to drive us out from Your possession which You have given us as an inheritance. O our God, will You not judge them? For we are powerless before this great multitude who are coming against us; nor do we know what to do, but our eyes are on You.

Then the Lord answered through Jahaziel:

Listen, all Judah and the inhabitants of Jerusalem and King Jehoshaphat: thus says the Lord to you, "Do not fear or be dismayed because of this great multitude, for the battle is not yours but God's. Tomorrow go down against them. Behold, they will come up by the ascent of Ziz, and you will find them at the end of the valley in front of the wilderness of Jeruel. You need not fight in this battle; station yourselves, stand and see the salvation of the Lord on your behalf, O Judah and Jerusalem." Do not fear or be dismayed; tomorrow go out to face them, for the Lord is with you.

The next day Jehoshaphat appointed singers to march before the army of Judah singing, "Give thanks to the Lord, for His lovingkindness is everlasting." Judah won its battle that day without unsheathing a sword or throwing a spear. By the time they came to the enemy, the armies Ammon, Moab, and Mount Seir had turned upon one another and destroyed each other.

{ L I V I N G   I T ! }

Today, in our age of nuclear weapons and laser-guided missiles, we need to remember more than ever that the battle is not ours but the Lord's. Battles and revivals are always won in the spirit first; then they manifest in the natural world. What battles are you waging in prayer today? Or have you forgotten this principle and instead trust in your own intellect rather than trusting in God?

★　　★　　★

A lot of confusion has been spread about "spiritual warfare" among believers today, but probably only because it has always been such an important part of expanding God's kingdom on the earth. What is spiritual warfare really? It is praying as God directs you to pray for the people and places He directs you to pray for. It is coming together with other believers to pray that God's light would be revealed to all and would expose that which needs exposing and open blind eyes that need to be opened to the Truth. Are you open to God for Him to pray such prayers through you? If so, what are you going to do to start?

An incredible movement is starting around such prayer today through a book called *Red Moon Rising* by Peter Greig and Dave Roberts. It is about what is being called 24-7 prayer. This is when a room is made available in a community for prayer 24 hours a day, 7 days a week, and people take hour time slots to go there and pray for the community. On the Internet, search "24-7 prayer" and your city name to see if there is somewhere in your community already doing this. If not, get a copy of the book and ask God if He wants you to help start something like this in your area.

Allegiance to a "Heavenly Country"

They did not keep thinking about the country they had left; if they had, they would have had the chance to return. Instead, it was a better country they longed for, the heavenly country. And so God is not ashamed for them to call him their God, because he has prepared a city for them.

HEBREWS 11:15–16 GNT

ROBERT MORRIS (1734–1806)

Robert Morris was one of the signers of the Declaration of Independence, but his signing was not the first time he had committed his all to the new country that would become the United States. More than a year earlier, Robert was at a dinner party when news of the Battle of Lexington reached his ears.

Disturbed by the news, most of the party guests soon left, but Robert and a few others stayed to discuss the implications of the attack. That night Robert and these few men, by a solemn vow, dedicated their lives, their fortunes, and their honor to the sacred cause of creating a new nation free from European tyranny.

Robert Morris was a warm and generous man with a talent for earning money. He was a partner in one of the top business houses in Philadelphia and owned a fleet of trading ships. His many friends included Alexander Hamilton, John Jay, and George Washington. Because of his talents and reputation, Robert was looked to time and again by Washington and others when American troops needed financial support. Such was Robert's reputation that on one such occasion Robert was able to secure ten thousand dollars simply on his promise that, "My note and my honor will be your only security." Historians have said, "Had it not been for Robert Morris's services in raising funds, it is hard to see how the Revolution could have succeeded."

In 1781 Robert agreed to serve as Superintendent of Finance for the young United States, but only on the condition that no more paper money be issued. He explained, "The United States may command everything I have except integrity, and the loss of that would effectually disable me from serving them now." This proved true. Many who did not trust Congress to repay its obligations instead accepted the word of Robert Morris. Robert went on to serve as a framer of the Constitution, helped form the Bank of North America, and was one of the first senators for Pennsylvania.

By the end of the war, Robert Morris had given much of his fortune to his new country, money that perhaps would have kept him secure when he later lost what wealth he had left on a land speculation in western New York. He died in relative poverty; however, he regretted nothing of what he had done in pledging his life and resources to "another country"—one based on freedom and trust in God rather than the English aristocracy into which he had been born.

ABRAHAM AND HIS DESCENDANTS

Abraham took his family and left a promising future in the land of Ur when God told him to search for another country—a better one—and live there under Him. Abraham longed for a city and a land God alone had prepared for him. Abraham's son Isaac clung to that same promise, living in the very place his descendants would eventually call their own, but under the authority of foreign kings. Jacob and his sons would also live there, hoping for the same promise, until famine drove them from the land and into eventual slavery in Egypt. There, for four hundred years, the sons and daughters of Abraham would live in bondage, calling out for deliverance and the country that God had promised them.

When God answered their call by sending Moses to deliver them, and they finally stood at the borders of that Promised Land, only Caleb and Joshua of the twelve spies acknowledged that God was able to give it to them. As a result of their unbelief and inability to pledge their lives to obtain what God had promised, the children of Israel wandered another forty years before entering into what God had promised Abraham centuries before.

{ LIVING IT! }

Robert Morris lived his life and pledged his all for the sake of a country different from the one in which he was born, a nation that didn't even exist yet but cost him much of his fortune and the lives of many friends. He was willing to sacrifice everything to make that country a reality—everything except what conflicted with living by biblical integrity. Yet it was specifically because Robert lived for heaven first that he was of such great value to the United States in some of its earliest times of need.

In a similar way, Abraham and his descendents lived for God, and as a result, the kingdoms they lived in as foreigners were blessed. The Bible tells us they "admitted openly that they were foreigners and refugees on earth. . . . They are looking for a country of their own" (Hebrews 11:13–14 GNT).

What kingdom do you live for today? Is your all pledged for "another country, a heavenly one"? Or do you live for your day-to-day, doing what seems practical for finite blessings instead of infinite ones? Can you look past your allegiance to your own country, your school, your church, your clique, your team, or any other group you belong to and live by the allegiance to your true home—with Jesus?

★   ★   ★

When measuring where your true allegiance lies, a good place to start is considering how you spend your money, how you spend your time, and what you dream to accomplish in your life. Take a week and write down everything you spend your money on and then what you do every half hour of your day. Then think for a while about what you want to accomplish in your life. What do these say about where your true allegiance lies?

If these show that your allegiance is somewhere else besides God, how can you change that? What should your week, your spending, and your dreams look like if you are living for heaven?

A Time for Revolution

*I only regret that I have but one life
to lose for my country.*

ATTRIBUTED TO NATHAN HALE AS HE STOOD BEFORE
THE GALLOWS ON WHICH HE WOULD BE HUNG AS A SPY
AGAINST ENGLAND ON SEPTEMBER 22, 1776

PETER MUHLENBERG (1746–1807)

"To every thing there is a season, and a time to every purpose under heaven," Pastor Muhlenberg proclaimed, reading from Ecclesiastes 3. "A time to be born, and a time to die. . . . A time to weep, and a time to laugh. . . . A time of war, and a time of peace." He stopped and looked at the people God had put in his care—hardworking farmers and their wives, merchants, and recent immigrants. The tiny town of Woodstock, Virginia, was a long way from the fighting in the colonies of New England. In early January 1776 the Blue Ridge Mountains had kept its citizens from hearing the news of events taking place in their own state.

"It is a time for war!" Pastor Muhlenberg declared. "And not only in New England. War has come to Virginia! The British have marched on our own city of Williamsburg, seizing our supply of gunpowder and munitions. Soldiers are entering private homes, homes just like ours.

"It is time for war! 'We are only farmers,' you may say. Patrick Henry has rallied five thousand men—farmers just like you—to fight back and drive the British out. It is time to act! Many of us came to this country to practice our religious freedoms. It is time to fight for those freedoms that we hold so dear. It is time for war!

"Let us pray." With that, Pastor Muhlenberg bowed his head and offered the traditional closing prayer. Then, breaking with all tradition, while still standing in the pulpit, he began to remove his pastor's robes and vestments. "I am a clergyman, it is true. But I am also a patriot—and my liberty is as dear to me as to any man. Shall I hide behind my robes, sitting still at home, while others spill their blood to protect my freedom? Heaven forbid it!

"I am called by my country to its defense. The cause is just and noble. I am convinced it is my duty to obey that call, a duty I owe to my God and to my country."

With that, he threw off the final layer of his robes—and now stood before his stunned congregation in the full uniform of an officer of the Continental militia. He marched to the back of the church, declaring to all, "If you do not choose to be involved, if you do not fight to protect your liberties, there will soon be no liberties to protect!"

Just outside the church army drummers waited. At Pastor Muhlenberg's command, they began to beat out the call for recruits. God's conviction fell on the men of the congregation. One by one they rose from their pews and took their stand with the drummers. Some three hundred men from the church joined their pastor that day to fight for liberty.

JESUS CALLED PETER AND ANDREW (*Matthew 4:12–20*)

Soon after He was baptized in the Jordan River by John the Baptist, Jesus began his public ministry by going from place to place proclaiming, "Turn from your old ways to God's ways, for the kingdom of heaven is at hand!"

As he traveled and taught this message, he came to the Sea of Galilee and saw two brothers, Simon (whom Jesus would later name "Peter"—"The Rock") and Andrew, casting their fishing nets into the sea. Jesus caught their eyes, and also the cry of their hearts. While they were fisherman, they also knew that there was something more, something bigger that they were supposed to do, but they didn't know what. That day it was revealed to them in one look and one phrase from the mouth of Jesus, "Follow me, and I will make you fishers of men."

So they did. They dropped their nets and immediately followed Him.

{ LIVING IT! }

When God calls, it is best to answer and follow right away. For Peter and Andrew, following Jesus would lead them to live two of the most incredible lives ever recorded in writing. The things they saw! The things they did! The way God moved through them to touch others! Most of us envy them today in some way or another because they had the chance to walk on earth with Jesus.

For Pastor Muhlenberg and his congregation, there was a call to defend their country and their ideals that would not wait another day. Peter Muhlenberg and the men who joined him became the Eighth Virginia Regiment. They fought valiantly in many of the battles of the Revolutionary War.

Yet either of these two groups also had another option. They could have refused to follow.

During the Revolutionary War, Muhlenberg was promoted to major general. After the war he was a hero second only to General George Washington among the Germans of his native state of Pennsylvania. In 1785 he became vice-president of Pennsylvania alongside Benjamin Franklin, who was elected its president. He worked hard to influence others to adopt the Federal Constitution in 1787 and served in the First U.S. Congress in 1789–1791.

It is not hard to believe that because of Pastor Muhlenberg's answer to his national duty, America became free. Certainly he did not do it alone, but just as certainly, it probably wouldn't have been done without him.

Jesus could have won the world without Peter and Andrew, yet our heritage is all the richer today for these "fishers of men" who became pillars of our faith because they did obey.

What is God calling you to do today? What obligation is your nation calling you to? While there may be a time for war and a time for peace, there is never a time to disobey God. Answer His call—just as immediately as Peter, Andrew, and Pastor Muhlenberg's congregation did.

A call of duty is always a call of service. It is a call of obligation for the liberties and privileges we have, both a call to give back because of them and a call to protect and preserve them. Take time to pray today for those who have answered that call on your behalf, whether they be people in the military, police or firefighters, government or elected officials, missionaries and ministers, or any others you can think of.

Take time yet again to pray about what God is calling you to do for His kingdom and your nation. Are you learning anything new each time you pray along these lines as you work yourself through the stories of this book? If so, record them somewhere to meditate upon later; if not, keep praying! God is simply leading you step by step rather than through big-picture thinking.

Holding to God's Plan

May I never boast except in the cross of our Lord
Jesus Christ, through which the world has been
crucified to me, and I to the world.

GALATIANS 6:14

Humility

JOHN WITHERSPOON (1723–1794)

On December 31, 1775, combined Canadian and British forces routed
a colonist battalion that had been pushing its way north at the Battle of
Quebec. The battalion's resigned retreat back into upstate New York
served as a sharp warning to many throughout the colonies that their
God-given vision for freedom might be in trouble. What was the threat
to all their grandest dreams? It wasn't danger from the Crown, but the
colonists' own pride.

Ministers from Massachusetts to Virginia preached in warning
against trusting too much in their own strength, their own plans. The
push for Quebec had marked the notable effort to expand the colonial
territories and may have been an overstepping of what God had called
them to do. Such prideful actions were surely steps to forsake God, and a
path without God could only lead to peril and calamity.

The fledgling Congress sensed the need to rededicate themselves to
God's vision, and on March 16, 1776, they put forth a proclamation setting May 17, 1776, as a "day of Humiliation, Fasting, and Prayer."

When that day arrived, Dr. John Witherspoon, a Presbyterian minister, president of the College of New Jersey (which later became Prince-
ton University), and one of the eventual fifty-six signers of the Declaration of Independence, gave a sermon that was the most widely
reprinted of all those delivered on that day.

> While we give praise to God, the supreme disposer of all events,
> for His interposition on our behalf, let us guard against the dangerous
> error of trusting in, or boasting of, an arm of flesh. . . .

I look upon ostentation and confidence to be a sort of outrage upon providence, and when it becomes general, and infuses itself into the spirit of a people, it is a forerunner to destruction. . . .

But observe that if your cause is just, if your principles are pure, and if your conduct is prudent, you need not fear the multitude of opposing hosts.

What follows from this? That he is the best friend to American liberty who is most sincere and active in promoting true and undefiled religion. . . .

Soon his sermon was finished and Witherspoon stepped from the podium. As the service ended and his church cleared, he found himself alone. In the last pew he discovered one of the printed copies of Congress's proclamation that had been distributed to every hand that would accept one. *A day of fasting and repentance.* Who knew if it would be enough? He scanned the page and came to the final words: *God Save These People!*

Not *God Save the King!* as across the ocean. Not *People Save Yourselves!* as so many seemed to want. But *God Save These People!* It was the best and only hope, and Witherspoon clutched the paper to him as though it were God's promise itself.

PAUL IS CALLED TO MACEDONIA (*Acts 16:6–10*)

Paul was frustrated. It had been days now, and he felt lost. All of his efforts seemed futile. He had felt in his heart that he should head farther east into Asia after he had preached in Galatia, but the Spirit of God had forbidden him to continue in that direction. When he instead tried to go north to Bithynia, he again felt uncomfortable with it as the Holy Spirit told him he was not to go in that direction either. Now, passing Mysia, Paul was at Troas on the coast. But there was nothing to do there—no ministry, and all that was ahead of them was water. What were they to do? Where exactly was it that God was trying to lead them?

Despite his frustration, that night Paul would have his answer.

As he slept, a man came to him in his dream. By his clothes and the shape of his face, Paul could tell he was Macedonian (from northern Greece). In his dream, the man said: "Come over to Macedonia and help us."

Immediately Paul awoke and knew what to do. The next day they caught a boat headed for Macedonia. Their journey was back on track!

No matter who we are, we all make the mistake from time to time thinking we should be doing one thing but later realizing that God actually had a different plan. And then sometimes we don't even get a different direction to go in, only that the direction we *were* going in was the wrong one.

This is exactly what Paul faced on his first missionary journey, but notice that when he got a "No!" he didn't just sit and wait, but he devised a new plan in a new direction that he would follow until God either corrected him again or gave him the okay. Paul knew his overall purpose and mission was to take the gospel to as many as he could, so he just stuck to the overall plan when his smaller plans were cancelled. He knew, though it may have been frustrating in the midst of it, that God was guiding him and teaching him patience and humility. He would stick to that rather than go back to rely upon his own ways and his own plans.

For the early colonists, it seemed to be God's will to free the thirteen colonies, but in their ambition for more—to push into Quebec and take a bit more territory—it also appears they had overstepped their bounds. Through wisdom from such men as Dr. John Witherspoon, they knew to pull back and regroup rather than give up—to return to the original plan as outlined rather than try to add their own desires to it.

Humility is not putting yourself down or never trying to achieve anything, but rather knowing who is in charge and not overstepping that boundary. Humble people can accomplish great things, as we will learn later with people such as Roger Sherman and George Washington Carver. How do you define humility in your own life? How do you walk in it? Are you open to God's changing the course of your life, or do you get wrapped up in your own plans?

Have you ever taken a "day of Humiliation, Fasting, and Prayer" before the Lord to listen more closely for His direction and guidance in your life? If so, what did you learn from it? If not, why not take one, even if it is only for half a day? See if some others might join you in a time of seeking and worshiping God for the sake of letting Him lead you more directly.

Freedom for All

*Faith in Christ Jesus is what makes each of you
equal with each other, whether you are a Jew or a
Greek, a slave or a free person, a man or a woman.*

GALATIANS 3:28 CEV

Equality

ABIGAIL ADAMS (1744–1818)

The day's chill soon broke and glorious spring seemed to fully take
hold of the Massachusetts countryside. The farm's first growth already
showed above the soil, and nature seemed clothed in its most splendid
attire. Abigail Adams had been warned about smallpox in Boston and
had put off visiting the family home in the city, but friends and neighbors mostly came by with good news over the next few days. All of this
made it into her letter when she finally returned to her writing on the
last day of March 1776. A post would be leaving for New York and
Philadelphia tomorrow, and if she wanted her letter on it, she needed to
finish tonight. Which meant finally asking the question she'd been
toiling through in her heart.

> I long to hear you have declared an independancy—and by the way
> in the new Code of Laws which I suppose it will be necessary for you
> to make I desire you would Remember the Ladies, and be more gen-
> erous and favourable to them than your ancestors. Do not put such
> unlimited power into the hands of the Husbands. Remember all Men
> would be tyrants if they could.

Once started, she could barely contain herself. Would her husband,
John, scold her for calling all men tyrants? Would he hear her passion in
the words, or would the letter be read only halfheartedly in the midst of
one of Franklin's digressions or Jefferson's eloquent speeches?

> Men of Sense in all Ages abhor those customs which treat us only
> as the vassals of your Sex. Regard us then as Beings placed by

providence under your protection and in immitation of the Suprem [sic] Being make us of that power only for our happiness.

She signed, as she always did, *Portia*, dated the letter, and sealed it with wax. She had put forth the question with eloquence and evenhandedness to one of the best men in the colonies. That women should stand equal and free, as God himself intended, alongside their husbands, seemed only natural to Abigail, and she thought John might feel the same way.

But even the best men in the Union could not change centuries of customs overnight. Nor did they feel particularly inclined. One revolution, it seemed, was more than enough at the moment for John, who responded to his wife's sincere call for equality as though she might be jesting.

> As to your extraordinary Code of Laws, I cannot but laugh. We have been told that our Struggle has loosened the bands of Government every where. That Children and Apprentices were disobedient—that schools and Colledges were grown turbulent—that Indians slighted their Guardians and Negroes grew insolent to their Masters. But your Letter was the first Intimation that another Tribe more numerous and powerfull than all the rest were grown discontented.— This is rather too coarse a Compliment but you are so saucy, I won't blot it out.

Abigail's disappointment in her husband was sharp but focused. On so many things he followed God's leading, and the cause of emancipating the colonies was vast and great. Yet on this single issue he had failed to see what her eyes could. He would not budge, and so she chastised him wryly in her next letter, warning of the coming days when the *next* revolution would come and women would subdue their masters.

That letter was posted May 7, 1776.

In 1869, ninety-three years later, Susan B. Anthony helped form the women's suffrage movement. Fifty-one years after that, in 1920, the Nineteenth Amendment to the Constitution—the Constitution John Adams himself helped draft—was ratified and women gained the right to vote.

Abigail returned to her empty bedchamber the evening after her letter found its way south, weary and already chilled. Great things, it seemed, were coming, her husband at their very fulcrum. And yet even great men can be blinded or need reminding of their true cause from time to time. It was not the goals of men for which they were fighting, but for God's own purpose—a design that included all his faithful men, women, and children. All called to Him.

PETER AND PAUL (*Acts 15* NASB; *Galatians 2:1–21* THE MESSAGE)

Supposedly the issue had been settled by the church fathers in Jerusalem. The question had arisen not long after Jesus had ascended to heaven: Would there be two classes of Christians? Would Jewish believers be the "True Believers," sanctified because they followed all of the laws of Moses, and would Gentiles become "Proselytes," meaning they must convert to Judaism first to become Christians? Was Christianity going to be a Jewish sect or a universal religion?

Paul and Barnabas brought the question before Peter and James in Jerusalem, as they saw that God showed no such favoritism between Jews and Gentiles—those circumcised and those not circumcised—in giving the Holy Ghost. Their argument was that what Jesus had done on the cross had fulfilled the law, and now making Jesus one's Lord and Savior and believing He was risen from the dead to the right hand of the Father in heaven was all that was needed to be saved. The church fathers seemed to concur, saying "For it seemed good to the Holy Spirit and to us to lay upon you no greater burden than these essentials: that you abstain from things sacrificed to idols and from blood and from things strangled and from fornication; if you keep yourselves free from such things, you will do well." Paul and Barnabas then returned to Antioch, Syria, feeling that God's will had been done and the decision was scriptural and sound.

It took longer for others to adjust, however.

While the decision was that all were one in Christ, all equally important with equal access to God, there were still many Jewish believers who would not give up their "higher station" as God's chosen people from the calling of Abraham. Although they acknowledged Gentile believers as Christians, they still practiced a form of segregation: They would not eat with Gentiles or associate with them, if possible.

When Peter came to Antioch to see how things were going, he was pulled in by this sect and ate with them regularly, reinforcing their segregation as legitimate and thus accepting that there were in fact two classes of Christians, with one better than the other.

While Paul seemed to have tolerated this from the immature Jews of the area, when Peter reinforced it, he felt compelled to confront him on the issue before them all: "If you, a Jew, live like a non-Jew when you're not being observed by the watchdogs from Jerusalem, what right do you have to require non-Jews to conform to Jewish customs just to make a favorable impression on your old Jerusalem cronies?"

Though it is not directly stated in the Scriptures, it appears that Peter repented on the matter. He had forgotten himself and fell into custom rather than working to change the cultural norms of the time with the truth of the gospel. As he acknowledged later in his second general letter to the churches, giving the writings of Paul his endorsement: "Bear in mind that our Lord's patience [His work on the cross] means salvation, just as our dear brother Paul also wrote you with the wisdom that God gave him" (2 Peter 3:15). In other words, what Jesus did was enough—there were no other requirements but faith in Him to be saved—and there was only one class of Christian, all "equal with each other, whether you are a Jew or a Greek, a slave or a free person, a man or a woman" (Galatians 3:28 CEV).

{ LIVING IT! }

It is one thing to believe all people are equal before God; it is another to live it. As Abigail Adams learned, while her husband was a good man and fought for the freedom of all, he was still somewhat confined by tradition. Although he was willing to break with Great Britain to secure "freedom" for the colonies, he was not yet ready to drop the similar shackles men had over women. While Peter had acknowledged that all were equal in Christ, when practicalities arose, he also fell into tradition rather than push for the truth of Christ's freedom for all.

While in today's American government sanctioned segregation is gone, do we as Christians cross the color and gender line in our churches, youth groups, and friendships? Are there special privileges for one group over another? Do our leadership committees reflect integration over subtle segregation?

As we already said, it is one thing to believe all people are equal before God; it is another to live it.

Do you have friends of other races and ethnicities? Why or why not? Are there barriers in your personal thinking that are blocking such relationships?

In the places you work or in your classroom, do you see subtle forms of discrimination based on gender, race, ethnicity, body size, attractiveness, or some other characteristic people don't really control? What can you do to change such things? What does it really mean that all of us are "equal with each other before Christ"?

Equality

Declaring Dependence—Upon God

I am well aware of the toil and blood and treasure
that it will cost us to maintain this Declaration, and
support and defend these States. Yet through all the
gloom I can see rays of ravishing light and glory.
I can see that the end is worth more
than all the means.

JOHN ADAMS

THE SIGNING OF THE DECLARATION OF INDEPENDENCE (AUGUST 2, 1776)

The choice to declare our independence from Great Britain in 1776 was not a decision that our Founding Fathers made lightly—in fact, they had tried everything else first. A year earlier, on July 5, 1775, just a few weeks after the Battle of Bunker Hill, Congress had sent the "Olive Branch Petition" directly to King George III, asking for his help in making peace. The king refused to even look at it.

Famous British parliamentarians argued for America's cause, but none of their arguments moved King George. In his eyes there was only one way to deal with rebellion: crush the rebels by military force.

But never in Britain's history was recruiting volunteers so difficult. The recruiting officers were tarred and feathered in Wales and stoned in Ireland; previously, in the French and Indian War, three hundred thousand men had volunteered, and now not even fifty thousand had come forward. King George was forced to hire mercenaries from Germany to fight the Americans.

Despite the fact that England had declared war, many congressional delegates were still hoping for a way to reconcile. Only eight of the thirteen colonies had voted to declare independence at that time.

Then, on June 7, 1776, news came that King George's hired mercenaries were coming to America to fight. In response, Richard Henry Lee of Virginia formally proposed to Congress that the colonies at last declare their independence. Congress postponed its decision until July, so those delegates who were uncertain could check with the constituents they represented.

When they reconvened, the Resolution for Independence was adopted by twelve of the thirteen colonies, with New York abstaining. Congress then began to discuss the wording of the Declaration. The changes demonstrated Congress's strong reliance upon God—as delegates added the words "appealing to the Supreme Judge of the World for the rectitude of our intentions."

In the center section are the complaints against King George that made independence necessary. Surprisingly, the reason given by modern history books—"taxation without representation"—is not at the top of the list. In fact, it was seventeenth in a list of twenty-seven grievances, including eleven points on abuse of representative powers, seven on abuse of military powers, and four on abuse of judicial powers.

The revisions continued into the late afternoon of July 4, when, at last, church bells rang out over Philadelphia; the Declaration had been officially adopted.

One of the most widely held misconceptions about the Declaration is that all the delegates in attendance signed it on July 4, 1776. In fact, it wasn't officially signed until August 2. On that day, John Hancock, the president of Congress, was the first to sign. He signed with a flourish, using a big, bold signature centered below the text.

Then, one by one, the other delegates were called upon, beginning with the northern-most states. Each man knew what he risked: To the British this was treason, and the penalty for treason was death by hanging. Benjamin Franklin said, "Indeed we must all hang together. Otherwise we shall most assuredly hang separately."

William Ellery, a delegate from Rhode Island, inched his way to stand near the desk where the delegates were signing their names. He was curious to see their faces as each committed this act of courage. Ellery later reported that he was not able to discern real fear on anyone's face. One man's hand shook badly: Stephen Hopkins, also from Rhode Island, was in his sixties and was quick to explain, "My hand trembles, but my heart does not."

A pensive and awful silence filled the room, as one delegate after another signed what many at that time believed to be their own death

{ *The Signing of the Declaration of Independence* }

warrants. The only sound was the calling of the names and the scratch of the pen.

Then the silence and heaviness of the morning were interrupted by the tall, sturdily built Colonel Benjamin Harrison of Virginia, who told the slender Elbridge Gerry of Massachusetts, "I shall have a great advantage over you, Mr. Gerry, when we are all hung for what we are now doing. With me, it will all be over in a minute, but you, you'll be dancing on air an hour after I'm gone."

In the end, no signer was hung for treason, though many suffered greatly for their stand. For these men, who mutually pledged to each other their lives, their fortunes, and their sacred honor, this was more than a declaration. It was more than a document. It was a covenant, the most solemn, the most sacred of human agreements. They understood that God himself was a witness of their actions that day.

MOSES GOES BEFORE PHARAOH (*Exodus 7:14–20*)

The Lord told Moses, "Pharaoh's heart is unyielding; he refuses to let the people go. Go to Pharaoh in the morning as he goes out to the water. Wait on the bank of the Nile to meet him, and take in your hand the staff that was changed into a snake. Then say to him, 'The Lord, the God of the Hebrews, has sent me to say to you: Let my people go, so that they may worship me in the desert. But until now you have not listened. This is what the Lord says: By this you will know that I am the Lord: With the staff that is in my hand I will strike the water of the Nile, and it will be changed into blood. The fish in the Nile will die, and the river will stink; the Egyptians will not be able to drink its water.'"

When Moses and Aaron confronted Pharaoh again, it was just as the Lord had told them it would be—Pharaoh again refused to let God's people go. When he did so, Aaron struck the water of the Nile with his staff and it turned to blood—what would be the first of ten plagues that would ravish Egypt.

{ LIVING IT! }

In declaring their independence from earthly power and authority, our Founding Fathers declared their dependence upon Almighty God:

"with firm reliance on the protection of divine Providence." Like the Pilgrims before them, they fully expected God to keep His side of the covenant as they obeyed His Word and followed His Spirit.

They were not disappointed.

For Moses and Aaron, they came before Pharaoh with nothing but God's words to them and proclaimed the independence of Israel. Pharaoh, however, was every bit as stubborn as George III, and in his refusal the river ran red with blood. The American Revolution would see similar blood spilt until, like Pharaoh, George III agreed to let the American colonies go.

Had the American colonies, or even Moses and the Israelites, declared their independence by the strength of their own arms, disaster would have followed. For the Israelites, the work would have gotten harder and harder until the last bit of their wills was broken. For the Americans the great British military of the time could have easily routed the colonists had not several fortuitous military secrets been revealed—all of which led to American victories. Without that hand of providence, several key battles of the revolution would have gone the other way—as would have the war.

While many in America have turned their backs on God in our nation today, America is still strong because of those who have not. Too many make the mistake of looking at events of our time and blaming them on godlessness—and perhaps this is true to a point; however, it is even more important to look at where we stand among nations and realize that we are still a strong nation because of those who still declare their dependence upon God and pray for our nation regularly. Are you among them?

What do you think it really means to depend on God today? For the colonists, their dependence on God did not mean they were without defenses or refused to fight when it was necessary. Today we have the strongest military in the world, but it is important to remember that it means nothing without God on our side. How do we balance in our own lives the need to work to be prepared for the challenges of the future while at the same time trusting in God to lead and guide us? What work is ours, and what do we trust God for?

In your journal, write your own Declaration of Dependence upon God. What truths do you hold to be self-evident? What are your "unalienable rights"? And then what are your responsibilities to God to make sure you live correctly in this dependence? What will be your self-government?

"The Invisible Hand"

No people can be bound to acknowledge and adore the invisible hand which conducts the affairs of men more than the people of the United States. Every step by which they have advanced to the character of an independent nation seems to have been distinguished by some token of providential agency.

PRESIDENT GEORGE WASHINGTON,

INAUGURAL ADDRESS

THE EVACUATION OF LONG ISLAND (AUGUST 1776)

"We are expecting the final attack at any moment. Our men are surrounded and outnumbered almost four to one." Just returning from headquarters to the trenches, Major Benjamin Tallmadge spoke softly to his fellow officers so as not to be overheard by the soldiers around them. "We are low on powder—as always—and the British fleet is even now preparing to sail up the East River to cut off any chance of retreat."

It was August 27, 1776, only six weeks after the Continental Congress had voted to accept the Declaration of Independence, and things were not looking good for the Continental army. To fight would mean defeat. And surrender was out of the question.

"What are we going to do, then?" a lieutenant asked.

"Firmly rely on the protection of Divine Providence," was General George Washington's reply. "God has not brought us this far to desert us." Little did the officers know they were about to see the most amazing episode of divine intervention in the Revolutionary War.

The Americans waited all afternoon—and no attack came. The night passed quietly. They waited all the next day as well. Why had the British not attacked? They clearly outnumbered the Americans. Perhaps they were waiting for the winds to change so their warships could join in the battle.

While General Washington waited, he was inspired with a daring plan. By night, they would secretly evacuate the entire army—eight thousand men—across the East River. It was a desperate move. The East River was a mile wide. And wouldn't the British see them in the moonlight or hear the splashing of their oars—not to mention the sounds that eight thousand men would make, no matter how quiet they tried to be?

Was it a coincidence that just the day before, a regiment of Massachusetts fishermen had come over to reinforce Washington's army? Equally skilled mariners from Salem had also joined them. Together they would gather the necessary rowboats, and then all night long they would make the dangerous two-mile round trip, rowing expertly and soundlessly, back and forth, their boats loaded with men, supplies, cannons, carts, cattle, and horses.

But as the next day dawned, the retreat was far from complete. At least three more hours were needed. Major Tallmadge's unit was among those who remained. They watched—silent but anxious—knowing that without the cover of night they would be exposed to certain discovery and fierce attack.

Major Tallmadge described the scene: "At this time, a very dense fog began to rise out of the ground and off the river, and it seemed to settle in a peculiar manner over both encampments. I recollect this providential occurrence perfectly well, and so very dense was the atmosphere that I could scarcely discern a man at six-yard distance. . . . We tarried until the sun had risen, but the fog remained as dense as ever."

Against all odds, the fog remained until the last boat, with General Washington in it, had left the shore. As the fog lifted, the British were shocked to find the American trenches empty. They ran to the shore and started firing on the last four boats, which were now out of range of their guns. By the time the British were able to move their cannons into position, the Americans had completely escaped.

FOUR LEPERS ROUTE THE ARAMEAN ARMY
(2 Kings 6:24–7:20)

Ben-Hadad, king of Aram, and his army had invaded Israel and were laying siege to the city of Samaria. Being cut off from their fields and supplies from outside, people began to starve within the walls of the city while the Arameans gorged themselves outside, waiting for the city to surrender. It was so bad within the city that a donkey's head sold for eighty shekels of silver, and a quarter of a half pint of doves's dung for five shekels.

When all things seemed at their worst, however, Elisha prophesied: "Hear the word of the Lord. This is what the Lord says: About this time tomorrow, [seven quarts] of flour will sell for a shekel and [thirteen quarts] of barley for a shekel at the gate of Samaria."

The king's guard who heard this thought he was crazy, but God knew what He was saying.

While this was going on, four leprous men outside the city gates came to the realization that if they didn't do something, they would simply starve to death. They said among themselves, "Why stay here until we die? If we say, 'We'll go into the city'—the famine is there, and we will die. And if we stay here, we will die. So let's go over to the camp of the Arameans and surrender. If they spare us, we live; if they kill us, then we die."

So at dusk the four lepers made for the Aramean camp, yet when they arrived, they found it deserted.

As they had walked, God had made their feet walking across the ground toward the camp sound to the Arameans like a huge army and host of chariots. At the sound the Arameans panicked, thinking the king of Israel had hired the Hittites and the Egyptians to attack them. In hope of surviving the great army, they fled, leaving behind all of their provisions, weapons, treasures, and livestock.

After the lepers had eaten whatever they wanted from the camp, they returned to the city to tell the king what they had found. By the very hour he had mentioned, Elisha's prophecy was fulfilled exactly as God had told it to him.

{ LIVING IT! }

Providence is when natural events take on a supernatural quality. Footsteps become the hoofbeats of charioteers. A normal fog lasts unnaturally long and protects men against discovery. God subtly and almost invisibly intervenes, and history is changed forever. Doubters still have room to call it coincidence, but believers know the handiwork of their Father when they see it.

While we can't make miracles happen, we can trust in God and act accordingly. Our part is to have faith—miracles are up to God. Such miracles can also happen in many different forms: it can be a dense, unusual fog or a sudden insight into how to act, or even the revelation of an enemy plan or position. It is our part to be ready to act when God creates such opportunities, and that takes watchfulness and trust in Him.

Have you ever had such providential events—even on a lesser scale—happen to you? Did you see God's handiwork in them or did you just strike it up to coincidence? After reading these stories, do you really think God would leave your future to chance?

What does it mean to be watchful for providence and trust in God fully? What would such a life look like? How do you think men such as George Washington did these things?

What does providence have to do with destiny and God's plans for your life?

No Sacrifice Too Great

The kingdom of heaven is like a merchant seeking
fine pearls, and upon finding one pearl of great
value, he went and sold all that he had
and bought it.

MATTHEW 13:45-46 NASB

ABRAHAM CLARK (1725-1794)

"We have captured your sons!" The British officer's words hung in midair.

Abraham Clark staggered backward at the news. Three British soldiers stood on his front porch; two were armed with muskets. The third man, the officer, paused to let his words sink in, then continued. "Your sons are prisoners of the Crown—locked away in our prison ship, the *Jersey*. They will surely die there, unless you repent of this foolish rebellion against the king." The officer took a rolled-up letter out of his jacket and held it out to the stunned father. "Sign this paper. Admit you were wrong, Mr. Clark, and your sons go free!"

Clark turned his head away to hide his confusion. His sons—captured? Held as prisoners of the Crown? How could this be? They had done no wrong. He was the one who had taken a stand, who had signed the Declaration of Independence. He was the one who had pledged his honor, his property, and his life for the cause of liberty. But not his sons.

"Shoot me!" Clark begged the armed soldiers. "I'm the one you want! Shoot me and let my sons go free. They are so young. Their lives are still before them."

The officer's eyes gleamed. "No. Your sons remain our prisoners until you sign the paper."

Clark's head dropped and his eyes closed.

The British officer thrust the letter in Clark's face. "This rebellion is a lost cause. You backwoods colonists can never stand against the power of the British Empire. Don't be a fool," he sneered. "Your sons' lives—their freedom—is at stake!"

The officer's words cut through Clark's indecision.

He suddenly knew what he must choose. It was for freedom's sake that he had taken this stand for independence, so his sons could live free—free from tyranny and oppression—even, if, in the end, it only meant that they would die free. He refused to sign the letter and nothing further the young officer said had any impact on him.

ABRAHAM AND ISAAC (*Genesis 22:1–14*)

"Father, the fire and wood are here, but where is the lamb for the burnt offering?"

Abraham turned and looked at his son—the son God had promised even though he and his wife had been too old to bear children. Yet here he was. Standing strong and confident, a young man in his late teens. *How can I make him understand*, Abraham thought. Then he said simply, "God himself will provide the lamb for the burnt offering, my son."

When they reached the top of the mountain, they paused to survey the surrounding hills and rugged terrain. As Isaac looked on, Abraham piled rocks into an altar and stacked the wood so it could burn the offering to ashes. Then he turned to his son.

"Come." The boy walked to his father. "Turn around." The boy turned and Abraham bound his wrists together.

"Father, what are you doing?"

"It will be all right, Isaac. It is too hard to explain, but it will be all right. Just trust God."

Abraham steered him onto the wood and laid the boy down. He read the anxiety in his son's eyes but said nothing. *I must be quick.*

Abraham turned to snatch his knife from his side and raise it high over his son. He had not meant to hesitate, but he did, only for an instant, and he saw the sun's gleam off of the knife in his son's wide-open, terrified eyes.

"Abraham! Abraham! . . . Do not lay a hand on the boy."

{ LIVING IT! }

What are you willing to give up for what you believe in? How much will you lay on the line for your God?

Abraham Clark knew the sacrifice the patriarch Abraham had been willing to make in the hope of bringing God's kingdom to earth—could he do anything less for the cause of the liberty for which God had led him to lay his name on the line? Certainly freedom had its costs, and this was the greatest price that could be asked of a parent, but if this was the way God had led him, could he truly risk turning back even if it cost him everything?

His answer, as was the first Abraham's, was clearly, "No!"

And just as the patriarch Abraham had faith in God that, in order to keep His promise to him, God would raise Isaac from the ashes if He had to, so Abraham Clark trusted that the freedom of future generations for whom he had signed that declaration would be worth the possible loss of his family.

Yet like Abraham the patriarch, Abraham Clark also received his sons back from seeming death as all three miraculously survived their imprisonment in the worst of British jails and from harsher treatment than others received because of their father's signature on the Declaration of Independence. His faith in God had not been in vain.

Sometimes it is easy to believe we could give up the big things in life for God if He asked, yet we are fooling ourselves because, in reality, we don't even give up the little things. Are there things you have given up in the last week or month to please God that no one else has seen but you and God? Are there other things, in looking back, that you now wish you had?

Too often we look at the things we don't do and think that by denying ourselves those things, it has been enough to really please God—in other words, "I didn't do drugs, I didn't kill anyone, I didn't have premarital sex, so I am okay with God." Yet God is not looking for do-nothings or couch potatoes, but for those who will go out and risk it all to make His kingdom on earth a reality. For a similar cause, Abraham Clark signed his name on the Declaration and fought to secure freedom for others. What have you done this week to expand God's kingdom in your realm of influence? What will you do next week? Tomorrow? Today?

Deceived

Therefore, get rid of all moral filth and the evil that is so prevalent and humbly accept the word planted in you, which can save you. Do not merely listen to the word, and so deceive yourselves. Do what it says.

JAMES 1:21-22

BENEDICT ARNOLD (1741-1801)

It had all begun with a small affront. In 1775 Benedict Arnold had used his own personal savings and credit to fight in Massachusetts, but the colony refused to reimburse him. This was so unfair that Congress, despite its poverty, voted to pay him eight hundred dollars. However, rather than forgiving and forgetting, Benedict had let the incident fester inside of him. He had been embarrassed and belittled. In his estimation, he deserved better.

Then in 1777 Congress insulted him further by promoting five less-experienced men to the rank of major general, a position he had coveted for some time. He would have resigned if General Washington had not personally begged him to stay. Washington, the only one who believed in him and valued his bravery, immediately demanded an explanation from Congress and emphasized Arnold's extraordinary leadership.

Then, sorrow upon sorrows, Arnold remembered how he had betrayed Washington. He was not able to live on the small salary of a Continental officer, and his debts were piling up. He had diverted food and supplies bound for the starving, dying soldiers at Valley Forge and sold them, keeping the money to cover his personal expenses. At the time it had seemed such a small thing and justified. Later, however, he would see it as just one more step down a slippery slope into self-deception.

Once he had started down that path, Arnold found it became easier and easier to act against his conscience. It was a small step from embezzling American supplies to offering to sell military secrets to the British. As the war continued, he became increasingly convinced that the Americans would not win. So he justified in his own mind and against the righteousness of their cause that whatever he could do to shorten the war would win him favor with history, and if he profited financially from it, what harm would that do? Arnold knew British Major John André from a time when they had both lived in Philadelphia. He approached the British officer—and soon Arnold and his wife were both spying for America's enemy.

Within a short time, however, a plot he had concocted with André to hand West Point over to the British was discovered through a strange and seemingly accidental set of circumstances. Had the British won West Point, American forces would have been divided and the American rebellion would have been squashed. Providence, however, had other plans, and the war eventually went to the Americans instead.

Late in his life, Arnold looked back on his foolish decisions with regret and repentance. His greed, his shame, his personal hurts, and his unforgiveness had led to subtle wrong decisions that amassed over time like snowflakes on a tree limb. Eventually the weight of all his bad decisions finally cracked the plans he had for his future.

JUDAS ISCARIOT (*Matthew 26:14–16, 47–50; 27:1–5*)

Judas sat on his knees before the high priest. Never had a bag of silver weighed more in his hands. The events of the last few days—and the last few years—raced through his mind, and in an instant he saw the pattern. All he had hoped for had been built on the false assumption he had embraced because of his own selfishness and hope for advancement, and now it would lead to the death of the only person who had ever shown him love. It was beyond anything he could live with.

Of all who had walked closest with Jesus, Judas was the most personable and charismatic. His zeal was easily read and people tended to like and trust him almost immediately. He became a follower of Jesus because he had hoped to have a good position in the new government the Messiah would establish once He chased the Romans from Israel and reestablished the throne of God in Jerusalem. But he had miscalculated and never understood that Jesus' earthly kingdom was not for the present moment. First He needed to free the people spiritually, and then His reign would come later, when the time set by the Father in heaven was at hand. Blinded by his hope of power, Judas had wrongly interpreted much of what Jesus spoke.

Judas was so trusted, in fact, that he became the treasurer and guardian of the common purse of Jesus' ministry. Because of this status, Judas felt it necessary to secretly "pay" himself from time to time for his efforts, so he took what he wanted from the money and no one ever suspected him.

Then, when Jesus returned to Jerusalem on Passover, he felt the time was right to force the events of the Messiah's kingship. He would find a time to turn Jesus over to the Jewish leaders quietly so that they could question Him and realize who He was. He felt that before he knew it the revolution would begin and the Romans would be vanquished.

Now, however, he knew he had been wrong. With sudden unmistakable clarity, all of his selfishness and mistakes revealed themselves for what they were. He had deceived himself and fell into the trap of the religious leaders who weren't looking for the kingdom of God but for the security of their own positions in their own "kingdoms of men." He had brought back his reward for turning Jesus over to the high officials—thirty pieces of silver—to try to fix what he had done, but they only scoffed at him for his foolishness.

"I have sinned," he said, "for I have betrayed innocent blood."

"What is that to us?" they replied. "That's your responsibility."

With this, in anger, he rose up and hurled the bag of coins at them with all his might. The bag was so heavy, however, it did not sail far before crashing to the ground and bursting open, the coins scattering everywhere and the room filling with their clattering. When the room at last fell to silence and the priests again looked up, they were alone. Judas fled and found his end at the end of a noose.

{ LIVING IT! }

Hebrews 12:1 tells us that we should "throw off everything that hinders and the sin that so easily entangles, and let us run with perseverance the race marked out for us." In other words, those things that trip us up to make wrong decisions aren't generally big things that are obvious; sometimes they are things like little bits of unforgiveness, hurt, or selfishness that skew our ability to see things truly as they are. We wouldn't be deceived if it were obvious—it's in its subtlety that it catches us, slows us down, or eventually gets us disqualified from the race God has called us to run for Him.

Both Benedict Arnold and Judas were deceived into acting wrongly, yet in their own minds they felt what they were doing was perfectly right and justified—until they saw it from a larger perspective. They had both heard the truth and the word over and over again; however, they both failed because they never lived it but merely gave lip service to it until it was too late.

Take time to think through your life right now. Are there words of Scripture you know but have never acted upon? If so, now is the time to make those things right and do them, rather than falling into being a hypocrite—a person who acts like a Christian but never really does the things that Christ asks them to in His Word.

Ask God to reveal to you any areas of your life where you don't see things as He does. Then take the time to read His Word today so that you can start looking for the things to do to keep you in the race He has called you to run.

Just as a marathon runner would not put on a backpack of rocks before he or she started a race, we need to be sure we are free from things that would slow us down in our race for Jesus. Take time to pray today that the burdens and guilt of past mistakes are washed out of your life and mind, and then once you have received God's forgiveness for them, never pick them up again! Today is your day for a clean start! Pledge to run your race without the hindrances and condemnation that will slow you down or keep you from God's best!

{ John Adams }

A Man of Inflexible Integrity

Suppose a nation in some distant region should take the Bible for their only law book, and every member should regulate his conduct by the precepts there exhibited! Every member would be obliged in conscience, to temperance, frugality, and industry; to justice, kindness, and charity towards his fellow men; and to piety, love, and reverence toward Almighty God.... What a Utopia, what a Paradise would this region be.

JOHN ADAMS

JOHN ADAMS (1735–1826)

John Adams was known for his shrewd judgment of character and was one of the most persuasive members of Congress, exerting decisive leadership and often turning the tide of public opinion. For example, on July 1, 1776, when Congress entered what John called "the greatest debate of all," John Dickinson, a delegate from Pennsylvania, spoke long and eloquently against independence. When he finally finished, there was a lengthy silence. John Adams waited and waited for someone to speak up for independence. But when no one else did, he rose and gave a powerful speech that touched every heart in the room.

Before God, I believe the hour has come. My judgment approves this measure, and my whole heart is in it. All that I have, and all that I am, and all that I hope in this life, I am now ready here to stake upon it. And I leave off as I began, that live or die, survive or perish, I am for the Declaration. It is my living sentiment, and by the blessing of God it shall be my dying sentiment, Independence now, and Independence for ever!

But in 1777 John Adams retired from Congress, feeling it was time to step down from public life. He wrote, "I see my brothers, as lawyers, easily making fortunes for themselves and their families. . . . I see my own children growing up in something very like real want, because I have taken no care of them." He was home to stay.

Then came a packet of letters from Congress naming Adams as a commissioner to France, to work with Benjamin Franklin and Arthur Lee. One of the letters noted the extreme importance of the negotiations with France, expressed concern over Franklin's age, and stated, "We want one man of inflexible integrity on the embassy."

The packet arrived in mid-December, about the time General George Washington was moving his army to Valley Forge. John Adams was out of town on law business. Abigail opened the package, thinking it was urgent. She was stunned as she read it and asked herself, "How could these congressmen contrive to rob me of all my happiness?"

She immediately wrote in a letter:

> And can I, sir, consent to be separated from him whom my heart esteems above all earthly things, and for an unlimited time? My life will be one continued scene of anxiety and apprehension, and must I cheerfully comply with the demand of my country?

When John returned home, he and Abigail sat down to seek God's guidance, knowing it would be a turning point in their lives. They rose from prayer with a decision: This was God's will. John would accept this "momentous trust"—he would go to France.

Abigail wanted to go with him, despite her fear of sailing. But the risk of her, a woman, being captured by the enemy, the expense of setting up a household in Paris, and the need for someone to run things at home caused John to decide against it. Ten-year-old John Quincy Adams also wanted to go—and his parents agreed. It was the chance of a lifetime "for acquiring useful knowledge and virtue, such as will render you . . . an honor to your country, and a blessing to your parents."

The trip afforded time for John Adams to wonder about *why* he was going to France. He felt ill suited for the position. He knew nothing of European politics or diplomacy, he could not speak French, and he had never even seen a king or queen. All he had to offer was courage, a passion for freedom and the American cause, and a sensitivity to the will and timing of God.

His friend Benjamin Rush had assured him, "Your abilities and firmness are much needed at the Court of France, and though dressing fashionably, powdering one's hair, and bowing well may be seen by some as necessary accomplishments for an ambassador, I maintain that knowledge and integrity with prudence are of far more importance."

The American diplomatic mission was a great success. While John Adams was in Paris, the French declared war on Great Britain. Historians agree that America had little chance of winning the war without France's help, as France was *the* major source of military supplies to Washington's army. They also provided us with trained soldiers and a fleet of warships.

The Calling of Isaiah (*Isaiah 6:1–8* CEV)

Isaiah gives the following account of how God called him to be a prophet to the people of Israel:

> In the year that King Uzziah died, I had a vision of the Lord. He was on his throne high above, and his robe filled the temple. Flaming creatures with six wings each were flying over him. They covered their faces with two of their wings and their bodies with two more. They used the other two wings for flying, as they shouted,
>
> "Holy, holy, holy, Lord All-Powerful! The earth is filled with your glory."
>
> As they shouted, the doorposts of the temple shook, and the temple was filled with smoke. Then I cried out, "I'm doomed! Everything I say is sinful, and so are the words of everyone around me. Yet I have seen the King, the Lord All-Powerful."
>
> One of the flaming creatures flew over to me with a burning coal that it had taken from the altar with a pair of metal tongs. It touched my lips with the hot coal and said, "This has touched your lips. Your sins are forgiven, and you are no longer guilty."
>
> After this, I heard the Lord ask, "Is there anyone I can send? Will someone go for us?"
>
> "I'll go," I answered. "Send me!"

{ Living It! }

John Adams had an overriding sense of duty and a need to serve, and he was passionate about America. He did the right thing, even when it made him unpopular. He took a long, historical view of the decisions that faced the young nation. He is famous for saying things like "Think of your forefathers! Think of your posterity," and "I must study politics and war that my sons may have liberty to study mathematics and philosophy." A patriot's patriot, John Adams had the humble heart of a servant, saying, "If we do not lay out ourselves in the service of mankind, whom should we serve?"

When God called him, Isaiah felt he was unworthy to speak God's words; however, when he "asked" God about it, God made up the difference so Isaiah could obey. When it came down to it and He saw the need, his answer was very similar to John Adams' response: "I'll go! Send me!"

We need to be willing to make the same response when duty calls us.

Ask not what your country can do for you; ask what you can do for your country.
—John F. Kennedy

The Bible tells us "Real religion, the kind that passes muster before God the Father, is this: Reach out to the homeless and loveless in their plight, and guard against corruption from the godless world" (James 1:27 THE MESSAGE). This speaks of a duty all of us have. Do you give to organizations that help orphans and the needy? What opportunities are there in your area to volunteer to make a difference in the lives of others?

Citizens of a nation have many duties that keep their freedoms—one example is that we keep the laws of the land. Another is that we vote. Are there other areas in which you can serve your country from where you are now? What are they? Do you feel God calling you to do more? What exactly?

A Prayer Upon Which
to Build a Nation

Your kingdom come.
You will be done,
On earth as it is in heaven.

MATTHEW 6:10 NASB

GEORGE WASHINGTON (1732–1799)

In a letter to the governors of the thirteen states, upon the close of
the Revolutionary War on June 14, 1783, George Washington offered the
following benediction:

> I now make it my earnest prayer that God would have you, and
> the State over which you preside, in his holy protection; that he would
> incline the hearts of the citizens to cultivate a spirit of subordination
> and obedience to government, to entertain a brotherly affection and
> love for one another . . . and finally that he would most graciously
> be pleased to dispose us all to do justice, to love mercy, and to demean
> ourselves with that charity, humility, and pacific temper of mind,
> which were the characteristics of the Divine Author of our blessed
> religion, and without an humble imitation of whose example in these
> things, we can never hope to be a happy nation.

WHAT PAUL TAUGHT ABOUT PRAYER
(*1 Timothy 2:1–4, 8*)

When Paul taught Timothy about prayer, he told him:

> I urge, then, first of all, that requests, prayers, intercession and
> thanksgiving be made for everyone—for kings and all those in author-
> ity, that we may live peaceful and quiet lives in all godliness and holi-
> ness. This is good, and pleases God our Savior, who wants all men to

be saved and to come to a knowledge of the truth. . . . I want men everywhere to lift up holy hands in prayer, without anger or disputing.

{ LIVING IT! }

Prayer changes things. Are you part of the praying church that is making change in our nation today?

In his prayer for the colonies, General Washington asked for some very specific and interesting things:

(1) "That God would have you, and the State over which you preside, in his holy protection . . ." There is perhaps no one in American history that understood the protective power of trusting in God better than "bulletproof" Washington, who was in countless battles without suffering any wounds. His prayer here is that they would never forget upon whom they truly relied or where their only sure protection came from.

(2) "That he would incline the hearts of the citizens to cultivate a spirit of subordination and obedience to government . . ." With revolution having just rocked the land, it would be difficult for the colonists to willingly put on the yoke of a new government, having just fought so valiantly and long to throw off the yoke of the old. Yet as always, it was not just freedom that was needed but unity as well, for no colonist could stand without the strengths and protection of others. The transitional period to a new government would be a critically important and difficult time. Washington's prayer was that it would go as smoothly as possible.

(3) "That he would incline the hearts of the citizens . . . to entertain a brotherly affection and love for one another . . ." Not only would citizens of the new union need to accept the dictates of government, but now more than ever neighbor would need to depend on neighbor to build and prosper. As love is the guiding principle of the kingdom of God, Washington prayed it would also be the guiding principle of the United States.

(4) "That he would most graciously be pleased to dispose us all to do justice [and] to love mercy . . ." Justice and fairness form the foundation of any organization that hopes to survive. Even a school club that does not treat its members with equality and fairness will soon crumple because no one trusts it or wants to be part of it. While justice is crucial,

however, it can also be doled out heavily and have an equally destructive effect. For that reason, justice must be balanced with mercy; only then can government and community prosper.

(5) "That he would most graciously be pleased to dispose us all . . .

a. "to demean ourselves with that charity . . ." Washington prays for charity—that we would be giving to others and willing to volunteer to lend a helping hand when needed.
b. "humility . . ." He also prays we would be humble—living in the place God has put us, respecting authority in its proper order with God first, and "not thinking more of ourselves than we ought."
c. "and pacific temper of mind . . ." Finally, he prays that we live with a temperament aimed at living peacefully with all around us.

These are exemplified by Christ himself—"which were the characteristics of the Divine Author of our blessed religion, and without an humble imitation of whose example in these things, we can never hope to be a happy nation."

Washington's prayer was full of hope, but also full of the realism and wisdom that had made him a great leader throughout the war. He balanced trust in God that all would work together for the good with the knowledge of the virtues of American citizens that would be necessary to make the new nation succeed.

Such prayers are needed as much today as they were then, and the instructions of Paul to pray for our leaders so "that we may live peaceful and quiet lives in all godliness and holiness" applies equally to all periods of history. Take the time to pray for them today.

★　　　★　　　★

What "virtues"—such as those things George Washington prayed for— do you feel are important to our nation and citizens today? Use them as part of your prayers for leadership and others you feel you should pray for.

Make a list of your local government leaders, law officials, judges, area representatives to your state congress, members of the United States Congress, our president, and any others you can think of, and carry it in your Bible or journal so that you can pray over it regularly.

"Sober and Frugal Virtues"

Getting wisdom is the most important thing you can do! And whatever else you do, get good judgment. If you prize wisdom, she will exalt you. Embrace her and she will honor you.

PROVERBS 4:7–8 NLT

Education

BENJAMIN RUSH (1743–1813)

As a patriot, Dr. Rush was a signer of the Declaration of Independence. Many of the delegates were disappointed with the number of compromises that had been made in writing the Constitution. But Dr. Rush saw the solid structure that had been achieved: the genius behind the system of checks and balances between the legislative, executive, and judicial branches; the creativity of having two bodies of Congress—the Senate with two votes per state and the House with votes based on population. He pronounced it "a masterpiece of human wisdom."

As a physician, Dr. Rush has been called the most eminent American physician of his generation. He served as physician-general of the Continental army. He also heroically attacked a deadly yellow fever epidemic in Philadelphia in 1793 that claimed over four thousand lives in one hundred days. By studying old manuscripts, he rediscovered a cure that saved the lives of six thousand.

He was also the medical advisor/trainer to Meriwether Lewis before Lewis and William Clark embarked on their quest to explore the Northwest Territories. Dr. Rush spent two weeks training Lewis for medical emergencies that he might encounter on the expedition.

As an educator, Dr. Rush served as professor of medicine at the University of Pennsylvania. He helped establish five universities and colleges. In 1791 he founded the First Day Society, an early form of today's

Sunday schools. He also helped start America's first Bible society.

Known as the Father of Public Schools, he called for free public education supported by a property tax. He wrote a pamphlet giving twelve reasons why the Bible needed to be the central textbook in schools. In his concluding remarks, he states, "I lament that we waste so much time and money in punishing crimes and take so little pains to prevent them. . . . We neglect the only means of establishing and perpetuating our republican forms of government; that is, the universal education of our youth in the principles of Christianity by means of the Bible . . . equality among mankind . . . respect for just laws . . . and sober and frugal virtues."

As an abolitionist, Dr. Rush was one of the black community's strongest white allies. He worked alongside Anthony Benezet to organize the Pennsylvania Society for Promoting the Abolition of Slavery and later served as its president. He also wrote a scathing pamphlet exposing the evils of the entire institution of slavery.

In 1787 Dr. Rush had a dream in which he was on a beach with a group of Africans who had been relating stories about the horrors of slavery, when the ghost of Benezet (who had died in 1784) came walking down the beach to meet with them. Rush awoke determined to continue Benezet's work and dedicated himself afresh to the cause of his "black brethren." Though still a slave owner himself, he promised freedom to his slave, William Grubber.

Rush was heavily involved in promoting the African Methodist Episcopal (AME) Church in Philadelphia. Richard Allen, founder and first bishop of the AME Church, acknowledged his great debt to Dr. Rush in his memoirs: "[He] espoused the cause of the oppressed and aided us in building the house of the Lord for the poor Africans to worship in."

When Benjamin Rush died in 1813, Thomas Jefferson wrote to John Adams: "Another of our friends of [1776] is gone, my dear Sir. . . . And a better man than Rush could not have left us, more benevolent, more learned, of finer genius, or more honest." Adams wrote in reply, "I know of no character living or dead, who has done more real good in America."

SOLOMON PRAYS FOR WISDOM (*1 Kings 3:5–14* CEV)

While Solomon was in Gibeon, the Lord appeared to him in a dream and said, "Solomon, ask for anything you want, and I will give it to you."

Solomon answered,

> My father David, your servant, was honest and did what you commanded. You were always loyal to him, and you gave him a son who is now king. Lord God, I'm your servant, and you've made me king in my father's place. But I'm very young and know so little about being a leader. And now I must rule your chosen people, even though there are too many of them to count.
>
> Please make me wise and teach me the difference between right and wrong. Then I will know how to rule your people. If you don't, there is no way I could rule this great nation of yours.

God was so pleased with his answer that He told Solomon,

> Solomon, I'm pleased that you asked for this. You could have asked to live a long time or to be rich. Or you could have asked for your enemies to be destroyed. Instead, you asked for wisdom to make right decisions. So I'll make you wiser than anyone who has ever lived or ever will live.
>
> I'll also give you what you didn't ask for. You'll be rich and respected as long as you live, and you'll be greater than any other king. If you obey me and follow my commands, as your father David did, I'll let you live a long time.

{ LIVING IT! }

Dr. Benjamin Rush was a man who profoundly respected and honored God, putting Him first in everything he did. Though well known and greatly respected, he never separated himself from the cause of the common man. Throughout his life, he diligently served others—as a patriot, a physician, an educator, and an abolitionist. May his name never be forgotten among us. When he could have had many different things in life, he instead chose to seek wisdom so he could serve others, just as Solomon had.

Wisdom and knowledge are just as important for us today. While many look down on schooling and education, as Christians we should instead love it and squeeze as much knowledge as we can out of our teachers. We should be just as able to defend what we believe in our science, history, English, math, and other classes as we do in our Sunday school classes. We need to look at these subjects and all of life through God's perspective. The world tries to take God out of education. When that happens, education becomes a hollow, empty shell. Education is not for getting a good job and making money. It is so that the world may grasp a glimpse of the awesome magnificence of God through a deeper understanding. Wisdom, knowledge, and understanding come from God. The more we seek Him and get to know Him and His creation, the greater He will be glorified.

What is school like for you? Are you anxious to learn, or are you one of those just trying to get through? Do you look at learning as a way to understand more about God? Which attitude honors God more? How will you live that attitude?

Far too many people think that science and religion oppose one another, but the truth is that most of the greatest scientists and inventors the world has seen were first great Christians. Take the time to pray for those you know are trying to worship science as if it were God, that God would show them the truth through His light. What does God tell you about how you should relate to them? After you've prayed for them for a while, what differences do you now see in them? How about in yourself?

Education

First Things First

The first thing I want you to do is pray. Pray every way you know how, for everyone you know. Pray especially for rulers and their governments to rule well so we can be quietly about our business of living simply, in humble contemplation.

1 TIMOTHY 2:1–2 THE MESSAGE

BENJAMIN FRANKLIN (1706–1790)

It was hot and humid in Philadelphia in the summer of 1787. At General Washington's personal, urgent appeal, delegates from all thirteen colonies had come to Philadelphia to "form a more perfect union." Instead, they were discovering their differences—and tempers flared. Just as they were about to adjourn in confusion, Benjamin Franklin stood to address General Washington and the assembly:

> How has it happened, Sir, that we have not hitherto once thought of humbly applying to the Father of lights to illuminate our understandings? In the beginning of the contest with Great Britain, when we were sensible of danger we had daily prayer in this room for the Divine protection.
>
> Our prayers, Sir, were heard, and they were graciously answered. All of us who were engaged in the struggle must have observed frequent instances of a Superintending Providence in our favor. . . . And have we now forgotten that powerful Friend? Or do we imagine we no longer need His assistance?
>
> I have lived, Sir, a long time, and the longer I live, the more convincing proofs I see of this truth—that God governs in the affairs of men. And if a sparrow cannot fall to the ground without His notice, is it probable that an empire can rise without His aid? We have been assured, Sir, in the Sacred Writings, that "except the Lord build the house they labor in vain that build it." I firmly believe this. I also believe that without His concurring aid we shall succeed in this

political building no better than the builders of Babel; we shall be divided by our little partial local interests; our projects will be confounded, and we ourselves shall become a reproach and byword down to future ages. And what is worse, mankind may hereafter from this unfortunate instance, despair of establishing governments by human wisdom and leave it to chance, war and conquest.

I therefore beg leave to move that henceforth prayers imploring the assistance of Heaven and its blessings on our deliberations be held in this Assembly every morning before we proceed to business.

Franklin's proposal was never adopted in the proceedings of the Constitutional Convention. But when the first Constitutional Congress convened in April of 1789, they implemented Franklin's recommendation. Two chaplains of different denominations were appointed, one to the House and one to the Senate, with a salary of five hundred dollars each. This practice continues today with prayer offered at the beginning of each daily meeting when Congress is in session.

JESUS, PAUL, AND PRAYER

From time to time throughout the Gospels the writers tell of times when the disciples could not find Jesus because He had withdrawn himself aside to pray. Or we get short verses such as John 8:1: "But Jesus went to the Mount of Olives" (NASB). While everyone else was busy with life, He needed time to pull aside and get with His Father.

Paul was also a man known for his prayers. In fact, in most of his letters, he didn't take time to stop, lay down his pen, and pray, but just wrote his prayers right into his letters. These are some of the most powerful prayers ever recorded: Ephesians 1:17–23; 3:14–21; Philippians 1:9–11; and Colossians 1:9–12 are four of the most well known. In these he prayed that those he was writing for would know the reason God had called them and that they would stay faithful until the day they had accomplished that calling.

It was also Paul who wrote: "Pray without ceasing" (1 Thessalonians 5:17 KJV) and "Continue earnestly in prayer, being vigilant in it with thanksgiving" (Colossians 4:2 NKJV). By this he seemed to mean that there was never a time when we shouldn't be able to pray or be in communication with God—even if it were to throw up brief prayers just mentioning individuals or concerns that come on us throughout the day. His model seemed to be that if we had any concerns at all, we should pray and leave them with God. In fact, in Philippians 4:6–7 he said,

"Instead of worrying, pray. Let petitions and praises shape your worries into prayers, letting God know your concerns. Before you know it, a sense of God's wholeness, everything coming together for good, will come and settle you down. It's wonderful what happens when Christ displaces worry at the center of your life" (THE MESSAGE).

{ LIVING IT! }

If Jesus and Paul needed to have time in prayer, how much more do we?

If the Founding Fathers of our nation knew that creating the union of the original colonies into the United States was impossible without first dedicating the cause to prayer, how much more do we need to pray in the complex times we live in?

Prayer can be a difficult thing to get into, however. Often when we pray, we don't feel the presence of God; we just feel alone. It can seem like a meaningless waste of time. But the Bible promises us that it isn't. In fact, 1 John 5:14–15 says, "This is the confidence we have in approaching God: that if we ask anything according to his will, he hears us. And if we know that he hears us—whatever we ask—we know that we have what we asked of him." How do we know His will? Well, we have His Word on it. If it is a promise in the Bible, then we have a right to pray that Scripture to Him and expect that He will honor it.

It is through prayer that anxiety is traded for peace, shyness is traded for boldness, uncertainty is traded for confidence, and that which is meant for evil is traded in for God's good!

Take time to start your day with prayer and see what a difference it makes. And it will make a difference—you have His Word on it!

If you are still having trouble praying, get with some friends and pray once a week, or gather somewhere at school at the beginning of the day or some other neutral place to pray together every day if you dare. Sometimes praying with others can be a great way to get into it.

Do you think prayer is important? Why? How do you make it a part of your life, or do you at all?

In your Bible reading times, look for promises you can pray for yourself or for others. If you are having particular problems or concerns, ask God to give you a Scripture to pray. Then write down what happens or log onto *www.undergodthebook.com* and share your testimony.

Thinking Outside of the Box

"My thoughts are completely different from yours,"
says the Lord. "And my ways are far beyond
anything you could imagine. For just as the heavens
are higher than the earth, so are my ways higher
than your ways and my thoughts higher
than your thoughts."

ISAIAH 55:8–9 NLT

ROGER SHERMAN (1721–1793)

It was summer in Philadelphia, June 11, 1787, and the heat made it almost impossible to think, let alone be reasonable and accommodating to debate. Yet hour after hour, Roger Sherman and his Constitutional Convention colleagues toiled away, charting the course of freedom in a document that would govern the nation.

Of any in the room, Sherman truly could claim to have seen it all. He'd played a part in the creation of all four major founding documents the country had yet seen—the Articles of Association in 1774, the Declaration of Independence in 1776, the Articles of Confederation two years later in 1778, and now this, the Constitution. He had watched these great men whom he considered brothers go gray under their powdered wigs.

Sherman himself did not stand on such ceremony. A cobbler by birth and without much in the way of education as a young man, he nevertheless had worked diligently at bettering himself and eventually earned an honorary degree at Yale University, even serving as the school's treasurer. His common background, though, showed in his speech, his dress, and even the clipped style in which he kept his hair. Now, however, was one of those times he wished for a wig, if only to pull it over his eyes. He couldn't stand any more of the bickering.

It all came down to voice. Whose voice would stand out strongest in Congress? Delegates from Pennsylvania, Massachusetts, and Virginia argued that since their states contained the lion's share of the people, shouldered the lion's share of the tax burden, and would carry the weight of the new republic on the backs of their cities and citizens, they should have the most say.

"Representatives based on population," one began, in yet another redundant summary.

He was quickly followed by Delaware's representative, who pointed out that the lion's share of struggle and sacrifice was technically born equally per capita. They paid less as a whole, but the individual obligation of their citizens was no different than in any other state. Why should their people be punished for living on one side of an imaginary line? "We've always stood as equals before," he said. "We'll stand as equals always!"

Sherman could take it no longer.

"Gentlemen," he addressed his colleagues, and they all quieted. Sherman hadn't yet spoken during this debate—unusual, as he was one of the Convention's most loquacious delegates, and from New Hampshire to Georgia his peers respected his commonsense approach to difficult impasses. "Gentlemen, my fellow statesmen from Pennsylvania and Virginia are correct."

The room fell silent. By siding with the large states, he'd effectively taken equal voice away from his own people. But he wasn't finished.

"Gentlemen, my fellow statesmen from Delaware and Rhode Island are correct too. Every point each makes is undeniably true. And therefore we must heed them all."

What followed was the proposal of a bicameral system by which Congress would consist of two halves: the Senate, which put all states on equal footing, and the House of Representatives, which gave states with larger populations greater representation. In the end, a system nearly exactly as he proposed made it into the final draft of the U.S. Constitution, and we continue to see the results of his thinking today.

It is most fitting that this man, with God-given talents to serve as a politician in the truest sense—as a wise representative of his people's common good—was the only man to sign all four founding documents of America's birth. Called to serve his faith and his country, he did both beyond reproach. A true patriot, a true Christian, Roger Sherman is a powerful example of a man of God doing great, and often unseen, things for this country.

It was just like being between the proverbial "rock and a hard place"; however, there was even less room to maneuver. Between a rock and a hard place, you can stay were you are and be safe, but where the Israelites were at the moment would only be safe for a little bit longer.

In their flight from slavery in Egypt, Moses had led them right up to the shores of the Red Sea. There was no going forward. And now Pharaoh's army, chariots, and foot soldiers, were pounding down upon the Israelites from the other direction. They could see the clouds of dust rise high into the sky as the great force descended toward them like a horde of locusts. There was no going back; there was no going forward.

The people cried out to Moses in anger, "Was it because there were no graves in Egypt that you brought us to the desert to die? What have you done to us by bringing us out of Egypt? Didn't we say to you in Egypt, 'Leave us alone; let us serve the Egyptians'? It would have been better for us to serve the Egyptians than to die in the desert!"

But what they saw was not what Moses saw. Where they saw no way out, Moses knew God would make a way if they called upon Him. He called back to them, "Do not be afraid. Stand firm and you will see the deliverance the Lord will bring you today. The Egyptians you see today you will never see again. The Lord will fight for you; you need only to be still."

Then Moses turned to God in prayer and God answered him, "Why are you crying out to me? Tell the Israelites to move on. Raise your staff and stretch out your hand over the sea to divide the water so that the Israelites can go through the sea on dry ground. I will harden the hearts of the Egyptians so that they will go in after them. And I will gain glory through Pharaoh and all his army, through his chariots and his horsemen. The Egyptians will know that I am the Lord when I gain glory through Pharaoh, his chariots and his horsemen."

And with that, Moses turned and raised his staff to the waters of the Red Sea. What others had previously seen only as a roadblock, God made a route to safety and victory.

{ LIVING IT! }

Roger Sherman's voice was heard not only on political matters but on religious topics as well. Sherman took the same insightful, straightforward, commonsense approach to faith as he did to politics. A member of the White Haven Church pastored by Jonathan Edwards Jr., son of the famed Puritan theologian, Sherman once penned a creed in his own words, spelling out the core beliefs he held so dear. So eloquent were his words that White Haven adopted the creed as its own. At Sherman's death, Rev. Edwards gave the eulogy, reaffirming what all who knew him understood: Roger Sherman had lived God's calling in his life.

Sherman was a man like Moses—when push came to shove and no one else could see a way forward, he turned to God in his own mind and found God had already provided the answer.

★　★　★

Are we willing to live like that today? When you face an impasse (a place for which it seems there is no way forward), what do you do? Do you quit, do you just live with it, or do you look for a creative new answer? When faced with A and B as the only alternatives, we need to realize that sometimes the answer is still C, or maybe even something farther out like M. God is in the creative answer, not just settling for the "lesser of two evils." How do you plug in to God for His better and higher way?

Do you run away from responsibilities because you don't like to make decisions? Being a Christian, Roger Sherman saw it as his obligation to serve and let Christ inside of him make a difference for his nation. What do you do with the responsibility of knowing Jesus? What are you doing with His wisdom in your life? Are you bottling it up and sitting on it like the foolish steward, or are you multiplying it and spreading it around so that all around you benefit from it?

Ingenuity

A Heritage of Fighting
for Freedom

I have a dream that one day this nation will rise up
and live out the true meaning of its creed: "We hold
these truths to be self-evident: that all men are
created equal." . . . I have a dream that my four
children will one day live in a nation where they
will not be judged by the color of their skin
but by the content of their character.

MARTIN LUTHER KING JR.

JOHN JAY (1745–1829)

Elected to the First Continental Congress in 1774, John Jay would later become the group's fifth president. He was one of three Americans who negotiated the Treaty of Paris that helped end the American Revolution, and later, when he was Secretary of Foreign Affairs (1784–1789), his Jay Treaty helped avoid a second war between England and the United States. During this crucial period of American history, Jay played other important roles. Together with Alexander Hamilton and James Madison, Jay helped pen the *Federalist Papers*, a series of passionate and reasoned letters defending the Constitution that were published in newspapers and helped to turn public opinion toward this powerful document.

Later he would serve as First Chief Justice of the United States Supreme Court (1789–1795), and he even spent two terms as governor of New York. Trusted by many to fill crucial positions during our nation's founding, Jay was known as a man of honor and his word. He was a man of God's Word too, as he'd also been the president of the American Bible Society. And nowhere in God's Word could he find any defense for upholding the practice of slavery. Yet still it remained, a lawful policy of the land. For the time. John's own opinion of the matter was stated most concisely: "We have the highest reason to believe that the Almighty will not suffer slavery and the gospel to go hand in hand. It cannot—it will not be."

Yet he still regretted not pushing harder during the framing of the Constitution to formally declare an end to the hateful institution. His antislavery group, the New York State Society for Promoting the Manumission of Slaves, had been prepared to petition the Constitutional Convention, but when colleagues as sympathetic as Benjamin Franklin—who presided over the Pennsylvania Antislavery Society—warned that such a move would jeopardize the group's brittle unity, Jay held his sharp pen and the Constitution moved forward with slavery still intact.

The Jay family story told that they knew what persecution was and the value of freedom—his ancestors were Huguenots who'd settled in La Rochelle, France. Henry IV's Edict of Toleration still held the land, and despite their Catholic neighbors, they practiced their religion in freedom, in quiet peace. But then came Louis XIV, whose wife insisted that the heretics living in her country be punished. In 1685 the Edict crumbled.

Pierre Jay, John's great-grandfather, helped his family escape but had himself been imprisoned. He finally just made it out of the country alive. Auguste Jay, John's grandfather, had escaped from a prison fortress one stormy evening. Once, men with the same blood as his had nearly died because of their faith and had found freedom only on American shores. God had led them here. Not that it was a blessed land, but rather a chance for a new beginning—a chance for man to worship God without shackles. John hoped this would be the legacy he left as well.

Near the end of his life, John Jay might have expected that turning the tide of slavery would come swiftly, although he would never see it. Certainly the legacy he left would never stop fighting for freedom for all until it was realized.

LOIS, EUNICE, AND TIMOTHY (*2 Timothy 1:3–12* NKJV)

When Paul wrote his second letter to Timothy from prison in Rome, He opened it by reminding Timothy of the heritage of faith he had through his mother and his grandmother:

> I thank God, whom I serve with a pure conscience, as my forefathers did, as without ceasing I remember you in my prayers night

and day, greatly desiring to see you, being mindful of your tears, that I may be filled with joy, when I call to remembrance the genuine faith that is in you, which dwelt first in your grandmother Lois and your mother Eunice, and I am persuaded is in you also. Therefore I remind you to stir up the gift of God which is in you through the laying on of my hands. For God has not given us a spirit of fear, but of power and of love and of a sound mind.

Therefore do not be ashamed of the testimony of our Lord, nor of me His prisoner, but share with me in the sufferings for the gospel according to the power of God, who has saved us and called us with a holy calling, not according to our works, but according to His own purpose and grace which was given to us in Christ Jesus before time began, but has now been revealed by the appearing of our Savior Jesus Christ, who has abolished death and brought life and immortality to light through the gospel, to which I was appointed a preacher, an apostle, and a teacher of the Gentiles. For this reason I also suffer these things; nevertheless I am not ashamed, for I know whom I have believed and am persuaded that He is able to keep what I have committed to Him until that Day.

{ L I V I N G   I T ! }

Revolution doesn't always come in the flash of a musket as it did at Lexington and Concord. Sometimes it can take generations. But if the legacy is strong and the cause is of God, who could stand against such a turning of the tide?

For Timothy his godly heritage was a source of inspiration to greater things. For John Jay's son, William, it became the foundation upon which he rose up to become one of the greatest minds and voices in America's abolitionist movement in the 1800s. Both would be part of something that took generations to accomplish, but because of their faithfulness to their causes, William would be a major contributor to seeing slavery abolished before the end of his century, and Timothy would see one of the strongest churches of the first century grow in Ephesus under his leadership.

We are not in the fight for truth and right alone—and not only are we in it with many others around the world, we are also in it with believers from all of the other generations before us—and that will follow. Hebrews 12:1 tells of the "great cloud of witnesses" who have gone on before us—leaving us a legacy of enduring hardships and persevering

through the worst of circumstances to do what God called them to do—
and are now watching us to see how we carry on the race they began.
Like the heritage John Jay left his son, we need to keep in mind that
there is a great deal to learn from those who went before us, and that
many of the freedoms we have today they never saw, though they
fought for them their entire lives.

In your own family, do you have a heritage of faith or fighting for
what is right that you carry on? How about in your church or community? What historical struggles do you feel part of? How are you carrying
on for what others have done before you?

What have you learned about heritage from reading the stories in
this book so far? How have they impacted your attitudes about who you
would like to be?

What do you feel still needs to be done for freedom in your community or state? How will you be part of that effort? What heritage will you
leave to those who follow behind you?

"Lord, How Do I Lift My People?"

Whoever wants to be the most important must be last of all and servant of all.

MARK 9:35 NCV

RICHARD ALLEN (1760–1831)

"It is one thing to be free from slavery. It is another thing to find your place in society," Richard Allen observed, looking at the growing number of freed African-Americans in Philadelphia after America had finally won her independence from the British. "These people are like sheep without a shepherd."

His friend Absalom Jones agreed: "The slave system has kept them ignorant. But look what God is doing! The Methodists are taking the gospel to the slaves on the plantations."

Richard knew there were various levels of freedom. It was one thing not to be another man's property, but it was quite another to be one's own boss and working as an important part of the community. This latter part, whether the person was a slave or not, was the real freedom he had found in Christ. Considering this, Richard added, "I remember how God's love transformed me as I learned His commandments and His ways. Forgiveness, diligence, honesty all became part of my life."

"God's power transformed my life," Absalom again agreed.

Considering all of this, Richard said decisively, "That is the key to lifting our people. It is done one heart at a time."

With this resolve, for the rest of his life, Richard Allen worked for the freedom of his people on all levels, starting with the most important first, their spiritual freedom. His constant prayer was, "Lord, how do I lift my people?" Richard knew true freedom, because he knew his true Master. Throughout his entire life he worked for no man but Jesus.

Before the American Revolution, Richard had been a slave, but his master gave him the opportunity to work for others to earn money to buy his own freedom. For years he struggled doing whatever work he could find to earn the two thousand continental dollars it would cost to buy his freedom—a tough thing to do in a time when such work was scarce and low paying. However, as Richard never shied away from hard work, his diligence began to pay off.

While Richard worked, he also had the opportunity to travel, delivering salt by wagon. Along the way, he would stop and preach the gospel to any who would hear him. Over the years be became a powerful speaker who God used time and again to bless his hearers, both black and white alike. For six years he worked and traveled, until he finally bought his freedom and could throw all his energies into building God's kingdom!

Around 1785, Richard was asked to preach regularly to the black congregation at Saint George's Methodist Church in Philadelphia. But when St. George's decided to start segregating blacks from whites in 1787, Richard and the other black leaders walked out with every African-American member of the congregation. In a few short years they built their own church, Bethel Methodist Church, which grew to 1,272 members by 1813.

From the start Allen recognized the importance of education to the future of the African-American community. In 1795 he opened a day school for sixty children and in 1804 founded the "Society of Free People of Colour for Promoting the Instruction and School Education of Children of African Descent." By 1811 there were no fewer than eleven black schools in the city.

By 1816 Allen realized that to fully meet the needs of his people and lift them up to the place where God wanted them to be, he would need to break with the white establishment and start a new denomination. Representatives from four other black Methodist congregations met with Bethel to organize the African Methodist Episcopal Church, the first fully independent black denomination in America. Allen was named the first bishop.

At the core of Allen's beliefs was his trust that as the lives of church members were transformed by God, they would forge a new identity for their people and would lift the prospects for all blacks. Throughout his life, Richard exhorted all freed blacks to help their enslaved brethren by being exemplary citizens:

If we are lazy and idle, the enemies of freedom plead it as a cause why we ought not to be free, and that giving us our liberty would be an injury to us. By such conduct we strengthen the bands of oppression, and keep many in bondage. Will our friends excuse—will God pardon us—for the part we act in making strong the hands of the enemies of our color?

As Richard sought God for a way to bring his people out of poverty and shame, God guided him through a process that made a tremendous difference in many lives—not only of the citizens of Philadelphia in the 1790s and early 1800s, but also of many black heroes to come. Sojourner Truth, Harriet Tubman, Frederick Douglass, and Biddy Mason all attended the AME church.

THE GREATEST OF ALL (*Matthew 18:1–4*)

"Who is the greatest in the kingdom of heaven?"

Jesus looked up at his disciples from where he sat on the end of a well in the midst of the Capernaum city square. Around them the hubbub of life went on with little notice of them. As he looked into their eyes, he knew they had been debating about position again—about who was second-in-command behind Jesus, and who would have which offices in His kingdom once they threw the Romans out of Israel. He sighed slightly, but he also knew he had another opportunity to teach them something they needed to know.

So in answer to their question, he stood up on the steps that led up to the lip of the well and surveyed the square. He saw a young boy who was crossing the square on what seemed to be an urgent task. Jesus called to him, "Young man, come here a moment."

Without hesitation, the boy stopped in his tracks and came to stand before Jesus. Jesus smiled, took the boy by the shoulders, and turned him to the disciples to stand before Him. Then, standing with a hand on the boy's shoulder, he said, "I tell you the truth, unless you change and become like little children, you will never enter the kingdom of heaven." Here he paused to let his words sink in. He knew it was not what they had expected, but he wanted them to see that the way up was not to fight over authority but to look for opportunities to serve.

But he still had not answered their question. "Who is the greatest?" they wanted to know. So to do this, He continued, "Therefore, whoever humbles himself like this child is the greatest in the kingdom of heaven."

{ LIVING IT! }

What was so special about this one child that Jesus made a special example of him as the "greatest in the kingdom of heaven"? It was very simple: When Jesus called him and asked him to come, the boy simply obeyed without hesitation. Greatness in the kingdom of heaven is measured simply by that: When Jesus calls, do we humbly and immediately obey, or do we start making excuses and looking for reasons we can't serve as He has asked us to?

For Richard Allen, greatness came because he simply and humbly obeyed God's voice time after time after time. And not only did he obey, but when he was called to a task, he did it with all his might as if he were working for Jesus instead of other men.

When you approach a task, do you do just enough to get by, or do you give it your all?

What do you think Jesus means when He says, "I tell you the truth, unless you change and become like little children, you will never enter the kingdom of heaven"? How does that apply to the greatness He is talking about? How does it apply to you?

Take a moment to think about your church, school, or community—are there areas that need help, but everyone else thinks they are too "below them" to help out? Many times these are opportunities in disguise to do something for others. Take some time to pray about them. What do you feel in your heart about them?

American Underground

These who have turned the world upside down have come here too. . . . And these are all acting contrary to the decrees of Caesar, saying there is another king—Jesus.

ACTS 17:6–7 NKJV

THE UNDERGROUND CHURCH IN AMERICA (1800s)

By the late 1840s many slaves belonged to what we would today call an underground church. It was similar in many ways to churches in today's "closed" nations such as China. In the South before emancipation, there were independent black churches with slave members, as well as racially mixed churches, where it was not uncommon for slaves to outnumber masters in attendance at Sunday services.

But outside of these visible, Sunday morning meetings, the slave community worshiped in their own manner. Hidden from the eyes of their masters, slaves gathered in slave quarters or out of doors in the woods or swamps for informal believers' meetings.

The persecution was real. Because of the fear of a slave revolt, many areas would not allow blacks to congregate. Slaves often faced severe punishment if caught attending secret prayer meetings. One escaped slave told how he was threatened with five hundred lashes for attending a prayer meeting—without permission—that was conducted by slaves on a neighboring plantation. His master, incidentally, was a deacon of the local Baptist church.

Despite these dangers, slaves continued having their own meetings because they could pray and sing freely, as the Holy Spirit led them. They were willing to risk punishment by their earthly masters in order to worship their heavenly Master as they saw fit. Peter Randolph, a slave in Prince George County, Virginia, until he was freed in 1847, gave the following description of a secret prayer meeting:

The slaves assemble in the swamp, out of reach of the patrols. They have an understanding among themselves as to the time and place of getting together. This is often done by the first one arriving breaking boughs from the trees, and bending them in the direction of the selected spot. . . . The speaker usually . . . talks very slowly, until feeling the Spirit, he grows excited, and in a short time, there fall to the ground twenty or thirty men and women under its influence.

Their deep love for God and their desire to feel His embrace and experience the amazing peace that comes from His presence caused these believers to risk all to gather for corporate worship.

NEHEMIAH'S PRAYER (*Nehemiah 1:5–11* NLT)

When Nehemiah heard that the walls and temple of Jerusalem were but rubble in Judah, he fell to his knees and prayed the following prayer of repentance for his people:

O Lord, God of heaven, the great and awesome God who keeps his covenant of unfailing love with those who love him and obey his commands, listen to my prayer! Look down and see me praying night and day for your people Israel. I confess that we have sinned against you. Yes, even my own family and I have sinned! We have sinned terribly by not obeying the commands, laws, and regulations that you gave us through your servant Moses.

Please remember what you told your servant Moses: "If you sin, I will scatter you among the nations. But if you return to me and obey my commands, even if you are exiled to the ends of the earth, I will bring you back to the place I have chosen for my name to be honored."

We are your servants, the people you rescued by your great power and might. O Lord, please hear my prayer! Listen to the prayers of those of us who delight in honoring you.

{ LIVING IT! }

It is amazing to think that in our nation, which was built on Christian principles and the right of all to worship God as they saw best, we would be a nation that suppressed such expression in very similar ways to what the Communists did in the twentieth century and some are still doing today. While such a realization should bring some shame, it should also make us realize that we are truly no better than any other people group in the world or nation on earth. It should also give way to a call for repentance, that we are not bound by the shackles of the past but that we can learn from them and make our time and the time of our children and their children better for what we have learned.

While it seems futile and meaningless to some people, it is still right for our generation to seek forgiveness and reconciliation for things caused by generations before us. Certainly we are all new and forgiven on the day we accept Jesus; however, years of bloodshed and hatred do not go away by ignoring them. So it is with some of the atrocities committed in our nation by one group against another. No one is without guilt—though some groups may bear more—and no groups are without need of reconciliation to those they either harmed or were harmed by.

Take time today to pray for forgiveness for the things that happened in your area before you were even born, and pray for racial and ethnic reconciliation. Now find a way to live as part of that reconciliation and start paving new rights and freedoms for all regardless of race, gender, or ethnicity.

Pray for areas where the church is persecuted today and believers have to go "underground" in order to worship God. Visit *www.jesusfreaks.net* to find out more about such areas and organizations that reach out to them.

A Father's Advice

*Man shall not live by bread alone, but by every word
that proceeds from the mouth of God.*

MATTHEW 4:4 NKJV

JOHN QUINCY ADAMS (1767–1848)

John Quincy Adams, sixth president of the United States, was a
devout reader of the Scriptures. Adams frequently sent letters to his
family when work called him away from home, and these letters were
later published in the *New York Tribune*. The following excerpt comes
from a letter written by John Quincy Adams in 1811, while ambassador
in St. Petersburg, to one of his sons.

In your letter of the 18th January to your mother, you mentioned
that you read to your aunt a chapter in the Bible or a section of *Dod-
dridge's Annotations* every evening. This information gave me real
pleasure; for so great is my veneration for the Bible, and so strong my
belief, that when duly read and meditated on, it is of all books in the
world, that which contributes most to make men good, wise, and
happy.

I advise you, in whatever you read, and most of all in reading the
Bible, to remember that it is for the purpose of making you wiser and
more virtuous. I have myself, for many years, made it a practice to
read through the Bible once every year.

In your infancy and youth, you have been, and will be for some
years, under the authority and control of your friends and instructors;
but you must soon come to the age when you must govern yourself.
You have already come to that age in many respects; you know the
difference between right and wrong, and you know some of your
duties, and the obligations you are under, to become acquainted with
them all. It is in the Bible, you must learn them, and from the Bible
how to practice them. Those duties are to God, to your fellow-
creatures, and to yourself.

Joshua Takes the Leadership of Israel
(*Joshua 1:2–9* NLT)

After Moses' death, Joshua became the leader of Israel. When he did, God spoke to him:

> Now that my servant Moses is dead, you must lead my people across the Jordan River into the land I am giving them. I promise you what I promised Moses: "Everywhere you go, you will be on land I have given you—from the Negev Desert in the south to the Lebanon mountains in the north, from the Euphrates River on the east to the Mediterranean Sea on the west, and all the land of the Hittites." No one will be able to stand their ground against you as long as you live. For I will be with you as I was with Moses. I will not fail you or abandon you.
>
> Be strong and courageous, for you will lead my people to possess all the land I swore to give their ancestors. Be strong and very courageous. Obey all the laws Moses gave you. Do not turn away from them, and you will be successful in everything you do. Study this Book of the Law continually. Meditate on it day and night so you may be sure to obey all that is written in it. Only then will you succeed. I command you—be strong and courageous! Do not be afraid or discouraged. For the Lord your God is with you wherever you go.

{ LIVING IT! }

It may seem odd, but it is still true: just as our physical bodies need food to grow and survive, so our born-again spirits need God's Word to grow and stay healthy. The more of God's Word we *eat*—read, meditate upon, mull over in our minds (which is a lot like putting food in our mouths and then properly chewing it up)—the healthier our spirits are and the stronger we are in resisting temptation and doing what is right.

This is why John Quincy Adams' advice to his son looks very much like God's advice to Joshua: "Do you want to have courage and good success? Then read and think about My Word day and night and obey what it tells you to do." Just as physical exercise makes us stronger and better able to do the things we want to do—whether it is winning a basketball game, climbing a mountain, or just staying fit—the spiritual exercises of reading the Word, praying, and meditating on God's truths also make us stronger and better able to live and function with vitality spiritually—in other words, plugging into God's destiny and plans for our lives and living them out.

Do you have a regular time for Bible reading and prayer? If not, commit to trying it for a solid week and find one time during the day. At the end of that week, write in your journal about how that week was different from others. Just like it takes more than a week of physical exercise to get stronger, it also takes more than a week of spiritual exercise to get spiritually stronger, but you still should be able to feel some effects of the exercise. What did you notice?

Meditating on God's Word can take several different forms: You could quietly think about a Scripture or passage while alone, write about it in your journal, compose a song or poem about it, draw a picture—any number of things the Holy Spirit might inspire that fits you best. Try some of these and see which works for you. What did you learn?

Drawing the
Dividing Line

*Whilst sun and moon endure, America shall remain a
city of refuge for the whole earth, until she herself
shall play the tyrant, forget her destiny, disgrace her
freedom, and provoke her God.*

GEORGE DUFFIELD, AMERICAN REVOLUTIONARY

WAR CHAPLAIN

THE MISSOURI COMPROMISE (MARCH 3, 1820) AND THE FUGITIVE SLAVE LAW (SEPTEMBER 18, 1850)

The Old Testament book of 1 Kings tells a powerful story of two women who claim motherhood of the same baby. King Solomon, in his wisdom, decrees that he will simply cut the baby in half, but the real mother pleads with him to let the baby live, even if it means giving up the child. Knowing this, Solomon gives the baby to the true mother.

In 1819 the territory of Missouri finally had a large enough population to qualify for statehood. The problem: Would it be a slave or free state? Choosing political compromise, in 1820 Congress decided Missouri would be a slave state, while Maine would be admitted as a free state, thus retaining the balance of slave v. free states twelve to twelve.

Essentially, the baby nation was cut in half.

For more than thirty-five years the Missouri Compromise ripped open the midsection of the nation. Additionally, it decreed that above the 36° 30' parallel, freedom for blacks was the law. Below it, slavery reigned. This dark dichotomy, however, only created an atmosphere for the Underground Railroad to grow and thrive. Perhaps more than any other issue in the early 1800s, the Missouri Compromise awakened the nation to the divisiveness of slavery.

In 1850, in an attempt to appease the southern states, Congress once again cut the baby in half. That year the Fugitive Slave Law was passed—a law requiring all citizens in free states to report escaped slaves to the authorities under threat of fine and imprisonment. Bent on profit, dishonest slave hunters were known to kidnap free-born northern blacks and sell them into slavery. Fear and suspicion reigned, and even African Americans whose families had been free for generations were unsafe.

In 1857 a pro-slavery Supreme Court, via the Dred Scott decision, declared the Missouri Compromise, which restricted slavery in certain states, unconstitutional. It also decreed that slaves were not U.S. citizens and therefore were ineligible to bring a suit to federal court. This delighted southern slave owners and enraged northern abolitionists, accelerating the day when the divided nation would clash in civil war.

ISRAEL DIVIDES FROM JUDAH (*1 Kings 12:1–17*)

When Solomon died, his son Rehoboam became king. At his coronation, Jeroboam and other representatives came to him to ask for mercy, saying, "Your father put a heavy yoke on us, but now lighten the harsh labor and the heavy yoke he put on us, and we will serve you."

Rehoboam asked for three days to consult his advisors and think it over. In that time, he went to his father's advisors and asked them what they thought. They answered, "If today you will be a servant to these people and serve them and give them a favorable answer, they will always be your servants."

But Rehoboam wasn't satisfied with this wisdom. Instead, he went to the ambitious group of young men he had grown up with. When he asked them what he should do, bent on impressing him and asserting themselves to find positions in his court, they answered, "Tell these people who have said to you, 'Your father put a heavy yoke on us, but make our yoke lighter'—tell them, 'My little finger is thicker than my father's waist. My father laid on you a heavy yoke; I will make it even heavier. My father scourged you with whips; I will scourge you with scorpions.'"

When Jeroboam and the others returned as instructed on the third day, Rehoboam gave them the answer he had foolishly chosen: "My father made your yoke heavy; I will make it even heavier. My father scourged you with whips; I will scourge you with scorpions."

Because his laws were unjust and because his father had turned from the truth of God to worship foreign idols, God allowed all of the tribes of Israel to secede from their union with Judah to become their own nation, and nothing Rehoboam did could bring them back.

{ LIVING IT! }

The United States came to the brink of division for very similar reasons to Israel's: In the compromises at the Constitutional Convention that allowed slavery to continue, in the Missouri Compromise, and in passing the Fugitive Slave Law, the United States turned its back on God's truth and instead endorsed greed, racism, and "scourging others with scorpions rather than just whips." Under this mentality slavery grew and became more barbaric rather than diminished. The blood of slaves spilt by the lash and murder called out to God for justice just as the prayers of the enslaved Jews in Egypt called out to God for freedom. God had warned America again and again about what was right, but instead, we as a nation chose compromise with evil instead of eliminating it.

Compromise can be a valuable tool to govern if it is used over things that are not absolutes, but when truth is compromised so that injustice can continue and innocent blood is shed, God's protection over a nation is no longer sure. For the United States, God's mercy lasted almost a century, and then our hardened hearts turned on each other in the bloodiest war we have ever known.

To live this lesson today, we must never forget to continue to fight for truth and freedom, or to continue to fight for it lawfully as God has described in His Word. We must pull out the big guns of what He prescribes for a world choking on its own arrogance—God's love and creative power. We must pray for our leaders, but we must also pray for the right actions to take and win the lost to the Truth. If we will ask Him, He will answer and show us *His* salvation—or do we really think we can do it better on our own?

While we live in a time of grace and mercy, God still protects the innocent. If we are to be His advocates on the earth, we must side with His right ways as well, but in the same spirit of love Jesus lived by. Our part is to love the lost, not judge them. Only God can change their hearts. Are you doing your part? Or do you find yourself looking down on others rather than praying for them and serving them as Jesus advised us to do? (See Mark 10:42–45.)

In our lives, thinking we are right and being right do not always go together. How then should we argue our cases? Do we thump a Bible our opponents don't even believe in and scream "God says," or do we use wisdom to find other ways to prove the same things and allow God to change their hearts? Proverbs 11:30 says, "The fruit of the righteous is a tree of life, And he who is wise wins souls" (NASB), meaning that if we live righteously, we will be a source of life to others rather than dead religion, and if we are life to others, then we will "win souls"—in other words, change the minds of others. How can you apply this Scripture to the way you "fight" for what is right?

Unity Through
Differences

As iron sharpens iron, a friend sharpens a friend.

PROVERBS 27:17 NLT

JOHN ADAMS AND THOMAS JEFFERSON

Throughout their careers, Adams and Jefferson were from virtual opposite ends of the political spectrum, yet they were cordial and complimentary of each other. They served on the committee that drafted the Declaration of Independence, and despite their differences they worked together to draft one of the greatest documents in our history.

Adams and Jefferson differed on many things, although they both believed in the need for the colonies to be independent of Europe. Politically, Adams, a Federalist, was at odds with Jefferson, who would become the leader of the rival Democratic-Republicans. After George Washington left the presidency, a bitterly fought battle ensued between Vice-President Adams and Secretary Jefferson. Adams defeated Jefferson by a three-vote margin (seventy-one to sixty-eight electoral votes), becoming the second president in America's short history. In 1800 another rough campaign occurred again between the two men, except Jefferson ended up the winner. It was even reported that, on the day of Jefferson's inauguration, John Adams was on a carriage headed out of the city. His son had recently passed away in New York, giving him a convenient excuse not to attend the inauguration of the incoming president.

The two also didn't agree on religion. But as they say, "time heals all wounds," and in this case that might have been true. For as the two men took a step back from the public, their friendship was reconciled by Benjamin Rush in 1812. Through this they became very good friends, writing to each other quite often on a variety of topics such as philosophy and religion.

Both men eventually died within hours of each other on July 4, 1826—a half century to the day that they had joined together to put their names on the line for the cause of American independence.

PAUL AND JOHN MARK (*Acts 13:13; 15:36–41; Colossians 4:10; 2 Timothy 4:11*)

John Mark, Barnabas's nephew, deserted Paul and Barnabas on their first missionary journey when things looked like they were getting rough, but he had repented and asked to go along with them on their second journey to the north. Despite John Mark's repentance, Paul refused to let him come along because of his earlier desertion. Barnabas, however, stuck with John Mark much as he had stuck with Paul before the brethren in Jerusalem years earlier.

Thus Barnabas and Paul went separate ways. Paul took Silas and headed to Syria and Cilicia, and Barnabas and John Mark went to Cyprus.

Though John Mark must have been hurt deeply by Paul's rejection and must have felt responsible for the division between his uncle Barnabas and Paul, the rest of his life shows little sign of discouragement or the lack of resolve that had led to his desertion of Paul and Barnabas in Cyprus on Paul's first missionary journey. In fact, Mark preached boldly in Cyprus when he and his uncle returned there after they had split with Paul.

God even gave John Mark the opportunity to redeem himself in the eyes of Paul. It is believed by most historians that Paul was in prison twice in Rome: the first time being freer and during which he continued to preach; the second being more severe and ending in his execution. John Mark was present with Paul during his first imprisonment and so distinguished himself that Paul sent John Mark to the church at Colossae with his commendation. Later, when Paul was in prison for the last time, he wrote to Timothy, "When you come, bring Mark, for he is profitable to me for the ministry."

John Mark eventually traveled with Peter and, at the request of the church in Rome, wrote the gospel of Mark from Peter's teachings. Peter endorsed the writings and had them distributed to the churches for the encouragement and education of their growing congregations.

{ LIVING IT! }

The Bible tells us that while there are many different parts in the body, we are all one in Jesus. Sometimes, however, that oneness is not as obvious as the differences!

But we make a mistake if we assume that oneness comes from always getting along in all things. People have differences of opinion. They make mistakes. They get mad and walk out of the room on each other. Sometimes they don't speak to each other for weeks, months, or years! Despite their differences, though, they are still one in Christ. So how do you have it both ways?

Friends like Adams and Jefferson are a great example of this. Despite their extreme differences of viewpoints, they remained unified around America's need to be independent. Actually, they fought for the same thing in different ways, and at the end of the day they trusted the democratic process to make the best and final decision. Politicians today ought to take a peek into the past and catch a glimpse of these two stalwarts and see how divergent personalities can work together for the greater good. They both fought hard for what they believed in but refused to let it divide them—instead they each let the other make them sharper.

Paul and John Mark seemed to have a similar effect on each other. Perhaps John Mark would never have risen to be the man he did had Paul not refused to let him slip by with his desertion. But Paul was also big enough to forgive and readmit John Mark to fellowship when he later proved himself "profitable to me for the ministry."

History also tells us that Franklin Delano Roosevelt used to pick people of differing backgrounds and opinions on purpose—sometimes putting people of violently opposing viewpoints in the same groups—then let them fight it out in meetings. By so doing, he was sure he had heard all of the points that could be presented and thus had all the information he needed to decide on an issue.

Our nation—and our churches, for that matter—still needs people to strongly stand up for what they believe is right and express their views so that all points are covered. Yet at the end of the day, we need to be able to trust the process and come together again as one. We need to learn from examples such as these on how to disagree and still stand for the same things, respecting and honoring our differences while also appreciating that without each other we would never grow stronger and sharper.

Are there people who you find rub you the wrong way? In dealing with them, are you more motivated by the desire to avoid them or walk in love toward them? You may have very different viewpoints, but do you act respectfully to them so that when you speak they will listen respectfully to you?

How do you love someone who is antagonistic toward you? How does the Bible tell us to act toward them? (1 Corinthians 13 might be a good place to start.)

How do you treat someone who you are sure is just out for selfishness and seems to have no respect for the Truth? How do you bring such a person back to the love of Truth we have as Christians?

Giving to Establish God's Will on the Earth

You shall remember the Lord your God, for it is He who gives you power to get wealth, that He may establish His covenant which He swore to your fathers, as it is this day.

DEUTERONOMY 8:18 NKJV

ARTHUR TAPPAN (1786–1865) AND LEWIS TAPPAN (1788–1863)

Arthur and Lewis Tappan were millionaires back in the days when a million dollars was an unthinkable sum of money. Engaged in the silk business in New York City, their company made more than a million dollars every year. Yet Arthur and Lewis chose to live modestly, as they believed God had entrusted them with wealth so they could help their fellow humankind.

Deeply touched by the ministry of Charles Finney, they financially supported his revival work. Later they joined Theodore Weld in founding Lane Seminary and Oberlin College, to prepare Finney's converts for the ministry.

In 1833 the Tappan brothers organized the American Anti-Slavery Society. In those days it took courage to speak out against slavery, and Arthur and Lewis suffered for their convictions. Pro-slavery mobs burned Lewis's home to the ground in 1834. Lewis wrote that he wanted his house to remain "this summer as it is, a silent antislavery preacher to the crowds who will see it." In 1835 a church built by the Tappans was set on fire. Later that same year, fire destroyed a building that housed much of the brothers' business. Undeterred, the brothers continued their work. Lewis wanted to eliminate the "black pew" and caused an uproar in upstate New York when he and his family sat in the pews reserved for blacks.

In addition to their antislavery causes, the Tappans supported the American Bible Society, the American Tract Society, the American Home Missionary Society, the American Education Society, the American Temperance Society, and the American Sunday School Union.

By 1849 Lewis had accumulated enough wealth to retire. Instead he decided to devote the rest of his life to humanitarian causes. When he was sixty-four, Lewis was instrumental in a project that finally broke through the nation's complacency concerning the plight of African Americans. In 1852 one of the publications he financed, the *National Era*, published a series of stories titled *Uncle Tom's Cabin* by Harriet Beecher Stowe, stories God used to forever change how Americans viewed slavery.

THE PARABLE OF THE RICH FOOL (*Luke 12:16–21* THE MESSAGE)

When asked by a man to make his brother pay him some of the inheritance left by his father, Jesus told this parable:

> The farm of a certain rich man produced a terrific crop. He talked to himself: "What can I do? My barn isn't big enough for this harvest." Then he said, "Here's what I'll do: I'll tear down my barns and build bigger ones. Then I'll gather in all my grain and goods, and I'll say to myself, Self, you've done well! You've got it made and can now retire. Take it easy and have the time of your life!"
>
> Just then God showed up and said, "Fool! Tonight you die. And your barnful of goods—who gets it?"
>
> That's what happens when you fill your barn with Self and not with God.

{ LIVING IT! }

There is an old comparison that talks about the Sea of Galilee, which is full of life and has beautiful plants and vegetation around it, and the Dead Sea, which is so dense with salt that nothing lives in or around it. Both are in the same part of the world, roughly the same climate, yet one is full of life, the other is dead. What is the difference?

The Sea of Galilee takes in water, but it also gives it out into the Jordan River. The Dead Sea only takes in. Because it is actually below sea level, it has no streams or other waterways that flow out of it. The principle? Only that which takes in and also gives out produces life—that which takes in and keeps all produces death.

This is easily seen in contrasting the lives of the Tappan brothers with the rich fool of Jesus' parable. They used their industry and wealth to build freedom for others; the rich fool thought he was using it to build freedom for himself only to find that when he reached his goal, it was too late to do anything with it. As Martin Luther King Jr. said of this parable: "Jesus called this man a fool because he allowed the means by which he lived to outdistance the ends for which he lived. . . . Somehow he became so involved in the means by which he lived he couldn't deal with the way to eternal matters."

Don't make the same mistake. Though the Tappan brothers gave generously, they always had enough. Though the rich fool kept everything, in the end it wasn't nearly enough. Life is not about what you have but about what you build for your future, your family, your community, and your world. What are you using your resources to build? Bigger barns or a better world?

★　　★　　★

Author Randy Alcorn in his book *The Treasure Principle* asks a simple question: Are you living for the dot or the line? For him, the dot is our short, finite life on earth. The line is the everlasting life we have with God. Which are you securing for the future with the resources you have? Are you building up treasure on earth or treasure in heaven? Are you living for the dot or the line?

How do you manage the money and resources (time and talents, for example) God has entrusted you with? Does your church offer classes in financial management or stewardship? If not, ask your pastor for suggested resources to learn more about organizing yourself in this area.

"Liberty and Union, Now and For Ever, One and Inseparable!"

Our ancestors established their system of government on morality and religious sentiment. . . . Whatever makes a man a good Christian also makes a good citizen.

DANIEL WEBSTER

DANIEL WEBSTER (1783–1852)

Daniel Webster first served his nation representing New Hampshire in the House of Representatives between 1813 and 1816, and then representing Massachusetts in the Senate beginning in 1827. The focus of his legal and political career was his great love for the Constitution of the United States. The man who would become famous as the leading defender of the Constitution and the Union found his specialty early. When he was eight, he used his life savings to buy a cotton handkerchief on which was printed the Constitution of the United States. He studied it thoroughly, later recalling, "There is not an article, a section, a phrase, a word, a syllable, or even a comma of that Constitution that I did not study and ponder in every relation and in every construction of which it was susceptible."

In January of 1830, not only was Daniel still a senator from Massachusetts, but he was also deeply involved in arguing a case before the Supreme Court. Because of this he had not been following the Senate's debate for some time. The Supreme Court, however, had adjourned early that afternoon, and Daniel "just happened" to stop by the Senate chambers. As he listened to Senator Hayne from South Carolina, he became alarmed. Senator Hayne argued for "state rights" to nullify federal laws that their legislators did not see as favorable to them, but the real question was: Could a state decide which federal laws they would obey and which they wouldn't?

In response to this, Daniel felt he must defend the Constitution and the Union from being cut to pieces if Senator Hayne's arguments stood to make individual states laws unto themselves. A central government whose laws could be accepted or rejected would have no power to govern and hold the nation together as one.

During the next two days, Senator Hayne continued to give one of the greatest speeches ever heard in the Senate chambers. His magnificent delivery, combined with his logic and the progression of his reasoning, impressed everyone who heard him. Hayne had outdone himself, and Daniel had only one evening to prepare his rebuttal. Still, Daniel did not seem anxious.

When Supreme Court Justice Joseph Story stopped by to offer his assistance, Webster smiled and shook his head. "Give yourself no uneasiness, Judge Story: I will grind him as fine as a pinch of snuff." God had seen ahead and provided: Daniel had already prepared detailed notes on the subject for another purpose. Webster later said, "If Hayne had tried to make a speech to fit my notes, he could not have hit it any better."

The Senate chamber was filled to capacity the next morning. When Daniel rose to speak, an expectant hush fell over the room. He began to speak calmly and with great strength. Eyewitnesses later remarked, "A deep-seated conviction of the extraordinary character of the emergency, and of his ability to control it, seemed to possess him wholly."

Daniel reminded his audience that the power behind the Constitution did not come from the various state legislatures but from "We, the people of the United States." He showed the absurdity of having the laws of our national government subject to twenty-four different state governments, "each at liberty to decide for itself, and none bound to respect the decisions of others, and each at liberty, too, to give a new construction on every election of its own members."

In closing, he turned and looked at our flag. "Behold the gorgeous ensign of the republic, now known and honored throughout the earth . . . not a stripe erased or polluted, not a single star obscured, bearing for its motto, no such miserable interrogatory as 'What is all this worth?' nor those other words of delusion and folly, 'Liberty first and Union afterwards'; but everywhere, spread all over in characters of living light, blazing on all its ample folds, as they float over the sea and over

the land, and in every wind under the whole heavens, that other sentiment, dear to every true American heart, 'Liberty and Union, now and
for ever, one and inseparable!' "

Daniel sat down to complete silence. An observer remarked, "The
feeling was too overpowering to allow expression by voice or hand. It
was as if one was in a trance, all motion paralyzed." Under God's grace
Daniel presented the real issues so plainly and eloquently that no one
could argue or misunderstand. Webster's oration dramatically affected
many Americans, reminding them of the value and sacredness of union.

PAUL DESCRIBES THE CHURCH (*1 Corinthians 12:12–27* NLT)

In his first letter to the Corinthians, Paul tries to explain to them
how the body of Christ can have so many different-looking parts with
differing functions and purposes, yet at the same time function together
as one unit bringing the kingdom of God to earth:

> The human body has many parts, but the many parts make up
> only one body. So it is with the body of Christ. Some of us are Jews,
> some are Gentiles, some are slaves, and some are free. But we have all
> been baptized into Christ's body by one Spirit, and we have all
> received the same Spirit.
>
> Yes, the body has many different parts, not just one part. If the
> foot says, "I am not a part of the body because I am not a hand," that
> does not make it any less a part of the body. And if the ear says, "I
> am not part of the body because I am only an ear and not an eye,"
> would that make it any less a part of the body? Suppose the whole
> body were an eye—then how would you hear? Or if your whole body
> were just one big ear, how could you smell anything?
>
> But God made our bodies with many parts, and he has put each
> part just where he wants it. What a strange thing a body would be if
> it had only one part! Yes, there are many parts, but only one body.
> The eye can never say to the hand, "I don't need you." The head
> can't say to the feet, "I don't need you."
>
> In fact, some of the parts that seem weakest and least important
> are really the most necessary. And the parts we regard as less honor-
> able are those we clothe with the greatest care. So we carefully protect
> from the eyes of others those parts that should not be seen, while
> other parts do not require this special care. So God has put the body
> together in such a way that extra honor and care are given to those
> parts that have less dignity. This makes for harmony among the

members, so that all the members care for each other equally. If one part suffers, all the parts suffer with it, and if one part is honored, all the parts are glad.

Now all of you together are Christ's body, and each one of you is a separate and necessary part of it.

{ L I V I N G   I T ! }

Despite Daniel's historic speech, the nullification issue continued to gain momentum. In 1832 South Carolina nullified the Tariff of 1832, and President Andrew Jackson threatened to send in troops to enforce the law. John Calhoun and Henry Clay achieved a compromise tariff that pacified both sides and put off the question of nullification, which was ultimately decided by the Civil War.

Many thought Daniel Webster should have been elected president, but it was not to be. In 1852 he retired to his beloved home on the Massachusetts coast. For nine miles before he entered its gates, friends scattered flowers in front of his carriage to honor him and welcome him home. Just before he died, this great defender of the Union whispered, "My wish has been to do my Maker's will. I thank Him now for all the mercies that surround me."

Daniel's cry was that though the states and citizens of the United States were diverse and had different opinions and dreams, that they could be "one and inseparable"—just as Paul had described the church.

Unity, despite great differences of opinion and aim, is possible, if we keep the most important things first in our priorities and let other things fall to their lower places. Today that is more difficult than ever, not only because of larger populations, but because fewer are willing to agree on what those top priorities should be. Pray today our nation would again realize that diversity is strength rather than a weakness, and that unity is not so much compromising on our differences as it is emphasizing and prioritizing what we agree on.

Do you pray regularly for groups that are different from yours? Do you associate with them, or even with people outside of your usual cliques? If you don't, then take a week to do so and journal about what God teaches you. Do you have more in common than you first thought or less?

Unstoppable

Love does not delight in evil but rejoices with the
truth. It always protects, always trusts, always
hopes, always perseveres. Love never fails.

1 CORINTHIANS 13:6–8A

THEODORE WELD (1803–1895)

Theodore Weld was the most unstoppable voice for abolition the
country had ever seen, if only because so many had failed to stop his
words. Traveling from small town to small town, he would preach, for
days if necessary, on emancipation and God's call to Christian benevo-
lence, and usually his words of peace and holy kindness were greeted
with threats and violence wherever he went.

Much of his work in 1835 focused on the state of Ohio, and in town
after town Weld arrived, secured a location to speak, and would stay
until the area caught hold of the vision for the work God would do.
Each night the mob would grow smaller, the shouts quieter, and soon
men and women would listen to him. Communities throughout the state
accepted his message and, in his wake, formed antislavery societies to
carry on the work.

But Weld knew the impact of many small groups would never equal
the power of a larger unified group, so in the fall of 1835, he called for
a convention of the new-sprung societies to form a larger, more powerful organization. For a location, he felt God leading him to the very
lion's den itself, the town of Zanesville, notorious for being the most
anti-abolition area in Ohio.

Arriving early to begin preparations, Weld found not a single room
or hall for his purposes. If the convention was to be hosted there, hearts
would need to change. So, shut out but unbowed, he set up camp across
the Muskigum River in Putnam, Ohio. But that was not far enough
away for the citizens of Zanesville.

As Weld spoke, his powerful voice filling the hall, a growing murmur could be heard outside. There was a flickering light that could be seen through the space's windows as though of torchlight, and soon the din of angry voices nearly drowned Weld out. On he spoke, fierce and unyielding amid the sound of rocks smashing windows and the great wrenching crash of a fence being destroyed. Windows broken, the chants and threats were even more ominous, but Weld continued through to his end. Then he gathered himself and his few belongings and headed out to meet the mob.

He had done this before, always praying for God's protection. Often he would pass as if unnoticed through angry mobs that had been almost supernaturally stilled. Tonight, God barely kept him from death as angry men hurled rocks and swung at him with rude clubs they'd made from elm branches.

Beaten and battered, Weld refused to yield. When the Putnam hall's owner refused to let him return, he found another location. With bruises across his face and a voice raw from a wounded throat, Weld preached God's word of freedom for all. Again the mobs came and the rocks rained down and blows were landed. Night after night, Weld faced the wrath of Zanesville until he wore them out. Subdued by his perseverance, they finally listened to his words and soon welcomed him into their own town. Sixteen days after he'd first arrived, hundreds answered his call to join the abolition movement, and the town, with days to spare, readied itself for Ohio's great antislavery convention. Just as God had promised.

PAUL LEFT FOR DEAD (*Acts 14:19–23*)

When those who had driven Paul from Antioch and Iconium heard that he was preaching in nearby Lystra, they couldn't stomach it. They had chased him and those with him from their areas, thinking they had silenced him for good; however, they found out his message was growing stronger then ever! Presently, claims were that a lame man in Lystra had been healed and the people now revered Paul and Barnabas as the Roman gods Mercury and Jupiter.

Deciding to put an end to him, they incited a mob against him and stoned him until they were sure that he was dead. Then they dragged him outside of town and left his body in an open field.

When the mob had left, slowly those who were traveling with Paul and those who accepted Jesus because of Paul's words gathered around him in a circle and began to pray. Soon Paul began to stir and then rose up healed. Then, as if being stoned to death once for Jesus were not enough, Paul returned to the city. The next day he and Barnabas continued on to the town of Derbe.

After he'd preached the gospel there, rather than cowering in the face of his persecutors, he retraced his steps back through Lystra, Iconium, and Antioch to encourage the believers he had left behind. What a proof of God's hand upon his life that must have been!

After he had confirmed their faith and exhorted them to continue on until the day of Jesus' return, they ordained elders for each church and returned to Jerusalem.

{ LIVING IT! }

Theodore Weld's life is a tribute to perseverance and devotion to God's truth. For him, slavery was not a secondhand issue but a national sin that had been institutionalized. For Paul, the issue of salvation through Jesus Christ rather than the law was one well worth dying for. Yet at the same time, he wasn't willing to go before his task on earth was accomplished.

The perseverance of such men should be examples to us not only of how we should live but also of how much determination it takes to change our world.

Today as well, there are contradictions to God's Word that have been written or are about to be written into law. It is, as the book of Esther says, "for such a time as this" that God wants us to stand just and strong in the face of opposition for the salvation of our nation. How do we stand to oppose injustice in our time? Do we march once and consider our part done? Or do we shout until our voices give out, even though those who oppose us shout louder? Do we, with discipline and fervor, continue speaking until we are heard? Or do we give it up as hopeless and go back to sit on your couches and complain that our country is going to hell?

Just how much of God's will for your life are you willing to settle for? Are you satisfied with only accomplishing half or three-quarters of it? Or are you going to be like Theodore Weld or Paul, who wouldn't consider quitting until they had done all God called them to do?

Endurance

Meeting the Truth

I am the way, and the truth, and the life. The only
way to the Father is through me.

JOHN 14:6 NCV

SOJOURNER TRUTH (1797–1883)

She was born into slavery and named Isabella Baumfree. Describing
herself as "the pure African," she was an imposing woman, standing six
feet tall with thick, muscular arms. By law, on July 4, 1827, slaves in
New York were to be freed. Isabella's master had promised to free her
family one year earlier than the legal deadline. When he didn't keep his
promise, Isabella left anyway.

That same year, Isabella had a profound encounter with God that
changed her life forever:

> God revealed Himself to me, with all the suddenness of a flash of
> lightning, showing me that He pervaded the universe. Conscious of
> my great sin, I wanted to hide, but I plainly saw there was no place,
> not even in hell, where He was not. I exclaimed aloud, "Oh, God, I
> did not know You were so big."
>
> I desired to talk to God, but my vileness utterly forbade it. I began
> to wish for someone to speak to God for me. At length a friend
> appeared to stand between myself and an insulted Deity.
>
> "Who are you?" I asked, as the vision brightened into a form dis-
> tinct, beaming with the beauty of holiness, and radiant with love.
>
> "It is Jesus."
>
> Before this event, I had heard Jesus mentioned, but thought that
> He was like any other eminent man, like a Washington or a Lafay-
> ette. Now He appeared to my delighted mental vision—and He loved
> me so much! How strange that He had always loved me, and I had
> never known it! And how great a blessing He conferred, in that He
> should stand between me and God!
>
> My heart was now as full of joy and gladness, as it had been of

terror and despair. The very air sparkled as with diamonds and smelled like heaven.

After this overwhelming experience, Isabella was always aware of God and totally committed to do His will. She began attending church and, not long afterward, moved to New York City and soon began preaching at camp meetings throughout the city.

In 1843 Isabella had another profound religious experience. The Lord called her to serve Him by traveling around the United States and preaching against greed, alcohol, and other sins so prevalent in the city. It was at this time that Isabella received her new name. In her autobiography she explained: "I went to the Lord and asked him to give me a new name. And the Lord gave me Sojourner [which means 'wanderer'], because I was to travel up and down the land, showing the people their sins, and being a sign unto them." She later said that when she asked God for a new last name, "I heard the word 'Truth'—because I was to declare the truth to the people." From then on, Isabella was known as Sojourner Truth.

In her years of speaking and public service, Sojourner became one of the most famous black women of the nineteenth century. Blacks and whites both admired her courage, and people repeated lines from her speeches, words that cut through all the rhetoric and went right to the heart of what God wanted to say.

JESUS AND THE CONDEMNED WOMAN (*John 8:2–12* NASB)

Jesus could read the anger and zeal in their eyes. They were certain they had him this time, and in that certainty, as always, they had missed what He was trying to do. Their question, spoken as if an accusation, still hung in the air: "Teacher, this woman has been caught in adultery, in the very act. Now in the Law, Moses commanded us to stone such women; what then do You say?"

In response, Jesus knelt and began writing in the sand. It seemed to be some sort of list—or half a list really—to be read clearly by all who were there.

Again the stone-carrying mob persisted in wanting an answer from Jesus. Jesus looked up to meet them eye-to-eye. "He who is without sin among you, let him be the first to throw a stone at her." Then again, He stooped to write in the sand, finishing the other half of his list.

Slowly men in the crowd began to drop their stones to the ground. Convicted by Jesus' words or His writings on the ground, they no longer saw a "prostitute" before them but a young girl who could be their own daughter or their sister. The older men were the first to walk away, and then one by one the rest of the crowd who had come to "do this sinner justice" left. Somehow self-righteousness and the demand for punishment in the harshest interpretation of the law had given way to mercy.

"Woman, where are they? Did no one condemn you?"

For the first time since being flung to the earth at the feet of Jesus, the young woman looked up. The crowd was gone except for those Jesus had been teaching as the mob dragging her along had approached.

"No one, Lord," she answered.

"Neither do I condemn you; go your way. From now on sin no more."

Then Jesus turned to those he had been teaching, "I am the light of the world; he who follows Me shall not walk in the darkness, but shall have the Light of life."

{ L I V I N G I T ! }

Lies can go a long way, until the simple truth is known. For Isabella Baumfree, meeting the Truth himself was so earth-shattering it forever changed who she was and who she would be. She was never concerned with the eloquence or learnedness expressed in her words, and instead she strove to always speak the truth, plain and simple. Thus her words, filled with love and faith, silenced some of the most powerful speakers of her time. Truth rang out stronger than education and fine clothes and manners that often were used to cover angry and hateful hearts.

The men who confronted Jesus came with a similar anger and a bloodthirsty sense of justice like a mob to a lynching, but something Jesus said or wrote in the sand changed that. The truth He expressed to them changed their hearts, and they chose mercy instead of justice. For each of these men coming with murder in their hearts, His truth opened their eyes for an instant into the wonders of His kingdom, and they chose to live for that rather than the legalism they had grown up with. The Truth had set them free.

Today we live in what many call the information age, but though the truth may seem harder to find in the midst of all this contradicting information and "spinning" of facts to keep certain groups in power, the

Truth is just as strong as ever. If we are willing to keep seeking it until we truly find it—to keep seeking until we find Him as truthfully as Sojourner did—then we will be the force for God needed to keep His Truth setting people free.

What issues do you feel passionate about in your community or nation today? Are you praying about them on a regular basis and actively seeking God's truth about the matters?

It is not uncommon for the overload of information that we face each day to drive us further from getting involved in community service or political campaigns, but the truth of the matter is that evil only flourishes when good people do nothing. As a person who loves the Truth, you are in a better place to be part of the solution to any problem than others who are only motivated by what their volunteering will look like on their college applications or as a stepping stone to what they want to do in the future.

Take time this week to look through your local paper or the Yellow Pages for places to volunteer your time. Find something you are passionate about and see what you can do to help in that area. Find a place where the love of the Truth you have can start setting others free—you'll be surprised how much good you can do just by letting the love of God within you show up regularly to reach out to others.

"I Stand Before You ..."

If my people, which are called by my name, shall
humble themselves, and pray, and seek my face, and
turn from their wicked ways; then will I hear from
heaven, and will forgive their sin,
and will heal their land.

2 CHRONICLES 7:14 KJV

ANGELINA GRIMKÉ (1805–1879)

> I stand before you as a southerner, exiled from the land of my
> birth, by the sound of the lash, and the piteous cry of the slave.

Angelina Grimké spoke in a voice that had never been heard before
in the State House of Boston. It wasn't only her words, as many in the
legislature were sympathetic to the abolitionist cause, but her very presence. It was a cold day, February 21, 1838, sixty-two years after independence had been declared, and finally a woman was addressing a legislative body in the United States.

Angelina Grimké was indeed not only a southerner, raised in
Charleston, South Carolina, but part of an aristocratic slave-holding
family. When she spoke of the sound of the lash, the cry of the slave,
those images came not from a neighboring plantation but from her own
upbringing.

> I stand before you as a moral being, endowed with precious and
> inalienable rights, which are correlative with solemn duties and high
> responsibilities. . . .

For Angelina, her abolitionist views were not merely an emotional
feeling or a reasoned opinion; they were fully derived from her faith as

a Christian woman. Slavery was appalling to God, a sin from which our country needed cleansing and possibly even saving. Revolutionary in her thinking, however, was the notion that it was the nation's women who were duty-bound to end it. In 1836 she penned her *Appeal to the Christian Women of the South*, a sermon-like pamphlet that spelled out her evangelical call. The pamphlet's epigraph was taken directly from the book of Esther and the peasant queen's decision to ask for the deliverance of her people. It was the core scriptural example at the heart of Angelina's ministry, her voice, her cause.

> And as a moral being I feel that I owe it to the suffering slave, and to the deluded master, to my country and the world, to do all that I can to overturn a system of complicated crime, built up upon the broken hearts and prostrate bodies of my countrymen in chains, and cemented by the blood and sweat and tears of my sisters in bonds.

Following this speech, Angelina Grimké and Theodore Weld, joined by Angelina's sister, Sarah, began a new phase of their abolitionist efforts. In 1839 Weld, with his wife's assistance, wrote *American Slavery As It Is: Testimony of a Thousand Voices*, a chilling, honest, and brutal look at the deep horrors that slaves faced daily. This foundational book for the antislavery movement inspired *Uncle Tom's Cabin*, by Harriet Beecher Stowe, motivating even more men and women to the cause. Now seen as mentors for the upcoming generation, Grimké and Weld turned their strengths to teaching others and equipping many for the spreading of both God's Word and the cause of freedom. Together this couple never wavered in leading the cause of abolition. They faced abuse and threats and beatings but continued to find their strength in God's cause, living with a tenacity that continues to inspire.

JONAH WARNS NINEVEH (*Jonah 3* NASB)

"Arise, go to Nineveh the great city and proclaim to it the proclamation which I am going to tell you."

When Jonah heard the word of the Lord, however, he tried to do everything he could except obey. God's warning, however, had to be delivered.

So it was that, after meeting a pretty big fish and finally realizing there was no escaping God's instructions to him, Jonah delivered the message: If they did not repent, in forty days Nineveh would be destroyed.

And then the most surprising thing happened to Jonah—Nineveh turned back to God and repented! As a result, the judgment that God had been ready to give to the city was stayed. Nineveh was saved because Jonah obeyed the word of the Lord to warn Nineveh, and Nineveh obeyed the word of the Lord given to them by Jonah.

{ LIVING IT! }

Neither the Civil War nor the civil rights movement came to the United States without warnings. Time and again, like the Jonahs of their time, people such as Angelina Grimké called out to America to repent of their ungodly ways, only much of America neither listened nor turned back to God.

Today we hear many warnings about the future of our nation, perhaps the most important ones being fresh calls for people to repent, turn back to God, and accept His salvation before Jesus returns again. Whether Jesus comes back tomorrow or a century from now, this message is always relevant. Is our response to that call also relevant to our society today?

★　★　★

Today Christians and non-Christians are at odds as they have never before been in our nation. We are on such divergent paths, in fact, that many of the questions Christians offer answers to are questions the world isn't even asking. How can we take our faith and make it relevant to a generation that defines itself so differently? Perhaps we should be listening more than preaching. What questions do your non-Christian friends seem to be asking about how to live? What answers would you provide them from the truth you know?

"Why do bad things happen to good people?" has always been a major question in religious thinking, but perhaps a better question for us as believers is, "Why don't more good people happen to bad things?" How can you get involved in "bad things" to make a difference for good?

Where True Bravery Comes From

The Lord has promised that he will not leave us or desert us. That should make you feel like saying, "The Lord helps me! Why should I be afraid of what people can do to me?"

HEBREWS 13:5B–6 CEV

HARRIET TUBMAN (1820–1913)

It was now or never. It had been decided: Tomorrow—or the next day at the latest—Master Brodas would sell Harriet Tubman and her three older brothers to a plantation far to the south in Georgia. Harriet knew that the farther south they lived, the more impossible it was for them to escape. She had heard about the Underground Railroad that took slaves to freedom in the northern states. She convinced her brothers to come with her, that this was the night they had to make their escape to the North—and freedom.

Harriet did not dare tell the rest of her family they were leaving. She had once talked with her husband about running away, and he had threatened to tell her master. And her mother was an expressive sort—if Harriet told her, everyone on the plantation would soon know. So off they went without a word, leaving behind everything and everyone.

The Maryland woods seemed especially dark that night as Harriet led her brothers through the trees. The farther they went, the more fearful Harriet's brothers became—afraid of the bloodhounds used by the patrollers to capture escaping slaves, of being whipped for running away, of being sold even farther south if they were caught. The brothers decided to turn back—but Harriet refused.

"You can't go alone," they told her.

"I can't go back," she said. "And I'm not alone. Jesus is here with me."

She later said, "I had reasoned this out in my mind: there was one of two things I had a right to, liberty or death; if I could not have one, I would have the other; for no man should take me alive; I should fight for my liberty as long as my strength lasted."

Every time she was afraid or did not know what to do next, she prayed the same simple prayer: "Lord, I'm going to hold steady on to you. You've got to see me through." Every time she asked for help, God answered. This was the beginning of Harriet's adventures in being guided step by step in a supernatural way. She hid in a haystack, in a root cellar, and in an attic. She traveled in a wagon, hidden under a load of vegetables. Once she found the next "station" along the way, friendly people would feed her, hide her, and tell her how to find her next stop. In all, Harriet walked a total of ninety miles.

At the end of her trip, she was given new shoes, fancy women's clothes and, since she couldn't read, a paper with the word *Pennsylvania* written on it so she could recognize the sign when she crossed the state line.

Finally she made it—Pennsylvania and freedom! What a wonderful feeling. Harriet said, "There was such a glory over everything, the sun came like gold through the trees and over the fields, and I felt like I was in heaven. I looked at my hands to see if I was the same person now that I was free."

DAVID IN THE WILDERNESS (*Psalm 11:1–2, 4, 7*)

Despite that fact that David fled for his life from Saul, he never turned his back on doing good for the people of Israel or the house of Saul. He could have easily fled to a place of refuge and just hid, but his heart did not permit him that luxury of safety while his family, friends, and nation were in danger. Instead, time and again, he returned to a place of personal danger for the sake of God's people, trusting his life and future to God.

Perhaps this was because he knew that he truly had no safer place than in the center of God's will for his life. His calling was to be king of Israel, its protector and guide, and regardless of who actually wore the crown inside the palace in Jerusalem, he had no choice but to do what God had called him to do. Of this he wrote in Psalm 11:

In the Lord I take refuge.
How then can you say to me:

"Flee like a bird to your mountain.
For look, the wicked bend their bows;
they set their arrows against the strings
to shoot from the shadows
at the upright in heart. . . ."
The Lord is in his holy temple;
the Lord is on his heavenly throne.
He observes the sons of men;
his eyes examine them. . . .
For the Lord is righteous,
he loves justice;
upright men will see his face.

Regardless of what evil men would do to him, David had to be the man God had called him to be, even if that meant throwing himself into obvious danger for the sake of others. Being anywhere else would be foolishness, no matter how safe it looked.

{ LIVING IT! }

With the experience of freedom came a new realization—Harriet had escaped only to find herself alone in a strange city. She remembered: "Oh, how I prayed then, lying on the cold, damp ground, 'Oh, dear Lord, I ain't got no friend but you. Come to my help, Lord, for I'm in trouble!'" She missed her family, who were all still slaves in the South. She came to a solemn resolution: She would make a home for her family in the North and, with the Lord's help, bring them there. "I was free, and my family should be free also."

With similar resolution of will, David pledged his all to the safety of Israel, even though the government of Israel at the time had a price on his head. He would not rest easy, however, while others were in danger of war or enslavement at the hands of the Philistines or other enemies.

Bravery is often not so much a matter of facing danger without flinching as it is following the dictates of conscience without swerving. Once Harriet Tubman found her freedom, she realized that it was better to be in harm's way and struggling for the freedom of others than it was to stay safe. David felt much the same way. Should we live any differently today?

★　★　★

Is there something God is calling you to do today that might seem a little dangerous, even though it may only be your reputation that is at stake and not your life? Which do you think is safer: obeying God even though it looks a bit risky or ignoring what your conscience is telling you to do?

There are many men and women around the globe putting themselves in harm's way for our American freedom today. Do you know any in particular? Take time to pray for these people today, that God would protect them as they follow the dictates of their conscience to keep democracy and freedom safe for others.

Supernatural Direction

The sheep know their shepherd's voice. He calls each of them by name and leads them out.... They follow, because they know his voice. The sheep will not follow strangers. They don't recognize a stranger's voice, and they run away.

JOHN 10:3–5 CEV

HARRIET TUBMAN (1820–1913)

Harriet gave the familiar knock at the door, but there was no answer. She knocked again.

A voice said, "Who is it?"

"A friend with friends," said Harriet, giving the password.

The frightened voice answered, "Slave catchers searched my house yesterday. Go away! Quick now!"

Harriet looked at the ten slaves and babies standing behind her on the country road. She had to do something—and fast. She prayed her familiar prayer, "Lord, I'm going to hold steady on to you. You've got to see me through." Suddenly she remembered an island in a nearby swamp. No one would think to look for them there. She hurried the group along, carrying the babies herself. They waded through the water and crawled under the bushes just before full daylight. They were so tired and hungry—but Harriet couldn't leave them in order to get food.

Over and over again she prayed. As night fell, they heard someone coming. The others shrank back in the bushes while Harriet moved closer to hear. The man was muttering as though to himself: "My wagon stands in the barnyard across the way. The horse is in the stable. The harness hangs on a nail." Still muttering, he soon was gone.

Harriet silently thanked God—once again He had made a way. As soon as it was dark, she crept to the barnyard. There stood a wagon loaded with blankets and baskets of food. Harriet quickly harnessed the horse and drove the wagon back to the swamp. Her passengers greeted her with joyful whispers.

JOSEPH AND MARY (*Matthew 2:13–15* NASB)

Joseph must have felt better going to bed that night than he had in some time. It seemed a long while since they had left the stable where his son had been born because there was no place else to stay. Now they were living in a nice rented house and sleeping on warm clean beds instead of the hay that had served them that night.

Not only that, the unexpected visit of the eastern kings and their bountiful gifts would take care of them for some time. Gold, frankincense, and myrrh were valuable commodities that were easily transported and sold wherever they might eventually travel. God was truly providing for them to care for His Son, the small child wrapped warmly in blankets and lying not far from them.

Yet despite his comfort, in the middle of the night, Joseph had a disturbing dream. In it an angel appeared to him and said, "Get up! Take the Child and His mother and flee to Egypt, and remain there until I tell you; for Herod is going to search for the Child to destroy Him."

Immediately upon hearing this, Joseph awoke, beads of sweat trickling down his forehead. Could it have been just a silly dream? No. It had been too clear. God was warning them, just as he had the kings, that Herod was a danger to the child.

Joseph turned and woke Mary, whose eyes filled with fear as he spoke. Though he himself was also greatly disturbed about what the angel had told him, he still spoke reassuredly to her, "Mary, don't worry. God would not have warned us too late to escape. Let us work quickly and go, but don't fear. God is watching out for us—and for His Son."

Later that night, when the soldier broke down the door of the house because no one answered when they had called, they found it empty except for the beds on the floor that had been too bulky to pack and take with them. The soldiers looked around without giving it much thought. They had moved so swiftly through the village that no one would have had time to warn anyone, so the house must have been empty for days. Finding nothing, they hurried out and on to the next house, leaving in the dust behind them any clues to the whereabouts of the Child for whom Herod was actually searching.

{ LIVING IT! }

Over the years Harriet Tubman experienced many more narrow escapes, but the Lord always sent help. Sometimes deliverance came through a friend on the Underground Railroad, while other times God would warn her and instruct her on exactly what to do.

Once, a premonition warned her she must immediately leave the path she was on and cross a swollen stream. Not knowing how deep the river was, the men with her hesitated. Harriet stepped in the water boldly and found it never came above her chin. When the men saw she was safely across, they followed her. Later Harriet learned that a group of men had been waiting just ahead to seize them. If she had not obeyed the whisper of warning in her mind, she would have been captured.

Harriet always gave God the credit for her escapes. Sarah Bradford, a white schoolteacher in Auburn, New York, who helped Harriet write the story of her life, recalled, "Sudden deliverance never seemed to strike her as at all mysterious; her prayer was the prayer of faith and she expected an answer." Whenever Sarah expressed surprise at Harriet's courage and daring or at her unexpected deliverance, Harriet would always reply, "Didn't I tell you, Missus. It wasn't me. It was the Lord!"

Just as God had protected Joseph, Mary, and the child Jesus, He had also protected Harriet in her journeys.

Harriet made nineteen dangerous trips back to Maryland, not counting her exploits later during the Civil War to help the Union to victory, risking her life countless times to help others. She led more than three hundred slaves to freedom before the war, including her elderly parents and all of her living brothers and sisters. During the Civil War she led several hundred more to freedom. Like Moses, who led the Israelites out of slavery in Egypt, Harriet led many out of bondage in the American South.

Today, though our times may seem less dramatic or adventurous, God's leadership in our lives is just as real, if we would only take the time to ask for and listen to it. Harriet's ability to hear God was not a special gift only she had, but one refined through practice and the fire of adversity. Yet God led her in her life's purpose every step of her journey. Are you open to God's leading you into what He has for you in a similar way?

The Bible is full of examples of how He leads us, but one of the strongest seems to be wrapped up in Psalm 37:4–5, "Delight yourself in the Lord; and He will give you the desires of your heart. Commit your way to the Lord, trust also in Him, and He will do it" (NASB). What desires do you have in your heart that God may have put there? Make a list of them and keep it in your Bible to pray over and think about when you get the opportunity.

Another way God leads us is in our talents and things we like to do. Are there areas of your life in which you feel as if God is smiling on you as you do them? Take time to pray over these areas as well and see what God is trying to teach you through them. They may be skills you need for doing something completely different, but if you are faithful in them, then finding that other area will be a lot easier. Are there things like this in your life that you can think of? Prayerfully make a list.

Called and Enabled

We are to use our different gifts in accordance with
the grace that God has given us.

ROMANS 12:6A GNT

HARRIET BEECHER STOWE (1811–1896)

It came to her in a flash. One minute Harriet Beecher Stowe was taking communion in her home church in Brunswick, Maine, surrounded by her six children. The next minute she was somewhere else, transported in a vision to another time, another place. Before her eyes, as real as life, came a scene of a black man being brutally beaten and dying under the lash because he would not act against his conscience nor deny the existence of his true master, Jesus Christ.

That afternoon Harriet went to her room and wrote down exactly what she had seen. As she wrote, the words flooded out, taking a form and a life of their own.

Later, as she read the vision to her husband, Calvin, they could both feel the power of the Holy Spirit in the words.

Calvin was quiet for a moment, then said, "Harriet, that is by far the best thing you have ever written."

"Calvin, I wish I could explain how I could see every detail—the angle of the sun through the trees, the sounds, the smells. All I had to do was write it down. I remember reading an article about this—I know it really happened." She paused. "But this was so much more real than any article. It was as if I were really there."

"Harriet, the details were there because God himself was there, an unseen witness of the tragedy. He knows everything that happened, the thoughts and feelings of everyone involved. He let you see the scene through His eyes."

"Yes!" Harriet replied. "It was as though God was speaking through me, telling me exactly what He wanted to say."

"You must go on with it, Hattie. You must write a story with this as the ending. It's what the Lord wants you to do."

Harriet agreed. For a long time she had felt God wanted her to use her writing talent to turn the tide against slavery. The stories that became Harriet's book, *Uncle Tom's Cabin*, were based on actual events. Harriet did extensive research to make her story of slavery and its horrors as authentic—and convincing—as possible. Some of the events, such as the scene Harriet saw in her vision, she had read of in the book *American Slavery As It Is*, a collection of journalistic accounts drawn entirely from the southern press and published in 1839 by fellow abolitionists Sarah Grimké, Angelina Grimké Weld, and Theodore Weld. She also drew on firsthand accounts collected by Josiah Henson, an escaped slave who pastored a church comprised of escaped slaves in Canada, where British law protected them from arrest and return to slavery.

Uncle Tom's Cabin made Harriet an international celebrity and a wealthy woman and enabled her to meet the most famous people of her day. When Harriet was introduced to President Abraham Lincoln in 1862, he greeted her with the words, "So you are the little woman who wrote the book that started this great war!" It was said that with one book Harriet Beecher Stowe created two million abolitionists.

Stowe believed that a transformation through Christian love must occur before slavery could be abolished successfully. Inspired by God, Harriet's stories touched the heart, cut through arguments and debate, and accomplished more for the cause of abolition than one hundred years of sermons had been able to do. Historians have said, "After *Uncle Tom's Cabin*, objective analysis of the slavery issue was almost impossible." Truth, now embodied, was a force that could not be stopped.

THE PARABLE OF THE TALENTS (*Matthew 25:14–30* NLT)

In teaching His disciples of the end of the age, Jesus told the following story:

The Kingdom of Heaven can be illustrated by the story of a man going on a trip. He called together his servants and gave them money to invest for him while he was gone. He gave five bags of gold to one, two bags of gold to another, and one bag of gold to the last— dividing it in proportion to their abilities—and then left on his trip. The servant who received the five bags of gold began immediately

to invest the money and soon doubled it. The servant with two bags of gold also went right to work and doubled the money. But the servant who received the one bag of gold dug a hole in the ground and hid the master's money for safekeeping.

After a long time their master returned from his trip and called them to give an account of how they had used his money. The servant to whom he had entrusted the five bags of gold said, "Sir, you gave me five bags of gold to invest, and I have doubled the amount." The master was full of praise. "Well done, my good and faithful servant. You have been faithful in handling this small amount, so now I will give you many more responsibilities. Let's celebrate together!"

Next came the servant who had received the two bags of gold, with the report, "Sir, you gave me two bags of gold to invest, and I have doubled the amount." The master said, "Well done, my good and faithful servant. You have been faithful in handling this small amount, so now I will give you many more responsibilities. Let's celebrate together!"

Then the servant with the one bag of gold came and said, "Sir, I know you are a hard man, harvesting crops you didn't plant and gathering crops you didn't cultivate. I was afraid I would lose your money, so I hid it in the earth and here it is."

But the master replied, "You wicked and lazy servant! You think I'm a hard man, do you, harvesting crops I didn't plant and gathering crops I didn't cultivate? Well, you should at least have put my money into the bank so I could have some interest. Take the money from this servant and give it to the one with the ten bags of gold. To those who use well what they are given, even more will be given, and they will have an abundance. But from those who are unfaithful, even what little they have will be taken away. Now throw this useless servant into outer darkness, where there will be weeping and gnashing of teeth."

{ LIVING IT! }

In the *King James Version* of this parable, the word *talent* is used as the measurement of money given to each servant: ten talents to one, five talents to another, and one talent to the last, each "in proportion to their abilities." Over the years, based greatly on this parable, the meaning of the word *talent* changed to what we know it as today: "the natural endowments of a person . . . a special often creative or artistic aptitude [ability]."* In other words, though the parable talks of the diligence with which each servant used their money, it has often been more broadly interpreted as how we use all God has given us.

All of us have three things to invest for a return: our time, our talents, or our treasure. We often trade our time and effort for a paycheck—most people work to get paid by the hour. Our talents, education, and abilities often determine how much we are paid per hour—such as someone working in a fast food place making minimum wage versus a lawyer or a doctor making several hundred dollars an hour. Once we earn money, it can be invested for a return as well—starting with a couple of percentage points in a savings account to profits made from buying and selling real estate or companies.

The point is, how do each of us use the resources that we have to further the kingdom of God? Harriet Beecher Stowe had a talent as a writer, yet she could have squandered it by writing fluffy stories to earn some extra money. Instead, however, she used her talents *on purpose* as a fiction writer to show people what slavery was really like, and in doing so she used her God-given talents to turn the head of her nation away from indifference toward fighting for the freedom of all Americans.

Though God does care a great deal about how we use our money, He cares just as much about how we use the gifts and resources he has put at our disposal. Are we here to use them to build our own little kingdoms on earth, or to establish His kingdom here on earth?

Think for a moment and list some of the things you are good at or like to do. Sometimes our likes tell us more about our talents than anything we have yet accomplished because our talents are yet undeveloped. You may like music but have yet to learn to play an instrument, for example. Now look at your list. How can you develop these talents for God? How are you going to use them to serve God in the next year? Five years? Ten?

Do the same analysis with your time. Are you using it to serve God when you can? Are you using it to improve your talents? Or do you mostly waste it?

---

*Merriam-Webster, Inc. *Merriam-Webster's Collegiate Dictionary*. Includes Index. 10th ed. (Springfield, Mass., USA: Merriam-Webster, 1996, c1993), s.v. "talent."

What about your treasure? Do you give regularly to your church and missions? Do you save to be less dependent on others in the future? Or do you spend most of your money on stuff that pleases for today but in the long run won't last?

Stewardship

What Are You For?

If God be for us, who can be against us?

ROMANS 8:31 KJV

My great concern is not whether God is on our side.
My great concern is to be on God's side.

ABRAHAM LINCOLN

FREDERICK DOUGLASS (1818–1895)

Throughout his life two tenets stood as pillars of Frederick Douglass's beliefs and actions: The first was his Christian faith, the second his call to stand against the atrocity not only of slavery but of discrimination and oppression in general, be it of women, immigrants, or the working class. "All great reforms go together," he stated. He believed that to be the case because he took as his measuring rod the model of the Bible, in which in the eyes of Christ all were equal—there being neither Greek nor Jew, slave nor freeman, man nor woman. And he hated what some Americans had done in the name of Christianity, distorting and perverting religion to meet their own needs.

In an appendix to his *Narrative of the Life of an American Slave*, Douglass with fierce eloquence writes, "I love the pure, peaceable, and impartial Christianity of Christ: I therefore hate the corrupt, slaveholding, women-whipping, cradle-plundering, partial and hypocritical Christianity of this land. Indeed, I can see no reason, but the most deceitful one, for calling the religion of this land Christianity. I look upon it as the climax of misnomers, the boldest of all frauds, and the grossest of all libels."

He would never rest in his crusade, not against the church but against the religion of a country that would stand, at all, for slavery. He upbraided the hypocrisy of the church as a whole, castigated the slaveowners of the South who knew they stood opposed to God and the Constitution and yet continued to do so, and generally put forth as powerfully as ever before the whole awful mess that was slavery in the United States.

JOSHUA (*Joshua 24:1–15* NLT)

Joshua had seen much in his lifetime. He had been with Moses when he delivered the children of Israel from slavery in Egypt. He was there the day God parted the Red Sea and destroyed Pharaoh's army in its backwash. He saw Moses come down from Mount Sinai with the Ten Commandments, bring water from a rock, and fall to his face time and again in prayer when Israel was either in danger of enemies or their own arrogance. He had followed God as a pillar of cloud by day and a pillar of fire by night. He had gone into Canaan with the other twelve spies and saw a land flowing with milk and honey, and then saw the faithlessness of Israel in being able to take it with God's help. He had wandered with them forty years in the desert because of their unbelief, but then was also one of the only two—himself and Caleb—of that generation to enter the land God had promised them. He had seen the walls of Jericho fall when they followed God's plan, and then seen their defeat at Ai when they trusted the strength of their own fighting ability more than trusting in God. In his lifetime he had seen many incredible things, and now it was time to address the people one last time before he followed Moses and Caleb home to be with his Lord.

When he called the Israelites together for one last address as their leader, he told them of their history, from God's calling Abraham out of Ur to this land of promise and all these things that Joshua himself had witnessed to why God finally gave that land to the sons and daughters of Abraham as an eternal inheritance. He spoke eloquently and the crowd listened to him intently. He told again of God's miraculous delivering of His people from every enemy, famine, and hardship. Truly they had a glorious heritage and a wondrous God to call upon.

Yet they had one thing to fear—their own weaknesses and selfishness. While God had been mighty on their behalf, they could squelch His power through their own unbelief and by turning to other things as a priority over the one true God. So Joshua warned them and gave them this challenge:

> So honor the Lord and serve him wholeheartedly. Put away forever the idols your ancestors worshiped when they lived beyond the

Euphrates River and in Egypt. Serve the Lord alone. But if you are unwilling to serve the Lord, then choose today whom you will serve. Would you prefer the gods your ancestors served beyond the Euphrates? Or will it be the gods of the Amorites in whose land you now live? *But as for me and my family, we will serve the Lord.* (emphasis added)

{ LIVING IT! }

There are a lot of people against things in our nation today. All of this negative energy seems to be having its effect. While many of these people are right in their causes, they are forgetting a fundamental truth— we always gain our power from what we are for, not what we are against.

While men and women such as Frederick Douglass were righteous to stand against slavery, the effective ones did not forget that they first had to be *for God*. First in Douglass's mind was his Christian faith, and because of that he could stand against the evils of slavery, prejudice, racism, and inequality. Joshua had seen it all, and he saw that it was not enough just to stand against foreign gods and put down evil practices, but the people of Israel first needed to actively seek God and follow Him wholeheartedly if they were going to survive and prosper as a nation.

Today, we might be a country formed under God, but we are not living up to His standards. He reigns over us and we are called, at all times, to follow His path. But are we living for Him enough to develop the inner strength and conviction to stand for what is right as Douglass and Joshua did? Are we willing to seek His righteousness and kingdom first above all?

We definitely need Christians today willing to stand for truth no matter what. We need to look beyond the party affiliations of donkeys and elephants to the more lasting truth. But our strength to do so will never come from a legalism derived from pasting together Scriptures as a code of morality to impose on others. We need to know the Author of the Book. Only from knowing and following Him wholeheartedly will we know how to apply His Scriptures correctly to our times and bring righteousness back to the forefront of our nation—and only that righteousness can protect us and right the causes for which we stand by the strength of His love.

Are there things that you feel are threatening our nation today from within? What does the Bible have to say about these things? Pray over the Scriptures you found in answering these questions and ask God to show you how to act upon them. Seek His will in this area and ask that it be done on earth as it is in heaven.

What are some areas of your life that you feel may drain your allegiance to God or the time you spend seeking Him? Certainly it would be wonderful to spend our every waking hour in prayer and Bible study, but God knows that is not realistic except for special times of getting away on retreats or at camps. In your day-to-day life, what can you cut out to be sure you are seeking God as the most important thing in your life?

How do you seek God every day? How do you put Him first in your life? (If you honestly feel that you don't, what are you going to do to change that?)

Refusing to Be
Silenced

We must obey God rather than men.

ACTS 5:29B NASB

KETTLE PRAYERS (1860S)

Silently, they opened the door to their cabin. By the moonlight, Mattie could see small groups of two or three adults stealing away to the barn. Mattie's father and one of the other men carried the large iron kettle. Others carried large rocks.

The men carefully opened the big barn door, moving it so slowly that it made no sound. Carrying the kettle, they slipped into the barn and shut the door behind them. Once inside, they turned the kettle upside down so the rim was placed on four rocks to create an open space underneath.

One by one, Mattie's family and neighbors lay on the ground around the kettle, their mouths close to the opening. Gramma motioned for Mattie to come lie beside her. Soon Mattie's father began to pray softly, the kettle muffling his voice. Taking turns, others joined in. They prayed and sang softly long into the night.

Whenever she prayed, Mattie asked God for help with something she faced that day. But as she listened, she noticed her family and neighbors were not praying for themselves. They didn't think they would see freedom in their time, so they prayed for the freedom of their children and their children's children. Mattie realized they were risking their lives to pray for her freedom and for children who would one day be born to her. She now had new questions: *How long do prayers keep? Do they last forever? Where does God keep them?*

Mattie dozed off wondering how many prayers it would take to fill the big kettle. She woke as the big folks were quietly getting up off the dirt floor. She was quickly alert, knowing that this would be her only chance to ask about all that she had seen.

Just then her favorite uncle, Robert, came over and gave her a hug. He whispered, "I betcha got a lotta questions. I did! Like, how does this thing work?"

Mattie nodded. "Yeah, how does it work?"

"I asked a lotta folks, and I got a lotta answers," Robert said. "Folks say God catches the sound of the prayin' and the singin' and keeps it in the kettle so the white folk can't hear us.

"You know, some families don't get down on the floor like we do. They just put the kettle on the doorstep to keep the sounds from escapin' out the door. They say that works just as well.

"Some say it don't matter *where* you put the kettle, 'cause the kettle is just a sign that shows God we're trustin' Him to be with us and protect us."

Mattie nodded. "Gramma says God can do anythin' if we trust Him."

At that moment Gramma joined them. Uncle Robert asked, "Mama, where did folks learn about prayin' into the kettle?"

"I don't know where they learned it," Gramma answered. "I kinda think the Lord put these things in their minds to do for themselves, just like He helps us Christians in other ways." She paused. "Don't ya think so?"

Robert smiled. "All I know is it works! I talk with folks from other plantations, and I never heard tell of anyone caught prayin' since our people started using them kettles."

Mattie noticed that most of the folks had already left. "Gramma, how long do prayers keep? Do they last forever? Where does God keep 'em?"

The old woman smiled. "I heard a preacher once tell that in heaven there was bowls full of the prayers of the saints. Them bowls sit right in front of the throne of God where He can see them all the time."

Mattie watched as her father and his friend picked up the big family kettle. "And our kettle is like our own secret bowl of prayers for our family forever."

Gramma reached out to hug Mattie. "I'm so proud of you, Mattie. Someday you'll be free, an' you will be able to pray wherever and whenever you want. Be sure to keep prayin' for your children. And be sure to tell your children how we prayed for them under the kettle."

Gramma noticed the men were waiting for them to leave so they could close the big barn big door. "Now hush, Mattie. No more questions about prayin' until next meetin'!"

PETER AND JOHN (*Acts 4:16–20*)

"What are we going to do with these men?"

The Jewish High Council was beside itself. Jesus was dead, yet He was gathering more and more followers every day! Only fifty days after His crucifixion—what should have been the last they heard of Him!—three thousand rose up one day to start following Him because of some commotion on the feast of Pentecost. Now, some cripple who had been begging at the temple gate called Beautiful was miraculously healed by these two uneducated fishermen named Peter and John. People were turning from their religious leadership to follow Jesus by the droves! What were they going to do?

"Everybody living in Jerusalem knows they have done an outstanding miracle, and we cannot deny it. But to stop this thing from spreading any further among the people, we must warn these men to speak no longer to anyone in this name."

Again the Council called the two men before them and commanded that they teach and speak no more in the name of Jesus. Their only response, however, was, "Judge for yourselves whether it is right in God's sight to obey you rather than God. For we cannot help speaking about what we have seen and heard."

The Jewish leaders warned them again but saw it would do no good. How could they punish men for healing a man who had lived crippled for over forty years? What were they to do about this Jesus talk?

{ LIVING IT! }

Intercessor and author William Ford III owns the prayer kettle used by his ancestors to pray for his freedom. He writes:

> One day, freedom did come. While many of those who prayed did not live to see freedom, their prayers were answered for the next generation. The young girl ["Mattie" in the above story] who passed down these stories attended these prayer meetings until slavery was abolished. . . . As a young teenager, she was set free. Can you imagine being that one that freedom fell upon, having listened to others pray

for your freedom for many years?

I believe this teenage girl saw fit to pass down this kettle because she knew that not only was she standing on the sacrifice of others' devotion to Christ, but so was everyone born after her in our family. She was careful to preserve and pass on both the kettle and its history. She passed it to her daughter, Harriet Locket, who passed it to Nora Locket, who passed it to William Ford, Sr., who passed it to William Ford, Jr., who gave it to me, William Ford III. It has been in our family for 200 years.

As Will continued to study generational prayer, he came to realize:

I could agree with the prayers made under our family's kettle by those who had gone before me. I thought, "Lord, I can agree with the prayers of my ancestors for the freedom of today's and the future generations in America." God was showing me in a new way that He is powerful, yesterday, today, and forever.

In his book, *History Makers*, which he coauthored with Dutch Sheets, Will speaks of the "synergy of the ages." He writes:

In God's kingdom, the prayers of Abraham are as immediate and relevant today as they were the day he prayed them. And so with the prayers of our forefathers. In other words, God is bringing together all the prayers of the saints to bear on the condition of America today. Connecting with this heritage can strengthen our prayers and heal our land, bringing revival and great societal change. No prayer is wasted. Our prayers count.

So when we pray, we can join our prayers with those of our founding fathers as well as the founders of our faith—early apostles such as Peter and John. When they were told to be silent and to never again mention the name of Jesus, instead they went out and prayed (see Acts 4:24–30). Mattie and her family did the same when she was told by her master not to pray. Today, we are told not to pray at school and often the same thing in the workplace. What are you going to do with that commandment of men?

What prayers of those who went before us can you join in with? What prayers do you think our ancestors prayed that have affected you? What can you pray that will affect your grandchildren and their children?

A legacy of prayer is a powerful thing. Does looking at the legacies left us by people such as Mattie and Peter and John change the way you see prayer? How?

What other traditions does your family have that affect you today? How can you preserve them so that they make an equally lasting impression on the generations that follow you, just as those in William Ford's family did for him?

God Is Just

The fear of the Lord is clean, enduring forever; The judgments of the Lord are true; they are righteous altogether.

PSALM 19:9 NASB

THOMAS JEFFERSON AND ABRAHAM LINCOLN

Etched into the third marble panel of the Jefferson Memorial is the following quotation:

> God who gave us life gave us liberty. Can the liberties of a nation be secure when we have removed a conviction that these liberties are the gift of God? Indeed I tremble for my country when I reflect that God is just, that his justice cannot sleep forever. Commerce between master and slave is despotism. Nothing is more certainly written in the book of fate than these people are to be free. Establish the law for educating the common people. This it is the business of the state to effect and on a general plan.

It is wrong to think that the issue of slavery did not rock the Constitutional Convention to the point that the United States could have disintegrated almost before it even began. While Jefferson and others like him owned slaves, it was not their desire to see slavery institutionalized anywhere the thirteen stars and stripes of the first American flag flew. But economic pressures from the South and their superior numbers forced compromise over the issue, a compromise that would eventually have to be solved by the bloodiest war the United States has ever seen— our American Civil War.

Some of the decisions made at this time have been misinterpreted today as racist, while in fact they were for the protection and hopeful eventual freedom of the slaves. One example of this is what came to be known as the "Three-Fifths Clause," in which slaves were only counted as three-fifths of a person. This was not decided to show that Congress saw slaves as less than a whole person, but so that slave states could not get disproportional representation in Congress by counting their non-voting slaves as "whole" citizens in their states. By reducing their count to three-fifths (five slaves being equal to three free men), free states had a closer number of state representatives and therefore more balance between antislavery votes and pro-slavery votes.

While God's grace is great, as Jefferson said, "his justice cannot sleep forever." Less than seventy-five years after the Constitution was ratified, the United States was nearly torn in half by the issues and differences slavery had propagated between the North and the South. At his second inaugural address in 1865, and at the height of the Civil War, President Lincoln described the events of the day in this way:

> If we shall suppose that American Slavery is one of those offences which, in the providence of God, must needs come, but which, having continued through His appointed time, He now wills to remove, and that He gives to both North and South, this terrible war, as the woe due to those by whom the offence came, shall we discern therein any departure from those divine attributes which the believers in a Living God always ascribe to Him? Fondly do we hope—fervently do we pray—that this mighty scourge of war may speedily pass away. Yet, if God wills that it continue, until all the wealth piled by the bond-men's two hundred and fifty years of unrequited toil shall be sunk, and until every drop of blood drawn with the lash, shall be paid by another drawn with the sword, as was said three thousand years ago, so still it must be said, "The judgments of the Lord are true and righteous altogether."
>
> With malice toward none, with charity for all, with firmness in the right as God gives us to see the right, let us strive on to finish the work we are in, to bind up the nation's wounds, to care for him who shall have borne the battle and for his widow and his orphan, to do all which may achieve and cherish a just and lasting peace among ourselves and with all nations.*

THE PARABLE OF THE FAITHFUL AND UNFAITHFUL SERVANTS (*Matthew 24:45–51* paraphrased)

When Jesus was talking of those who would be alive upon the earth in the latter days, He told this parable:

---

*Abraham Lincoln, "Second Inauguration Address." Available online at: *www.law.ou.edu/hist/lincoln2.html*. Accessed 21 March 2005.

When the Master returns to His household, who will be the wise and faithful servants he finds doing as He first instructed them to do and taking care of his household, ensuring all within it are getting their proper food at the proper times? How blessed will be those he finds doing what He called them to do! Truly I tell you, they will have greater responsibilities in His kingdom down the road.

However, what of those servants who say, "Oh, why worry? Our Lord will not be back for many, many days—in fact, He may never return!" Then those disbelieving servants will begin to abuse their privileges: They will take more for themselves than the Master appointed for them to have, and they will take the excess out of those they have rule over to the point of abusing and degrading them. He will begin to party and carouse with those out only to please themselves and satisfy their own desires at the expense of others. Then the Master of the household will come on a day the servant does not expect—because the servant is not looking for Him to return—and the Master will give Him retribution for the pain he has caused others. He will stand as a hypocrite with the hypocrites in a place where there will be great repentance, crying, and gnashing of teeth because the prizes that were lost can never be regained again in all the ages to come.

{ L I V I N G   I T ! }

Jesus died on the cross that all humanity might be saved. All the sins we have ever committed were washed away by His shed blood on the cross. Yet where does that put us in following His ordained laws of love? Though we are saved, can we overlook justice and fair treatment between all people groups of the world? Do we ever have a right to abuse our positions of authority, to put others down or treat them as inferior?

This may seem obviously wrong in a master/slave relationship, but what about a supervisor/employee relationship? Or with our younger siblings? Or others we may be working with at our church or other service organizations? Do we lord any authority we have over others because of our position or social standing? Or exploit the skills and talents of others for our own profit? What will our eternal reward look like if we are largely living for our own profit by ignoring God's standards of justice and brotherhood—or by ignoring His truth?

The moral principles and precepts contained in the Scripture ought to form the basis of all our civil constitutions and laws. All the miseries and evil men suffer from vice, crime, ambition, injustice, oppression, slavery, and war, proceed from their despising or neglecting the precepts contained in the Bible.

—Noah Webster

What does it really mean to be "faithful" to God? Is it just a matter of what we don't do: don't smoke, don't have premarital sex, don't drink, don't chew tobacco, and don't hang out with those who do? Or is there something more we should be doing? Is it enough just to not do wrong things, or are there good things we should be doing to make our world a better place through God's love?

What does it mean to be a good citizen of our nation? What does being a Christian have to do with being an American? Which should be more solid within us: the customs of our culture or the principles of God's kingdom?

Jesus told more than one parable where there was a master who went away for a while and then came back and called to accounting the things his servants had done while he was away. What things do you feel your Master is calling you to do before He returns? Are you actively seeking His purpose for your life so you can plug in to it and do it, or are you content to just hang around on the sideline until the game clock expires?

Turning Point

Do not fret or have any anxiety about anything, but
in every circumstance and in everything, by prayer
and petition ... with thanksgiving, continue to make
your wants known to God. And God's peace ...
which transcends all understanding shall garrison
and mount guard over your hearts and minds
in Christ Jesus.

PHILIPPIANS 4:6–7 AMP

ABRAHAM LINCOLN (1809–1865)

Union General Daniel Sickles asked President Lincoln, "Were you anxious about the battle at Gettysburg?"

President Lincoln replied that he was not worried and then explained:

> In the pinch of your campaign up there, when everybody seemed panic-stricken, and nobody could tell what was going to happen ... I went to my room one day, and I locked the door, and got down on my knees before Almighty God, and prayed to Him mightily for victory at Gettysburg.
>
> I told Him that this was His war, and our cause His cause, but we couldn't stand another Fredericksburg or Chancellorsville. And I then and there made a solemn vow to Almighty God, that if He would stand by you boys at Gettysburg, I would stand by Him.
>
> And after that ... soon a sweet comfort crept into my soul that God Almighty had taken the whole business into His own hands and that things would go all right at Gettysburg. And that is why I had no fears about you.

Lincoln was not the only one praying. He had proclaimed April 30, 1863, to be a national day of fasting, humiliation, and prayer. He requested that "all the people abstain on that day from their ordinary secular pursuits and unite ... in keeping the day holy to the Lord."

After victory at Gettysburg and in Vicksburg the day after, President Lincoln did not forget the One to whom the credit for those victories was due. On July 15, 1863, President Lincoln asked for a day of national thanksgiving, praise, and prayer, exhorting citizens to thank "the Divine Majesty for the wonderful things He has done in the nation's behalf, to invoke the influence of His Holy Spirit to subdue the anger which has produced . . . a needless and cruel rebellion, to guide the counsels of government, and to visit with tender care and consolation all those who [because of the war] suffer in mind, body, or estate."

THE BATTLE OF REPHIDIM (*Exodus 17:8–16*)

"Choose some of our men and go out to fight the Amalekites. Tomorrow I will stand on top of the hill with the staff of God in my hands," Moses told Joshua.

The Amalekites were not anxious to let Israel cross through their lands, feeling that such a great number would do great damage, and as a result they came out in force to stop God's people. The Israelites took up arms to defend themselves.

While Joshua led the arms, Aaron, Hur, and Moses went to the mountaintop to watch over the battle and pray for their victory. As Moses held his hands up to the Lord, Israel prevailed, but as he dropped them, the Amalekites took the advantage. Moses held his hands up as much as possible, but as the day and the battle wore on, Moses grew tired. To help him, Aaron and Hur set him on a rock and each took one of his wrists to keep his hands toward heaven until the end of the day. As a result, Joshua and his army overwhelmed the Amalekites and victory was theirs.

As a memorial to the battle, Moses built an altar and put the name *Jehovah-Nissi* on it, meaning, "The Lord is my Banner."

{ LIVING IT! }

It is easy to underestimate prayer. Even taking the time to pray five to ten minutes every morning can seem like drudgery and a waste of time, but God sees faithfulness. Just as exercise and practice are necessary to an athlete, so prayer is essential to our lives as Christians; and just as one teammate who exercises and practices to their fullest can be a help to their team, so one Christian who takes prayer seriously can be an incredible aid to the body of Christ.

Abraham Lincoln's prayers and the prayers of our nation at that time helped turn the tide of the Civil War. Moses' "intercession" to God by holding his hands up in worship turned the tide of the battle for Joshua. What are our prayers accomplishing today in our nation?

Make a list of people you should pray for. Don't just list the president, but go to the Internet and find the senators for your state and the representative for your area. List your mayor, Supreme Court judges, or friends or family you have in law enforcement, fire fighting, the military, or any other area you can think of. Keep this list in your Bible and from time to time when you think of it, pull it out and pray for these people. Your prayers don't have to be long, just heartfelt, and you can pray for them in the middle of a church service just as much as at home. Then note the change in you as you do this regularly. Does prayer make a difference?

Tell your youth leader you want to take time during a meeting just to pray for our nation. Make copies of your list for others so they know whom to pray for.

Remembering Our Foundations

By this time you ought to be teachers yourselves, yet here I find you need someone to sit down with you and go over the basics on God again, starting from square one.

HEBREWS 5:12 THE MESSAGE

THE GETTYSBURG ADDRESS

The tall, gaunt figure of Abraham Lincoln walked slowly to the podium. Hesitantly, he began:

Four score and seven years ago our fathers brought forth on this continent a new nation, conceived in liberty and dedicated to the proposition that all men are created equal. Now we are engaged in a great civil war, testing whether that nation or any nation so conceived and so dedicated can long endure. We are met on a great battlefield of that war. We have come to dedicate a portion of that field as a final resting-place for those who here gave their lives that that nation might live. It is altogether fitting and proper that we should do this. But in a larger sense, we cannot dedicate, we cannot consecrate, we cannot hallow this ground. The brave men, living and dead, who struggled here have consecrated it far above our poor power to add or detract. The world will little note nor long remember what we say here, but it can never forget what they did here. It is for us the living, rather, to be dedicated here to the unfinished work which they who fought here have thus far so nobly advanced. It is rather for us to be here dedicated to the great task remaining before us—that from these honored dead we take increased devotion to that cause for which they gave the last full measure of devotion—that we here highly resolve that these dead shall not have died in vain, that this nation, under God, shall have a new birth of freedom, and that government of the people, by the people, for the people shall not perish from the earth.

Lincoln delivered his two-minute Gettysburg Address on November 19, 1863, at the dedication of the cemetery at Gettysburg, the site of the battle that arguably turned the tide of the Civil War in favor of the Union. So short was his message that many in the crowd did not even realize he was speaking until he was done. But so powerful were the words that shed new light on the Declaration of Independence, a document espousing equality for all people. Just ten months before, on January 1, 1863, Lincoln's Emancipation Proclamation had declared freedom for the slaves. And whereas the Declaration of Independence put forth freedom for all as an idea, the Gettysburg Address was a bold step toward making a "new birth of freedom" for all, including slaves, a reality.

The last written draft of the Gettysburg Address contained 265 words. But as Lincoln stood to deliver the address, he added two words on the spur of the moment: *under God*. Lincoln's eloquent address is considered one of the finest speeches ever delivered by an American, and the addition of just two words reminds us of a truth that we must not subtract from America's equation: Our future will be assured and secured only as we remain under God—under His grace and guidance.

THE BOOK OF THE LAW IS REDISCOVERED
(*2 Kings 22–23*)

The nation of Judah had had such a long history of ungodly kings that the Word of God was no longer preached in the temple and no records of it remained anywhere that men knew of in all the land of Judah. Into this came an eight-year-old boy named Josiah, who took the throne when his father Amon was assassinated. Yet rather than follow in the tradition of his fathers, instead he chose to seek and follow God.

When he was twenty-six, Josiah called for the Temple of God to be renovated. In the repairs, the high priest Hilkiah found a book. He gave it to the scribe Shaphan, who took it before Josiah and read it. Suddenly the law that had long been the foundation of Judah's government and society was alive again. When he heard the Word of God, Josiah tore his robes in sorrow for what his nation had lost. Though he had sought the Lord all of his life, in their ignorance of God's founding principles, Judah had strayed far from the truth.

God overlooked the sins of Josiah's fathers and looked instead at his heart. Josiah called for a gathering of all in the temple and read to them all the words of God's laws. Then he stood before them and promised before God that he would walk after the Lord and keep His commandments with all his heart and soul. He would stick to the words of God's law and follow all that was written in the book. All of the people assembled there stood to show they would live by this promise as well.

Because of this, Josiah made sweeping changes in Judah to align his nation with the will of God as it was revealed through His Word, and for the reign of Josiah as king, Judah prospered.

{ LIVING IT! }

As Abraham Lincoln stood on the field of the bloodiest battle in American history, he felt it necessary to speak of why such a war had to be fought. What were they fighting for? Why was it necessary to shed so much blood? What could possibly justify the more than fifty-one thousand Americans killed in this single battle?

History records that President Lincoln was not even to be the main speaker that day. He was given just a few minutes, while a professional orator had been hired to speak for hours to try to do homage to those who had died. Yet it is only Lincoln's words that were remembered. Why?

Because Lincoln did not speak only to their bravery or their sacrifice but about the founding principle of America for which they fought: *the proposition that all men are created equal.* Nor did Lincoln call for the dead to be honored by dedicating a cemetery or a monument to them only, but that the living should *highly resolve that these dead shall not have died in vain, that this nation, under God, shall have a new birth of freedom, and that government of the people, by the people, for the people shall not perish from the earth.*

Lincoln's words stated simply that a nation that does not remember the founding principles on which it was built cannot survive. Josiah realized the same thing—if Judah did not return to a government and culture built upon the standards of the Word of God, it would fall. No nation can last built on inequality, nor can it deny the Word of God as the ultimate authority and endure the test of time.

What we need today are young people like Josiah who will "find" the book of the law upon which our nation was built and demand that it again be implemented as the foundation for both our laws and our practices. In the moral chaos of our modern society, God's truth still points to the best path forward—it is time for today's generation to undo the neglect of past generations just as Josiah did for Judah.

What principles from God's Word do you feel are most important for our nation today? Do you pray for these regularly? If not, add them to your regular times of prayer.

How do you apply these principles in your life? Are you living them as well as praying that others do?

In the Face of Evil

*'Tis the business of little minds to shrink, but he
whose heart is firm, and whose conscience approves
his conduct, will pursue his principles unto death.*

THOMAS PAINE

SILAS SOULE (1839–1865)

Silas was tired from a long night's ride. As dawn arrived, word came down the line that they had reached their destination: Sand Creek. Silas eased his horse to the edge of the bluff, peering over the escarpment at what lay below. "Chief Black Kettle's people," he said to Lieutenant James Cannon, a junior officer. "Old men, women, children—the braves are probably off hunting buffalo. No sign of any Dog Soldiers either." Below them lay the quiet winter camp of Black Kettle, White Antelope, Left Hand, and other friendly southern Cheyenne and Arapaho chiefs, about 550 people total.

Suddenly Silas heard the order from Chivington: "Attack! Attack!"

Silas paused, not wanting to accept what he had feared for days. "We can't attack," he said to himself. He was thinking out loud, more than he was giving a command. But he realized, reflexively, that he could not follow Chivington's order.

"No one attacks!" Soule shouted to his company. "I am ordering you to stand your ground." All around him, however, Silas saw the majority of the other 725 cavalry soldiers attacking as chaos erupted. Chivington himself approached Soule, red faced, demanding he attack—Chivington knew that Soule preferred peace with Black Kettle. But Soule refused Chivington's direct order. "This is murder!" yelled Soule. Chivington reared his horse and thundered down the embankment, cursing Soule.

Black Kettle, the peace-seeking Cheyenne chief who had personally met President Lincoln, had been told by a white officer to always fly the American flag while encamped. "If you do, no one will harm you," he had been promised.

Silas could hear the screams of the women and children and the look of realization as the old men and chiefs scrambled into action. The attack continued for about six hours, Silas recorded, over a distance of four miles up the creek bed. The massacre took place as a running engagement. In all, 163 Cheyenne and Arapaho were slaughtered, two thirds being women, children, and infants. The soldiers lost fewer than ten men.

Silas wrote:

> It is hard to see little children on their knees have their brains beat out by men professing to be "civilized." One squaw was wounded and a fellow took a hatchet to finish her, she held her arms up to defend her, and he cut one arm off and held the other with the one hand and dashed a hatchet through her brain. I saw two Indians hold one another's hands, chased until they were exhausted, when they kneeled down, and clasped each other around the neck and were both shot together. One woman was cut open and the child inside of her taken out, and scalped.

JOSHUA AND CALEB (*Numbers 13:26–14:10*)

As the twelve men stood before Moses and the entire congregation of Israel, they showed them the incredible clusters of grapes they had found in the land. The crowd gasped at the magnificence of it. Certainly this was an incredible place God was calling them to! At last they would enter the land promised to their forefather Abraham!

Or at least their optimism was high until the first man who had gone to spy out the land spoke: "We went into the land to which you sent us, and it does flow with milk and honey! Here is its fruit. But the people who live there are powerful, and the cities are fortified and very large. We even saw descendants of Anak [giants] there."

At this, the crowd murmured nervously. Nine of the other spies nodded. At that moment Caleb stepped forward and signaled for the people to be quiet. "We should go up and take possession of the land, for we can certainly do it."

Ten of the other spies didn't agree. And the crowd was growing surly and questioned who to believe. One of the ten answered Caleb's call to bravery with, "We can't attack those people; they are stronger than we are." Then another said, "The land we explored devours those living in it. All the people we saw there are of great size. . . . We seemed like grasshoppers in our own eyes, and we looked the same to them."

At this the crowd was lost. Despite the faith of Joshua and Caleb, who said, "The land we passed through and explored is exceedingly good. If the Lord is pleased with us, he will lead us into that land, a land flowing with milk and honey, and will give it to us. Only do not rebel against the Lord. And do not be afraid of the people of the land, because we will swallow them up. Their protection is gone, but the Lord is with us. Do not be afraid of them," the people still feared. In fact, rather than finding fault with the ten faithless spies, they wanted to stone Joshua and Caleb to death!

Yet because of their faith, God intervened. This generation would not see God's promise fulfilled because of their faithlessness. Instead, they would wander in the desert for forty years, and then come back to the very place they now stood, and Joshua and Caleb would lead their children into the land instead of them.

{ L I V I N G   I T ! }

On April 23, 1865, Charles Squiers, purportedly hired by Chivington's men, shot and killed Soule near his home in Denver, shortly after Soule had testified against Chivington. Soule had been married just weeks earlier. When Chivington took the stand just one day after Soule's burial, he tried to brand Soule a coward and drunkard. But men who served under Soule could stand it no longer and came to his defense, praising Soule for his unwavering courage in the face of the treacherous order to attack. First Lieutenant James Cannon, loyal to Soule, tracked down Squiers in New Mexico and brought him back to Denver to stand trial. Squiers escaped, and Cannon was poisoned. Squiers was never recaptured.

The incident is sad not because of the apparent futility of Soule's standing against the evil of his commander, but that in standing against the evil and the massacre of innocent, peace-seeking people, he stood alone. Of 725 soldiers, Soule was the only officer with enough moral courage to say "No!" to an inhuman order.

Decades later, at the Nuremberg trials that sought to find an explanation for the atrocities committed by simple German soldiers during the Holocaust, the hollowness of one answer rang out until it today stands as the ultimate cop-out: "I was just following orders."

In the face of two million people, Joshua and Caleb were the only ones willing to stand against the crowd because they wanted to stand for what was right—they wanted to stand on God's side. In the heat of battle, Silas Soule stood in a similar way, even in the face of threats and direct orders of his commanding officer. He knew that no matter what authority he faced, there was only one that really mattered, standing before the judgment seat of Christ when his eternal reward would be determined. The Bible says that "The fear of the Lord is the beginning of wisdom" (Psalm 111:10a KJV). This is true. It is also the beginning of courage. We are only valuable to our nation, or ourselves, if we hold God's laws above all others.

What better place to "take our stand" than on God's side?

There is an old saying: "If you don't stand for something, you will fall for anything." What do you feel passionate about standing for? How do you take that stand every day? Or do you?

Have you ever had a situation where you had to stand against the crowd, or at least should have? How did you handle it? If you had the chance to live through that moment again, how might you have handled it differently?

Are there places dedicated to Native American life near where you live? Have you ever visited there? If not, find the time to take some friends and go. As you walk through, pray quietly to yourself for the Native American people in our land and the reconciliation between all the different people groups of the United States.

A Faithful Steward

*Well done, good servant; because you were faithful in
a very little, have authority over ten cities.*

LUKE 19:17 NKJV

BRIDGET "BIDDY" MASON (1818–1892)

"We are free! We are really free!" Biddy Mason's three daughters,
ages seventeen, eleven, and seven, were laughing and dancing for joy.
Just a few hours earlier, a district judge had decided that Biddy and her
children were being illegally kept as slaves—and therefore set them free.

Now, as they celebrated their newfound freedom at the home of
their friend Robert Owens and his family, they realized that on this day,
January 21, 1856, their lives had changed forever.

Biddy soon found her skills as a midwife were in great demand. She
delivered hundreds of babies for women of all races and social classes,
working in the grandest Victorian homes and the lowliest of hovels. For
those who could not pay, she worked for free. During a smallpox epidemic, she nursed many people at the risk of her own life.

She had two goals during this time—to help others and to buy her
own land. Earning $2.50 a day, a good wage for an African-American
woman at that time, in ten years she was able to save $250. On Novem-
ber 28, 1866, Biddy bought two lots bounded by Spring, Fort (now
Broadway), Third, and Fourth Streets on the outskirts of Los Angeles.
She was one of the first black women to buy property in the United
States.

Biddy kept improving her property, first building small rental
houses and then a commercial building. Selling and buying pieces of real
estate, she began to build a fortune, which she used to help her community. A devout Christian, Biddy's passion was helping others in need.
She gave money and land to schools, where the poorest and most needy
children could be taught. In 1872 she and her son-in-law, Charles Owens,

formed the First African Methodist Episcopal Church in Los Angeles, building the first black church in the city on land Biddy provided. She helped establish day-care centers, stores, and eleven convalescent homes. After floodwaters destroyed sections of Los Angeles in the 1880s, Biddy went to a local grocer and set up open-ended accounts so people who lost their homes and jobs could get food and necessities. Biddy quietly paid the bills, helping people of all races. To Biddy there were no differences.

Biddy did not just give money and land. She also visited the poor, the sick, prisoners, and the elderly. A godly woman, Biddy taught her children the virtues of generosity and Christlike love. Her life demonstrated the biblical principle that if you give, it will be given to you, and that giving to others always brings back more than what you gave.

The city continued to grow, and within twenty-five years the main financial district of the city was just a block away from Biddy's property. By the late 1800s Biddy's shrewd investments had made her one of the wealthiest African-American women in Los Angeles.

JESUS TELLS HIS DISCIPLES OF THE END OF THE AGE (*Matthew 24 and 25*)

When His disciples asked Him about the signs of the end of the age in Matthew 24, Jesus gladly told them what they needed to watch for to know when His return to the earth would be approaching. Rather than simply answer their questions, however, He also taught them something they would need to know as the end of the age neared: His expectation that they would take care of one another while He was away.

After telling the disciples about end time events, Jesus told them four parables. The first was about a servant who had been left in charge of the household while his master was away. The question of the parable was, "Who then is the faithful and wise servant, whom the master has put in charge of the servants in his household to give them their food at the proper time?" Then He told them the parable of the ten virgins—the five who had extra were admitted into the Bridegroom's banquet, the other five were not. Then He tells the parable of the talents—those who faithfully used what their master left them were rewarded, those who sat on their "talents" were not. Then to wrap it all up, he told them the parable of the sheep and the goats. The sheep, those who helped others when they saw their need, were blessed. Those who ignored the needs of others were not.

{ LIVING IT! }

Biddy Mason did more with her freedom than just find a place to live on her own and secure a free future for her family. Rather than going from one form of slavery, with a human master, to another, working for a daily wage, she made money serve her so that others would benefit. Using God-given wisdom and patience, Biddy carefully saved and invested so that by the end of her life she had enough for her future, the future of her family, and enough to give to others as they had need.

In His answers to the disciples' questions, Jesus told them of the time to come when he would return to establish His kingdom on the earth, but in the meantime there would be a time "When the master would go away, and then return to take accounting of what his servants had done with what he had left them while he was gone." Jesus' message seems clear; the key was not to sit around watching for the signs of the end, but to work energetically in the meantime with all He had left at our disposal—our time, talent, ingenuity, and treasure as many people see it—being the best stewards of them that we can. To what end? As He says in His transitional question, that those in His household might receive "their food at the proper time." If this was not clear enough, he ends the sermon with the parable of the sheep and the goats: "Truly I say to you, to the extent that you did it [fed, clothed, or healed] to one of these brothers of Mine, even the least of them, you did it to Me" (NASB).

Do you have a plan for being a long-term blessing to the body of Christ? Many of us have plans to do well financially or run a business in our future, but how many of us do it with a similar motivation to Biddy Mason's? What is the "giving" plan for the "living" you will earn? Bill Bright, the founder of Campus Crusade for Christ, used to challenge donors to set a goal of giving a million dollars to the gospel in their lifetime. Have you ever considered doing something like that? Sit down for a minute and think about it. When you are called to account for how you used the resources that came through your fingers, what do you want to hear Jesus saying to you about how you used what He entrusted to you during your lifetime?

The Bible also tells us with respect to money that "He who is faithful in a very little thing is faithful also in much; and he who is unrighteous in a very little thing is unrighteous also in much" (Luke 16:10 NASB). You may have a little now or you may have much, but are you faithful in your tithing and giving *now*? If you are not, what do you think you will do when you get more? Take some time to sit down with a pencil and paper and look at your money and what you are giving. Are there changes you should make to show yourself faithful in how you manage whatever money you do have?

One Step Forward—Two Steps Back

If the power of the gospel is not felt through the length and breadth of the land, anarchy and misrule, degradation and misery, corruption and darkness will reign without mitigation or end.

DANIEL WEBSTER

THE COMPROMISE OF 1877

In 1876 Ulysses S. Grant still held the office of president, though most of the country, Republicans and Democrats alike, were tired of him. Corruption ruled during Grant's terms, and the great job of pulling together a fractured nation seemed lost in Washington's clamor for lined pockets and the fight for self-interest. If bribes were going to be paid anyway, they might as well be coming to you.

The issue of Reconstruction stood on the national agenda. It was now eleven years since the Confederate Army surrendered, and yet the work was still not done.

At the end of the Civil War, Union troops roamed the South, Southern states were forced to accept new amendments to the U.S. Constitution in order to be let back into the country, and a powerful Congress had overridden President Johnson's veto by passing the Reconstruction Acts of 1867–1868, dividing states into military districts.

The Freedman's Bureau, created in 1865, was given the enormous task of tackling the transition at a practical level. The jobs included finding work for freed slaves, setting up schools and educational systems, and much more. The Bureau had the power to enact laws to meet their goals and helped establish new state constitutions and governments for each reconstructed Southern state. Southerners, who watched their states be handed over to blacks and newly arrived "carpetbagger"

Yankees, hated the Bureau with a passion, and it's not surprising that members were often targeted by the newly emerged Ku Klux Klan.

Take all this unrest, let it fester for a number of years, and then add the Hayes-Tilden Election of 1876, and you have a rough idea of the state of the country at that time. Angry voices, pointing fingers, and outright threats filled the public discourse. We were still a nation divided.

The problem with the election was this: Democrat Samuel Tilden, champion of the white South, had won the popular vote, 4,282,020 to 4,036,572, and the day after the election the electoral returns stood at 184 for Tilden and 165 for Hayes. But the winner needed 185 votes, and four states' votes still remained—Oregon, Florida, South Carolina, and Louisiana.

Oregon's three votes soon went to Hayes, but the other three states were a debacle. In the end, under reciprocal charges of voter fraud, both parties produced their own sets of electoral results and sent the results to Washington, D.C. All the numbers contradicted each other, and when the government turned to the Constitution for help they found none. No manner of resolution for such a problem had ever been spelled out.

Days turned into weeks, then into months. It was now March 1877, and the inauguration, now merely theoretical, was just days away. A bill was passed calling an Electoral Commission consisting of five members of the Senate, House, and Supreme Court to review the election and vote for the winner. There would be seven Republicans, seven Democrats, and one Independent. Shortly after the bill, however, the one Independent left the Supreme Court for a Senate seat. In filling the remaining spot from the Supreme Court, the commission had no choice but to select a Republican; there were no Democrats left.

The Commission's vote, eight to seven, made Rutherford Hayes president of the United States. But Congress still needed to accept the decision. Securing the majority vote necessary to carry the measure seemed almost an impossibility until a compromise was reached. In return for accepting Hayes as president, his first tasks would be to provide more federal funds for rebuilding the ruined Southern infrastructure and also to end Reconstruction by officially removing federal troops and recognizing Democrat governors elected to numerous Southern states. The Republicans agreed. Their man took office, but in return for the Republicans' win, the Democrats, over the next decade, were able to erase most of the civil rights laws that had been passed in the preceding fifteen years. And so among blacks, the Compromise of

1877 became known as the Great Betrayal.

The South celebrated as if they'd actually won the war. As Northern troops boarded ships home, Southern citizens fired guns and rang bells. Meanwhile black citizens, free but unequal, watched in silence. The war that was fought seemed to have been won in vain. They were emancipated, but that freedom now seemed worthless as their other rights soon vanished without protection.

JOSHUA AND THE GIBEONITES (*Joshua 9*)

The word of the Lord had been clear to Moses, Joshua, and Israel: In possessing the land of Canaan as the land God had promised them, they were to utterly drive out or destroy all the inhabitants and the shrines of their gods.

When word came to the Gibeonites that both Jericho and Ai had fallen and that none had been spared, they feared their own destruction at the hands of the great army, since they were in the next valley into which the Israelites would travel. To try to protect themselves, they devised a plan to make a treaty with Israel. They took old, dry, moldy bread to show as their food, put old sacks and wineskins that were cracked and mended on their donkeys, and then dressed in clothes that were well worn and patched as if from a long journey. Then they set out as ambassadors to meet Joshua and the other elders of Israel.

When they arrived, they entreated him, "We have come from a distant country; make a treaty with us."

Being suspicious, the elders of Israel and Joshua asked them, "But perhaps you live near us. How then can we make a treaty with you? . . . Who are you and where do you come from?"

Slyly, they answered, "Your servants have come from a very distant country because of the fame of the Lord your God. For we have heard reports of him: all that he did in Egypt, and all that he did to the two kings of the Amorites east of the Jordan—Sihon king of Heshbon, and Og king of Bashan, who reigned in Ashtaroth. And our elders and all those living in our country said to us, 'Take provisions for your journey; go and meet them and say to them, "We are your servants; make a treaty with us."' This bread of ours was warm when we packed it at home on the day we left to come to you. But now see how dry and moldy it is. And these wineskins that we filled were new, but see how cracked they are. And our clothes and sandals are worn out by the very long journey."

The Israelites then made the mistake of trusting their own eyes and not inquiring of the Lord what they should do. They made a treaty with the Gibeonites only to soon find out that they had been fooled and thus compromised the instructions God had given them for possessing the land God had promised them. Thus for centuries to come the Gibeonites and their false gods would be a stumbling block to the people of Israel and cause them to fall away from God again and again.

{ LIVING IT! }

After the Civil War, Southern states had been forced to accept laws declaring blacks and whites equal, but when that threat of force vanished, segregation became enacted into law with the *Plessy v. Ferguson* decision calling for "separate but equal" treatment. And it was easy to ignore the "equal" part of that ruling. Poll taxes, literacy tests, and brutal force kept blacks from voting. Courts turned a blind eye to justice— often rendering convictions without trials or throwing out complaints made by blacks without even considering evidence—and with the eventual rise of the KKK, segregation turned into something more than separation. It turned brutal and violent. The KKK reigned with terror, and the lynch mob's noose struck terror for decades.

More than three thousand blacks would be lynched over the next forty years, and that doesn't even mark the tip of the mountain of those who were beaten, tortured, abused, stolen from, and treated as insignificant. In many ways, during Jim Crow a black southerner's life was, arguably, worth less than during slavery. Once again compromise of God's will for our nation cost us dearly, just as it did Joshua and the children of Israel.

As Frederick Douglass put it: "You have emancipated us. I thank you for it. You have enfranchised us. And I thank you for it. But what is your emancipation—what is your enfranchisement if the black man, having been made free by the letter of the law, is unable to exercise that freedom? You have turned us loose to the sky, to the storm, to the whirlwind, and worst of all, you have turned us loose to our infuriated masters. What does it all amount to if the black man after having been freed from the slaveholder's lash is subject to the slaveholder's shotgun!"

There is no denying Douglass's words. The North, tired and frustrated by the political quagmire in which it had become entangled, bailed when expedience called for it. For the sake of the executive office they traded the burgeoning rights of the African-American race. What might have been won over the next five years now took blacks nearly a century. There are no easy answers, but there are certainly bad choices—and the Compromise of 1877 stands as one of the worst in our nation's history. For it compromised very little that affected the people making the choices. It wasn't *their* freedoms they were surrendering or their rights they were chaining down. Our call is to look out for the powerless, not to sell them out for power.

When is compromise good and when it is bad? Should we ever compromise anything? Or are there some things that we need to hold to and others that we can let go of?

History is full of incidents that appear so incredibly wrong in retrospect that it is hard to believe anyone ever did them, and yet at the time the mistakes were not so obvious. As has too often been the case, it is easy to judge others for mistakes and then be blind in making the same mistakes ourselves. How can we be sure that our decisions are better? Is there something we can learn from Joshua's experience with the Gibeonites that can help us in this?

{ Chief Joseph }

``I Will Fight No More Forever''

It does not require many words to speak the truth.

CHIEF JOSEPH

CHIEF JOSEPH (1840–1904)

I am tired of fighting. Our chiefs are killed. Looking Glass is dead. Toohoolhoolzote is dead. The old men are all dead. It is the young men who say yes or no. . . .

It is cold and we have no blankets. The little children are freezing to death. My people, some of them, have run away to the hills, and have no blankets, no food; no one knows where they are—perhaps freezing to death. I want to have time to look for my children and see how many of them I can find. Maybe I shall find them among the dead.

Hear me, my chiefs. I am tired; my heart is sick and sad. From where the sun now stands, I will fight no more forever.

This now-famous speech was delivered on the morning of October 5, 1877. Later that day, Chief Joseph surrendered his rifle to Captain Nelson Miles, who had engaged the Nez Percé throughout the campaign. It is estimated that approximately 175 U.S. soldiers and citizen volunteers were killed, while as many as 200 Nez Percé lost their lives, and 90 were wounded—a casualty rate exceeding 30 percent.

Some survivors were able to escape to Canada, most joining the Sioux of Sitting Bull. Those who surrendered believed they would be returned to the Nez Percé reservation, but instead they were relocated to Oklahoma's Indian Country. Joseph later commented: "General Miles had promised that we might return to our country with what stock we had left. . . . I believed General Miles, or I never would have surrendered."

Chief Joseph was never allowed to live again in his ancestral homeland in the Wallowa Valley. His final years were spent at the Colville Indian Reservation in northeastern Washington. He died on September 21, 1904, at age sixty-four, of what the agency doctor determined was "a broken heart."

ANANIAS AND SAPPHIRA (*Acts 5:1–10* NASB)

Ananias and Sapphira had sold a piece of land and told the disciples that they had given the entire amount to the church, even though they had held some of it back for themselves. As a result, the Holy Spirit revealed to Peter what they had done and he confronted Ananias about the lie: "Ananias, why has Satan filled your heart to lie to the Holy Spirit and to keep back some of the price of the land? While it remained unsold, did it not remain your own? And after it was sold, was it not under your control? Why is it that you have conceived this deed in your heart? You have not lied to men but to God."

In response, Ananias fell dead at the apostle's feet.

Just a few hours later, when Peter confronted her, Sapphira also lied about the price of their land and their gift, and she also breathed her last as a result. Because of their deaths, the fear of the Lord fell on the church and all who heard about the incident.

{ LIVING IT! }

In 1986 the Nez Percé (*Nimíipuu*) Trail was established by the U.S. Congress as a National Historic Trail. The trail traces the 1,170-mile journey of the 1877 flight, stretching from Wallowa Lake, Oregon, to the Bear's Paw Battlefield near Chinook, Montana. Today, some Nez Percé make their home on the reservation at Lapwai, Idaho. Others, including some descendants of the 1887 Nez Percé, live in and around Chief Joseph's beloved Wallowa Valley, Oregon.

In 1805, during their push to the Pacific, Lewis and Clark stumbled upon a peaceable people they called the Chopunnish, or Pierced Nose Indians, a misleading name given them by the expedition for a practice that was never a large part of their culture. The Nimíipuu, or Nee-Me-Poo, came to be called the Nez Percé (pronounced *nez purse*) by the whites. That fall, with provisions running low and the expedition faltering, the Nez Percé came to the aid of Lewis and Clark, providing food, shelter, and honorable hospitality.

While these Native Americans treated our first ambassadors to them with such respect, it is grievous to look back on our history and see how we treated them in return. Truly if God's Spirit had been as present in those times as He was in the days of the early church in Jerusalem, could our judgment be any less than that of Ananias and Sapphira?

Living for the truth also means living by the truth—which, in short, means simply telling the truth and sticking to our word. Because of our deceit, America has lost a rich heritage of people whose ways actually greatly contributed to our system of government. Our original thirteen colonies were actually organized into a union of individual states based on the League of the Iroquois, which united six Native American nations. Our institution of caucuses was derived from the Algonquian word *caucauasu*, meaning "counselor." These informal meetings to discuss issues are much like the Indians' traditional powwows. All of this we gained from them, and yet we took their land and livelihoods.

To look back on such things does call for a cultural repentance, but it also calls for dealing differently with similar groups in the future. Today, America is not always known in the world as a people of our word, but instead many times people see us as a greedy nation that will take what it can and say whatever it needs to in order to gain that end. Whether this is completely true or not, we need to be the generation that changes that reputation—and we will never do it in a national forum until we can live it every day with those around us.

What does it mean to you to "keep your word"? How well do you feel you do in that? Do you know anyone who does? What kind of respect do you have for such people that is different from how you see others?

If you have the opportunity, visit a Native American exhibit or historical site. Take time to write in your journal about the experience. What are things about their way of life that you appreciate? Why do you think they lived like that? How can we benefit from such things in our modern society?

Many of the stories in this book have to do with people telling the truth in one way or another. How do you define "truth"? How are our modern attitudes about truth different from those of our Founding Fathers? Which do you want to live in your own life?

Exercising What Is Right

Freedom is what we have—Christ has set us free!
Stand, then, as free people, and do not allow
yourselves to become slaves again.

GALATIANS 5:1 GNT

JOHN PRENTISS "PRINT" MATTHEWS (1840–1883)

Elections were not free in Mississippi during the 1870s and 1880s. In 1881 "Print" Matthews lost reelection to the sheriff's office by eighty-four votes. The Democrats threw the election, claiming a hungry mule thrust his head through a window and ate the ballots in the nearly all-black precinct of Mount Hope. Still, Print's party won the majority of the seats on the powerful Copiah County Board of Supervisors. The Democrats swore this would not happen again.

By Election Day 1883, it was obvious that voters favoring Print's Fusion Independent Party were too terrified to come to the polls. Print himself was handed a written warning to stay at home. As a point of personal honor, he decided to ignore it. His wife and daughters listened as he told the messenger, "I think I have as much right to vote as any of you. I have never done any of you any harm. I have tried to be useful to society in every way that I could. . . . You have got it in your power to murder me, I admit. But I am going to vote tomorrow, unless you kill me."

The next morning Print walked to the polling place across the street from his home. He walked past several Democrats standing by the door with shotguns. Inside, he saw Ras Wheeler, the precinct captain and a family friend, and went over to sit next to him. The two talked in low voices for a minute. Wheeler said, "Print, I would not vote today if I were you."

Print rose, walked over to an election official, and handed him his ballot. As he was folding it, Wheeler picked up a double-barreled shotgun and, taking quick aim, fired both barrels. Print Matthews died instantly.

HANANIAH, MISHAEL, AND AZARIAH (*Daniel 3:4–18* NKJV)

The decree went throughout the land:

> To you it is commanded, O peoples, nations, and languages, that at the time you hear the sound of the horn, flute, harp, lyre, and psaltery, in symphony with all kinds of music, you shall fall down and worship the gold image that King Nebuchadnezzar has set up; and whoever does not fall down and worship shall be cast immediately into the midst of a burning fiery furnace.

To this call to squash religious freedom, most of the people willingly complied—but three young Jewish men named Hananiah, Mishael, and Azariah (the Babylonians knew them as Shadrach, Meshach, and Abed-Nego) refused to bow their knee to any god but the One True God. In Him alone they had freedom, and even at the threat of death, they would not relinquish it.

For this they were called before King Nebuchadnezzar, who was furious at their defiance. "Is it true, Shadrach, Meshach, and Abed-Nego, that you do not serve my gods or worship the gold image which I have set up? Now if you are ready at the time you hear the sound of the horn, flute, harp, lyre, and psaltery, in symphony with all kinds of music, and you fall down and worship the image which I have made, good! But if you do not worship, you shall be cast immediately into the midst of a burning fiery furnace. And who is the god who will deliver you from my hands?"

The three young men, however, were unmoved by either the King's anger or his threats. "O Nebuchadnezzar, we have no need to answer you in this matter. If that is the case, our God whom we serve is able to deliver us from the burning fiery furnace, and He will deliver us from your hand, O king. *But if not*, let it be known to you, O king, *that we do not serve your gods, nor will we worship the gold image which you have set up*" (emphasis added).

{ LIVING IT! }

Both Print Matthews and the three Hebrew young men faced a very similar ultimatum: Give up your freedom and rights or else we will kill you. And both of their responses were also very similar: Kill us if you want, and if you can, but we will not give up our freedom and duty to the Truth.

Print Matthews refused to back down for what is the most essential freedom of a democracy: the right to vote. Today our nation is plagued with apathy in this area. Where nothing stands between them and the ballot box except registering to vote, nearly half our nation doesn't exercise that right. For Print, though a shotgun stood between him and his right to vote, he still chose to vote. What has changed since his time and ours?

For freedom to remain, we must never forsake our duties and most basic rights of citizenship—and above all we must not forsake our right to voice our God-given opinion by voting every time we have the opportunity. Our forefathers fought and died for the right for us to choose our own leaders. Men like Print Matthews refused to back away from it even though it could cost them their lives. The least we can do is honor them by exercising that right. Inform yourself, pray for God's guidance, and vote as you feel led in *every* election. We need to do this even if others tell us we should not or that it is a waste of time.

Our nation is built on each person playing their part—some in bigger ways, some in smaller ways—using the gifts God has given each of us, whether it is like Robert Morris with his financial abilities, Phillis Wheatley encouraging Washington with her poetry, or Harriet Tubman leading slaves through the woods in the dark of night toward freedom. We, too, can follow God's leading—even if it seems insignificant or we can't preplan it or do it perfectly.

God's supernatural hand was upon our nation at its birth. He wanted a shining example of a nation "under God." He still does. But being a nation under God does not mean pointing fingers or cursing those with whom we don't agree. It starts with pointing our prayers to God, allowing Him to first judge our hearts and then acting in love and grace as we seek to fulfill the specific things He calls us to do. We must first talk to God about our neighbors before we talk to our neighbors about God. Pray, and then act as He directs.

Are you registered to vote? If not, go to your local post office the next time you have the chance and register. If you are, when is the next election in your area? What is it for? Say a brief prayer now, asking God to start leading you in how you should vote in these matters.

There are times when we must directly defy authority to do what is right—just as Hananiah, Mishael, and Azariah had to before King Nebuchadnezzar—yet most of the time it is just up to us to exercise our freedom of religion and freedom of speech quietly before God and men. And even when we must stand before authority figures to voice our faith, do we do it in love, telling the truth, or out of a spirit of rebellion and defiance? The Bible tells us that there are no laws against the fruit of the Spirit—"love, joy, peace, patience, kindness, goodness, faithfulness, gentleness and self-control" (Galatians 5:22–23). Is your goal to operate out of these so that God can change the hearts of others, or are you just trying to be right in the wrong way?

TERRORISM AT ELECTIONS

THE USE OF THE SHOT-GUN IN MISSISSIPPI.

MR. HOAR'S COMMITTEE AT WORK—THE BROTHER AND SON OF A MURDERED MAN TESTIFY—WITNESSES IN FEAR.

NEW-ORLEANS, Feb. 15.—In a pleasant room at the Custom-house, this afternoon, Senator Hoar's committee began its inquiry into the Mississippi outrages. A dozen reporters and a fringe of curious lookers-on heard the stories of the witnesses, one at least of which was truly pathetic. Senator Frye conducted the case for the Republicans, while Senator Saulsbury, tall and thin, said all that was to be said on his side. The first witness called was Leon H. Matthews, brother and partner of the murdered man. He is a rather good-looking man of 45 or 50, and was an Independent candidate for Sheriff in Copiah County. During the canvass the Independent meetings were broken up, and toward the last there were murders, whippings, and burnings. The outrages were committed by a mob armed with guns and numbering 150 men. Their organization was notorious. Three weeks before the election it began its work in the county. Two colored men and one woman were murdered. A colored church was burned the night after an Independent meeting had been held there. Whipping was frequent. Houses were fired into and burned and the colored people in many cases took to the woods. "We must win the fight if we do it with the shot-gun," shouted the Democratic voters on the stump, and they did it. Very few negroes voted, and the white Independents were terrorized by a secret gang, which was abetted by all the State officers. Wheelock, who killed Matthews, was one of its leaders, as was Meade, the editor of the *Copiah Signal* and Chairman of the County Democratic Committee.

The Matthews family were leaders in politics, and for years had done the largest trade of any house in the county. The one who was murdered had been Alderman and Sheriff. Under his management the Independents were in a fair way to win. He made good speeches and the mob finally determined that with him out of the way their success would be certain. Two days before the election, 150 of them rode into Hazlehurst and gathered around the Court-house, where they were addressed by Congressman Barksdale. They sent a delegation to Matthews's house bearing a note ordering him not to vote. Then the party left town. Matthews urged the Sheriff to break up the mob. Meade and others arranged to have him made a Deputy Sheriff, and shot when executing the process. This was charged in Meade's presence, and he did not deny it. Matthews refused the post. Then the warrants were given to the mob to serve. They have not been heard from since. The United States District Attorney at Jackson was called on, but refused to act, as he was powerless. On election day Matthews

was powerless. On election day Matthews was shot by Wheeler when voting. It was the first thing after the polls were opened. There are two voting precincts, and the witness went over to one to distribute tickets. When he returned his brother had been killed. Witness saw that a crowd had gathered and ran to the voting place. The door was shut and only three or four men were there. Witness asked who killed his brother. An Inspector said: "Wheeler did it." Both barrels of a shot-gun were emptied into his breast. Several white men had guns, but no colored men were armed. The mob held the streets all day. Wheeler and others, with guns, escorted the colored men to the polls. A public meeting was held afterward and resolutions approving the murder were passed. They were sent to Matthews's house, but as the funeral was taking place only one man was sent with them. All the time the streets were guarded and a band of music played. Nothing was said about it in the Copiah papers, save a notice of his death. The killing of Wallace and the whipping were not mentioned. The effect in Hazlehurst was that very few Independent votes were cast. Two weeks later the Aldermen, all Democrats, elected Wheeler to the office of Marshal. It is rumored that two or three days ago he resigned. He has never been tried. Witness has lived in Hazlehurst since the tragedy, but has kept mighty quiet about politics. No further violence has been offered.

John Matthews, son of the murdered man, was next called. He is a handsome young man of 21, a student at the University of Mississippi, and remarkably intelligent. He went to Jackson tol the State Fair the week before election. While there he was told by Judge Wharton, of that judicial district, and a Democrat, that his father was in danger, and that serious times were afoot at Hazlehurst. He started home that night. On Sunday he became cognizant of the fact that a conspiracy was in the air to kill his father. On Monday he went back to college at his father's request. On Tuesday he received a dispatch informing him of the murder. He started for home. At the station he met Mr. Meyers, Secretary of State. "What has happened?" said Meyers. "I am informed that my father has been murdered," the boy replied. "Ah," rejoined the Secretary, "I knew it was going to be done. Didn't know it had happened." Armed men met the boy at Jackson, and a squad was at the station, but he was not assailed. During the day of the funeral guns were fired and the band played and there were congratulatory speeches all day and at night. The roads were patrolled to prevent Matthews's friends from gathering. The burial was deferred one day because no one would work in the vault at night. Mrs. Matthews and the family have left Hazlehurst, but this boy swears that he will avenge his father's murder.

A. W. Burnett, Chairman of the Greenback Committee, who was shot and nearly killed by a Democratic rough, told his story and corroborated the other witnesses regarding the reign of terror last Fall. He said he was going to Kansas. About 50 witnesses have been summoned, but many of them say they do not dare to appear. The committee will go to Hazlehurst after the hearing here terminates.

Witty Inventions

I am simply trying as best I can and as fast as God
gives me light to do the job I believe He has
given me in trust to do.

GEORGE WASHINGTON CARVER

GEORGE WASHINGTON CARVER (1861–1943)

George Washington Carver was alone in the biology lab at Iowa
State College when the student brought him the letter that would change
his life. It had been a wonderful morning—summer break meant he was
free from his teaching duties, free to do what he loved best: commune
with God by examining the plant life around him.

He examined the letter: *That's curious*, he thought. *It's from Booker T.*
Washington. Washington was the founder of Tuskegee Institute in Alabama, a school dedicated to helping southern blacks through vocational
training and teaching the biblical virtues of hard work and thrift.

Washington wrote:

> Our students are poor, often starving. They travel miles of torn
> roads, across years of poverty. We teach them to read and write, but
> words cannot fill stomachs. They need to learn how to plant and
> harvest crops. . . .
>
> I cannot offer you money, position or fame. The first two you
> have. The last, from the place you now occupy, you will no doubt
> achieve.
>
> These things I now ask you to give up. I offer you in their place
> work—hard, hard work—the challenge of bringing people from degra-
> dation, poverty and waste to full manhood.

Suddenly George knew. This was God's plan for his life, the purpose
God had been preparing him for: He would teach his people to grow
food.

He traveled to Tuskegee, where, during the interview with Washington, he had a "mighty vision." He saw how, with God's help, he would turn the dusty campus into an oasis of hope and promise for the burned-out South.

After accepting Booker T. Washington's offer to work at Tuskegee, Carver set about to use the discoveries of science to transform southern agriculture. He said, "The primary idea in all of my work was to help the farmer and fill the poor man's empty dinner pail. . . . My idea is to help the 'man farthest down.' This is why I have made every process just as simple as I could to put it within his reach."

Carver noticed the soil was worn out due to years of growing nothing but cotton. So he introduced techniques of crop rotation, soil improvement, and erosion prevention. He showed the farmers how planting legumes such as peanuts would put nitrogen back into the soil.

Then he went to the laboratory to invent products that used the crops he was encouraging southern farmers to grow, including peanuts, sweet potatoes, and soybeans. Over the years he developed hundreds of food items; nine medicines; twelve animal feeds and fertilizers; twenty cosmetic items; dozens of dyes, paints, and stains; synthetic cotton, synthetic plastics, and synthetic rubber, which was used widely during World War II.

He wrote, "As I worked on projects which fulfilled a real human need, forces were working through me which amazed me. I would often go to sleep with an apparently insoluble problem. When I woke the answer was there. Why should we who believe in Christ be so surprised at what God can do with a willing man in a laboratory? Some things must be baffling to the critic who has never been born again."

Among the heroes of American agriculture, there has been no one more creative or more productive than George Washington Carver, the "Wizard of Tuskegee." Carver dedicated his work to improving life for African Americans, and his scientific applications helped feed hungry populations worldwide. He introduced new cash crops for southern farmers that would enrich the depleted soil. His innovations stimulated demand for those crops, greatly benefiting the southern agrarian economy. New industries were sparked by his genius. By the early 1940s, George's research and agricultural contributions resulted in a five-hundred-million-dollar peanut industry, with more than five million acres planted in peanuts. His life—from his humble beginnings as a sickly, orphaned slave to becoming a scientist of international reputation—is a testimony of what God can do through someone who is totally yielded to His purposes.

THE SHEEP AND THE GOATS (*Matthew 25:31–46* GNT)

After telling the parable of the talents, Jesus told the parable of the sheep and the goats so they would know what the purpose was for the wealth and the resources He would one day bless them with in a similar way:

> When the Son of Man comes as King and all the angels with him, he will sit on his royal throne, and the people of all the nations will be gathered before him. Then he will divide them into two groups, just as a shepherd separates the sheep from the goats. He will put the righteous people on his right and the others on his left. Then the King will say to the people on his right, "Come, you that are blessed by my Father! Come and possess the kingdom which has been prepared for you ever since the creation of the world. I was hungry and you fed me, thirsty and you gave me a drink; I was a stranger and you received me in your homes, naked and you clothed me; I was sick and you took care of me, in prison and you visited me.
>
> The righteous will then answer him, "When, Lord, did we ever see you hungry and feed you, or thirsty and give you a drink? When did we ever see you a stranger and welcome you in our homes, or naked and clothe you? When did we ever see you sick or in prison, and visit you?" The King will reply, "I tell you, whenever you did this for one of the least important of these members of my family, you did it for me!"
>
> Then he will say to those on his left, "Away from me, you that are under God's curse! Away to the eternal fire which has been prepared for the Devil and his angels! I was hungry but you would not feed me, thirsty but you would not give me a drink; I was a stranger but you would not welcome me in your homes, naked but you would not clothe me; I was sick and in prison but you would not take care of me."
>
> Then they will answer him, "When, Lord, did we ever see you hungry or thirsty or a stranger or naked or sick or in prison, and would not help you?" The King will reply, "I tell you, whenever you refused to help one of these least important ones, you refused to help me." These, then, will be sent off to eternal punishment, but the righteous will go to eternal life.

{ LIVING IT! }

From the very beginning, God stated His plan for the earth. As He told Abraham: "I will make you a great nation; I will bless you and make your name great; and you shall be a blessing. I will bless those who bless you, and I will curse him who curses you; and in you all the families of the earth shall be blessed" (Genesis 12:2–3 NKJV).

God blesses us with resources, gifts, talents, insight, and all that He gives us so that we can be a blessing to others. By this alone will those who belong to His kingdom be recognized.

How will you use the blessing God has given you? Will you be a sheep like someone such as George Washington Carver, or will you be a goat like the foolish rich man who was interested only in spending his wealth upon himself?

How do your plans and dreams for the future relate to the idea of your being a blessing to your world?

When you run into a problem, how do you handle it? Do you draw on the gifts and blessings God has given you to find a solution? How can you develop those gifts and talents to be even better resources for you in the future?

Get together with some friends and discuss some ways to be "sheep" in your area. Now, what are you going to do about those opportunities to be a blessing?

Ingenuity

Change Begins in Hope

We are saved by hope.

ROMANS 8:24A KJV

IDA B. WELLS-BARNETT (1862–1931)

In January 1922 Ida Wells-Barnett took up the cause of twelve black prisoners sentenced to death in Little Rock, Arkansas. Snuck in undercover, she interviewed these men who were wrongly accused of leading what would be called the Arkansas Race Riots. Black sharecroppers in Phillips County, Arkansas, had joined together in a union and demanded better prices for their cotton. Area whites were outraged. Armed gangs came from three neighboring states and murdered dozens of poor black farmers.

Instead of arresting the murderers, police arrested hundreds of blacks, both men and women, for planning a revolt and plotting to kill white people. The "trial" lasted only a few minutes—an all-white jury sentenced sixty-seven blacks to long years in prison and twelve to death. Once behind bars, the men lived in constant torment. They were beaten and tortured with electrical shocks in an attempt to force them to confess their alleged plot to murder whites. A lynch mob tried to seize them. Three times they were saved from execution by last-minute appeals to the courts.

When Ida had completed her interviews, the twelve men sang for her, beautiful songs about heaven and the wonderful life that awaited them. When they finished, they smiled at Ida, waiting for her approval. But instead she moved close to their cells and told them in a low voice, "I have listened to you for nearly two hours. You have talked and sung and prayed about dying, and forgiving your enemies, and of feeling sure you are going to be received in heaven. But why don't you pray to live and ask to be freed? . . . If you believe God is all-powerful, believe He is powerful enough to open these prison doors. . . . Pray to live and believe you are going to get out!"

Ida turned her notes from the interview into a pamphlet, *The Arkansas Race Riot,* which she sent to influential people in Arkansas. Thanks in part to her work, the U.S. Supreme Court ruled in 1923 that the twelve men had not received a fair trial and released them from prison.

PAUL AND SILAS (*Acts 16:22–34*)

It was really more a cave then a cell, though it did have bars for a door. There were no windows, and in the dead of night it was as dark as a coal mine, and the air seemed as stale.

The ground was cold, damp earth. Paul and Silas, stripped to their waists, could do nothing but sit or lie on it as their feet were fixed in stocks. They were in the innermost cell of the prison and could hear nothing but the breathing, or snoring, of other prisoners. They were still too uncomfortable to sleep, however, as the beating they had taken at the hands of an unjust magistrate still stung and it was too painful to lie down. For hours they had sat and talked, prayed, and wondered at their predicament. It was nearing midnight, and sleep still wouldn't come. Paul decided to change tactics.

Since they couldn't sleep or do anything else worthwhile, why not get back to the business of the expansion of the kingdom of God in Macedonia? While they certainly couldn't preach to anyone—they couldn't even see if anyone was awake to listen—they could still pray. They could still plow up the fallow ground and hearts of the region to prepare them for the gospel going forth once they were released. And they could still create an atmosphere of praise and thanksgiving that would welcome God's presence despite the horrible circumstances. Who could know— maybe that alone would allow them to save another soul or two before morning dawned.

At first they prayed and sang quietly, but gradually as the presence of God began to fill the little cell, they grew louder and more enthusiastic. Prisoners around them began to wake up and listen. Something was different to them—there was something about this singing and the atmosphere it created. The singers weren't particularly melodious, but there was something about it. It warmed the hearts of these criminals and made them wonder that anything so beautiful could be created in a place so dark and depressing. Tears came to the eyes of some of them. The presence in the room seemed to emote a love they had never experienced, and certainly if they had, they never would have ended up in prison as despised criminals. A deep sorrow for their past deeds began to wash over them.

Again, the songs grew louder and suddenly the two men seemed to be weeping in gratitude to some unseen god. They were thanking Him that they had been counted worthy of suffering for His sake! What were they saying? It seemed ludicrous! How could these men sing like this? Yet the presence in the room seemed to make it all make sense. It was that Love to which they were singing and in which they were rejoicing!

Suddenly the building and ground started to shake! Cell doors popped on their hinges as they were twisted and clattered to the floor. The stocks on Paul's and Silas's feet jumped on the ground and came crashing down, cracking and splitting open on impact. Unexplainably chains rattled and fell from prisoners' wrists and ankles.

In a moment it was over and silence filled the place. No one moved as the presence still filled the place and no one wanted to leave it. Then, with a bang, the front door of the jail flew open and the jailer burst in with a lantern—his own sword pointed at his chest so he could fall on it to end his life in case prisoners had escaped. When Paul saw him, however, he called out, "Don't harm yourself! We are all here!"

At that moment the Presence of God hit the jailer, he called to his family to bring more lights, and he crumbled at the feet of Paul and Silas with only one question on his lips: "Sirs, what must I do to be saved?"

Paul must have looked at Silas at that moment and smiled briefly. Yes, there was more yet to be done that evening. God was not finished with their work yet!

{ LIVING IT! }

In our darkest times we need to look to our hope. The men on death row who were interviewed by Ida Wells-Barnett set their hopes on heaven, but Ida convinced them that they could still hope for something closer to home and not leave their families fatherless yet. The same God who would welcome them to heaven was also the God of justice and would not gladly see them executed on false charges. Paul and Silas, who also hoped in heaven, set their eyes to continue the work they had been called to do in Philippi despite their circumstances. Because they rose up in praise and prayer rather than sink to the ground in tears and regrets, God moved the earth to answer their call for His gospel to continue to go out in the region, and in the very prison in which they sat!

Too often we overlook the simple power of hope. We struggle to have faith for God to act on our behalf, or struggle to love in situations that seem unsolvable, but we fail to realize that before we can do either, we must first have the hope that things can change for the better. Hope is the raising of the head sunk in despair to look upward for an answer. It is the first posturing of the spirit to have faith or be able to love. Hope gives faith its substance and tangibility; hopelessness drains our strength to do anything.

Ida B. Wells-Barnett hoped for change and persistently warned her nation of its wicked ways. As a result things did change: The violence of lynch mobs is largely a thing of the past today. What kind of change is God calling you to make?

What do you place your hope in today? Are you generally hopeful about your future, or do you feel that only bad and more bad is headed your way? If we don't have hope, do we really know God?

Is there a situation in your community or which you know about that seems hopeless, yet you still feel compassion for it? If so, this is likely God working on your heart to do something about it and bring hope to the situation. You might be the very light someone else needs to pull their situation through. Take some time today to pray over the situation and see what you think God wants you to do about it.

How are you helping your church or youth group spread God's hope to others? Are you more concerned with convincing others that God is real than letting them experience Him through your own attitude and optimism? Or are you self-consciously trying to get others to accept you rather than reaching out with the acceptance of Jesus that lives in your heart?

Breaking Barriers

*But what happens when we live God's way? He
brings gifts into our lives, much the same way that
fruit appears in an orchard—things like affection for
others, exuberance about life, serenity. We develop
a willingness to stick with things, a sense of
compassion in the heart, and a conviction that a
basic holiness permeates things and people. We find
ourselves involved in loyal commitments, not needing
to force our way in life, able to marshal and
direct our energies wisely.*

GALATIANS 5:22–23 THE MESSAGE

JACKIE ROOSEVELT ROBINSON (1919–1972)

It was Branch Rickey, the Dodger owner at the time, who'd seen the
path Jackie would take. Rickey talked God and money and the future as
though they were one thing, so Jackie never knew if it was a holy vision
or not. But the old man certainly had thought the thing through.

"I've spent years looking for you," Rickey told Robinson during one
of their first meetings while Jackie was still playing for the Negro
League's Kansas City Monarchs. Jackie had returned after three years in
World War II without a college degree, and baseball seemed his quickest
hope at earning a decent salary. Now he was being handed the hopes and
dreams of his race—to break the color barrier and play Major League
Baseball. Rickey didn't understate the moment. "This great experiment
lives and dies with you."

Rickey showed Jackie six factors that needed to be addressed. First
was the support of ownership. Now that Rickey owned the Dodgers,
that was no problem. Next were the actual nuts-and-bolts details of his
playing in the Major League. For instance, would cities allow a black
player onto their ball fields? Third was tempering the response of the

Negro race. Fourth was the acceptance by other ballplayers of the Dodgers. Fifth and sixth were Jackie's own conduct, both on the field and off. Rickey thought he had a handle on the first three. The fourth rested out of his hands. The fifth and sixth were up to Jackie.

As Jackie thought about this, he thought first of the words of his pastor, Karl Downs, who had been a father to young Jackie when his own father had left the family. Over the years that he and his family had attended Pastor Downs' church during Jackie's formative teen years, his message was a consistent one: "Live a life of courage. Be fearless in the face of worry. Be thoughtful and rational in the face of raging emotions. Be prepared to give up everything for the fight. Do everything with the will of God in mind and the spirit of Christ in your heart."

In the next few years, Jackie faced some of the toughest obstacles a man could face with the quiet resolve of Jesus before the Jewish Council on the night before the cross. Everywhere that he turned were the walls that had previously kept African Americans in a separate league from white Americans, and it was Jackie who was the battering ram to knock them down. Yet he did it again and again with a composure that would have made Rev. Downs proud of him.

Jackie Roosevelt Robinson proved to be the right man for the right time, and within a few years, other African-American players broke into the Major League. His courage and self-control in the face of opposition changed the face of American sports forever.

ESTHER (*Esther 3–5* NKJV)

In all his years Mordecai had never seen such an evil plan filled with such racism and hatred. Haman had coerced King Ahasuerus to sign a decree to murder all of the Jews, young and old, throughout his kingdom. All of this was because Mordecai had refused to bow before Haman as if Haman were a god. Mordecai had refused because he could give no such homage except to the one true God in heaven, yet because of this, he and his people were despised by the power hungry in King Ahasuerus's court.

At the announcement, the Jews throughout the land fasted in sackcloth and ashes before God, calling for His deliverance. Mordecai tore his garments and mourned before God as well, but then God gave him an idea, and he sent word to his niece within King Ahasuerus's palace to ask for her help.

Because of her beauty and grace, Mordecai's niece, Esther, had

{ *Jackie Robinson* }

married King Ahasuerus and become his queen. Her coveted place in the court put her in a unique position to help. Mordecai sent a message to prompt her help: "Do not think in your heart that you will escape in the king's palace any more than all the other Jews. For if you remain completely silent at this time, relief and deliverance will arise for the Jews from another place, but you and your father's house will perish. Yet who knows whether you have come to the kingdom for such a time as this?"

Esther saw in an instant that it was just for "such a time as this" that she had come to the position of privilege and favor that she was now in. Yet she set her resolve to do what she could and sent word back to her uncle: "Go, gather all the Jews who are present in Shushan, and fast for me; neither eat nor drink for three days, night or day. My maids and I will fast likewise. And so I will go to the king, which is against the law; and if I perish, I perish!"

A few days later, Esther entered the throne room of King Ahasuerus unannounced, an action that called for her death unless the king extended his scepter toward her. Yet because of her favor in his eyes, he extended his scepter, and Esther was able to later plea on behalf of her people for their protection in the face of Haman's plan. As a result, the Jews were allowed to defend themselves, saving the nation, and Haman was put to death.

"For such a time" Esther was called of God to save her people, and because of her response, the tide of a nation was changed.

{ LIVING IT! }

God placed Jackie Robinson before the eyes of the nation in the late 1940s and 1950s because He needed such a man of resolve and godly character to smash a wall of racism in his time. Esther was placed in the palace of King Ahasuerus for a very similar reason: to speak up for her people in one of their greatest times of need. If either of them had not been the people of self-control, discipline, and courage that they were, neither would have made the impact on their nations that they did. Because Jackie refined himself in his calling to be an athlete and disciplined himself to remain quiet in the face of open attacks on him, he broke the color barrier in Major League Baseball. Because Esther refined her beauty and poise, she was able to win the favor of the king and save her people from massacre. Each, doing as they were called to do, played an important part in fulfilling God's will upon the earth.

★　　★　　★

In what gifts and abilities could God be calling you to discipline yourself to have an impact on your world? Make a list of the things you truly love to do and have some God-given ability in. How could you use these talents and desires to impact your world? Are there skills you need to develop to be your best in these areas? Dedicate yourself to being the best you can be and using these talents for God as He shows you how.

In looking at growing in these areas, are there things you should stop doing that suck energy or time away from being your best? God expects a balance in our lives of work and recreation, exertion and relaxation. But are you correctly balancing them toward the accomplishment of God's goals for your life? Are you working more to be edified or entertained? Are you using all of the areas of your life to accomplish God's plan for your life, or are some areas moving forward while others are moving backward? How can you keep it all moving forward?

Remembering the Rock Upon Which Our Nation Was Built

Righteousness alone can exalt America as a nation.
Virtue, morality, and religion . . . [are] the armor . . .
that renders us invincible.

PATRICK HENRY

THE PLEDGE OF ALLEGIANCE

The Pledge of Allegiance was formed largely from the vision of three men: Daniel Ford, James Upham, and Francis Bellamy.

Daniel Ford was the publisher of a popular family magazine, *The Youth's Companion.* Ford's belief in Christ was a great influence on the content of his magazine, and he guided his life and business by Christian principles. With a circulation of nearly half a million, *The Youth's Companion* was the nation's most-read weekly magazine in the late 1880s and early 1890s.

James Upham, head of the magazine's premium department, was disappointed that most public schools did not have their own flags, so he launched a campaign wherein schoolchildren raised funds to purchase a flag from the magazine. As a result, about thirty thousand flags were sold and flown for the first time in front of America's schools between 1888 and 1891.

In 1892 the country prepared to celebrate the four hundredth anniversary of Columbus's arrival in America. President Benjamin Harrison declared Columbus Day, October 12, a national holiday for the first time. Upham wanted children across the country to participate, so he began planning the National Public School Celebration that would center on raising a school flag.

First, a proclamation from the president would be read, followed by prayer and Scripture reading, the singing of "America," and patriotic speeches. Wanting the children to participate more fully, Upham determined that they should recite a salute to the flag. He enlisted the talents of another magazine employee, Francis Bellamy, who had been pastor at the Boston church Daniel Ford attended. Bellamy labored for weeks and finally brought his composition to Upham: *I pledge allegiance to my Flag and to the Republic for which it stands: one Nation, indivisible, with liberty and justice for all.* It was published in *The Youth's Companion* on September 8, 1892. Thirty-four days later, twelve million schoolchildren across the country recited the Pledge of Allegiance for the first time.

In 1923 and 1924 the words *my Flag* were changed to *the Flag of the United States of America.* In 1948, a man named Louis A. Bowman proposed to his fellow Sons of the American Revolution that the words *under God* be added after *one nation*—following a precedent set by Abraham Lincoln, who had extemporaneously added those same words to his Gettysburg Address. Then, in 1952, William Randolph Hearst caught wind of the idea and began a campaign in his newspapers that helped bring about legislation to officially add *under God* to the Pledge. President Dwight D. Eisenhower approved this change on Flag Day, 1954, and proclaimed, "In this way we are reaffirming the transcendence of religious faith in America's heritage and future; in this way we shall constantly strengthen those spiritual weapons which forever will be our country's most powerful resource in peace and war."

THE PARABLE OF THE TWO HOUSES (*Matthew 7:24–27* THE MESSAGE)

At the end of the Sermon on the Mount, Jesus told this parable about the truths we build our life upon:

> These words I speak to you are not incidental additions to your life, homeowner improvements to your standard of living. They are foundational words, words to build a life on. If you work these words into your life, you are like a smart carpenter who built his house on solid rock. Rain poured down, the river flooded, a tornado hit—but nothing moved that house. It was fixed to the rock.
> But if you just use my words in Bible studies and don't work them into your life, you are like a stupid carpenter who built his house on the sandy beach. When a storm rolled in and the waves came up, it collapsed like a house of cards.

{ L I V I N G I T ! }

It is so important to build firmly on a solid foundation. For years the Pledge of Allegiance was said every day in every classroom across our nation to remind us exactly of that fact—and often with that, until it was ruled unconstitutional in 1962, a prayer was said. In the years prior to the pledge, it was standardly just the prayer. Both of these worked to let us know from the beginning of our days that it was not the strength of our armaments or the cunning of our scientists that we relied upon in our nation, but that we were a nation *under God*.

Today we are a nation of individuals more than ever before—with an emphasis on *individual* rather than *nation*. This balance between individual freedoms and unity has always been what has made our nation strong. For example, look at our coins: On the heads side, you will always find the word *liberty* somewhere; on the tails side you will find the inscription *e pluribus unum*—"out of many, one"—meaning "though we are many and different, we stand together as one." When this balance sways too far one way or the other, our nation is weaker—when it swings to conformity, our nation begins to look like a tyranny that loses the strength of diversity; however, when we swing as we are now to emphasize individuality over standing together as one, we begin to lose ourselves to the causes and voices of special interest groups who use their influence and money to create legislation and legal decisions that only benefit themselves and their constituents. The majority is limited for the sake of the minority, and our differences are emphasized rather than our unity. Instead of "united we stand," it has now become "united we come together to fight about our differences"—the intermediary step before "divided we fall."

The answer has always before been what is printed on our dollar bills—these larger denominations taking precedent over the less valuable coins—the words "In God We Trust." True unity does not come from conformity, but from all of us having an allegiance to a higher principle. While we may all be culturally and ethnically different, each family and person adding their own views and virtues to spice our lives, the fact that we are answerable to God over all is what has always kept us from pulling apart at the seams. God's laws are over all of our nation's laws, and as it says in Galatians, if we live by the fruit of the Holy Spirit, "Against such things there is no law" (Galatians 5:23b).

Where is the balance? While freedom and unity often seem to be opposites, they are truly found together in only one place: Jesus. You want to be truly free? Be like Jesus. You want to be truly unified with others? Be like Jesus. Do we want to remain "one nation, indivisible, with liberty and justice for all"? Then the answer is to be *under God*.

> Just as each of us has one body with many members, and these members do not all have the same function, so *in Christ* we who are many form one body, and each member belongs to all the others. (Romans 12:4–5 emphasis added)

What are you doing at the beginning of every day to remind yourself you need to be more like Jesus? If "nothing," then what should you be doing? Do you spend time daily reading and studying the Bible? Do you talk to God daily? Now is the time to start—every day!

The Jesus we let live through us has a tendency to rub off on those we are around. Yet if the people we are always around are already Christians, is that as effective as it can be? What are you doing to be around people who need Jesus? Are you remaining so strong in Jesus that He is rubbing off on those around you at school, during sports, or in serving your community, or are you letting their worldly and selfish ways rub off on you and fade the Jesus in you?

Blood Still Cries Out

What have you done? The voice of your brother's blood
cries out to Me from the ground.

GENESIS 4:10 NKJV

EMMETT TILL (1941–1955)

On Wednesday, August 24, 1955, while Emmett's uncle was at church, Emmett and his cousin Wheeler went to Bryant's grocery store to buy some candy. Emmett struck up a conversation with a group of black teenagers outside the store. Before long Emmett pulled out his new wallet to show pictures of his Chicago friends. Purchased for the trip, the wallet had come with a studio shot of actress Hedy Lamarr.

"That's my girlfriend," Emmett announced, pointing to the white actress.

The Mississippi boys were sure that this was the empty boasting of a city boy from Chicago. One of them challenged Emmett, "If you are so good with white women, I dare you to talk to the woman in there running the cash register."

Emmett went into the store and bought some bubble gum from Carolyn Bryant. Some say Emmett whistled at the twenty-one-year-old white clerk. Others say he said, "Bye, baby," as he left. Mrs. Bryant testified later that Emmett grabbed her and said, "Don't be afraid of me, baby. I been with white girls before."

Whatever Emmett said or did, it broke the "rules" that his mother had tried so hard to warn him about, and it started a chain of events that would focus the eyes of the nation and the world upon Money, Mississippi.

Emmett and Wheeler decided not to tell his uncle, Papa Mose, about the incident. Nothing had happened, really, and they didn't want to make Papa Mose angry with them. By the end of the week, the kids weren't even thinking about the incident anymore.

But word spread quickly. Roy Bryant, the store clerk's husband, returned to town on Saturday night and heard what had happened. He and his half brother, J. W. "Big" Milam, knocked on Papa Mose's door about two in the morning, Sunday, August 28. Big Milam had a flashlight in one hand and a Colt .45 automatic in the other. The two white men told Papa Mose they were looking for "the boy from Chicago, the one who had done the talking." They started searching the house for Emmett. Both Uncle Mose and Aunt Lizzy pleaded with the men—but they took the boy, threatening to kill Uncle Mose if he told anyone. Emmett would never be seen alive by his family again.

On August 29, Milam and Bryant were arrested and held without bond on kidnapping charges in connection with Emmett's disappearance. The two men said they had taken Emmett but had let him go.

On August 31, fishermen in the Tallahatchie River found the body of the fourteen-year-old from Chicago. It had been weighted down by a heavy gin fan tied around Emmett's neck with barbed wire. Emmett's face was so mutilated that his uncle could only identify the body by a ring Emmett was wearing.

Getting Emmett's body sent home became a legal battle. Officials in the South wanted to bury him in Mississippi, "to get the body in the ground as soon as possible." They finally released the body but had strictly forbidden the funeral director in Chicago to open the officially sealed coffin. But Mamie Till was determined to see her son. At her insistence, the coffin was unsealed. The smell of death was overpowering. This was the sixth day since Emmett's murder, and his body had been in the river for three days. To make matters worse, southern officials had packed the body in lime so it would deteriorate even faster.

Although she was horrified by the mutilation, Mamie courageously decided to have an open-casket funeral, saying, "Everybody needs to know what happened to Emmett Till." She later stated, "There was nothing more we could do for my baby, but we could honor him by recognizing that we all had a responsibility to work together for a common good. I could not accept that my son had died in vain. . . .

"With God's guidance, I made a commitment to rip the covers off Mississippi, USA—revealing to the world the horrible face of race hatred."

On September 23, an all-white jury acquitted the two white men charged with Emmett's murder after only an hour of deliberation. Their defense: The body found in the river was not Emmett Till. They admitted that they had taken Emmett but said they had let him go. They claimed that the National Association for the Advancement of Colored People (NAACP) and Mamie Till had dug up a body and pretended it was Emmett. According to their defense, Emmett was hiding out in Chicago.

Newspapers across the U.S. and in six European countries expressed shock and outrage over the Till verdict.

"This brutal murder and grotesque miscarriage of justice outraged a nation and helped galvanize support for the modern American civil rights movement," said R. Alexander Acosta, assistant attorney general for civil rights. "We owe it to Emmett Till, and we owe it to ourselves, to see whether after all these years some additional measure of justice remains possible."

CAIN AND ABEL (*Genesis 4:9–12* GNT)

"Where is your brother Abel?"

Though Cain knew the Lord's voice, he didn't even turn around to answer Him. "I don't know. Am I supposed to take care of my brother?"

God, however, was not shocked by his disrespect. Cain had long since hardened his heart to be selfish and disrespectful. Because he had chosen this path, he had become bitter to the point of jealousy, and in the jealousy he had murdered his own brother. The crime cried out to God for justice, and He came to Cain to let him know what would happen because of his choices and his actions.

God turned Cain to face Him, then confronted him: "Why have you done this terrible thing? Your brother's blood is crying out to me from the ground, like a voice calling for revenge. You are placed under a curse and can no longer farm the soil. It has soaked up your brother's blood as if it had opened its mouth to receive it when you killed him. If you try to grow crops, the soil will not produce anything; you will be a homeless wanderer on the earth."

{ LIVING IT! }

On December 1, one hundred days after Emmett's murder, Rosa Parks refused to give up her seat to a white passenger on a city bus in Montgomery, Alabama. When asked, "Why didn't you go to the back of the bus after such threats?" she said she thought of Emmett Till and knew she couldn't give in. Soon after this, Martin Luther King Jr. called for a citywide bus boycott that lasted 381 days. The civil rights movement was born.

Emmett Till's murder was the spark that set off that movement. The Supreme Court decision to integrate schools the year before (*Brown v. Board of Education*) marked a *legal* turning point in the war against racism. But the murder of Emmett Till was the *emotional* turning point. His death and his mother's courage shook the nation and awoke it to action. Putting the struggle for emancipation above her personal privacy and allowing Emmett's disfigured body to be displayed in an open casket resulted in the largest civil rights demonstration of its day. Those who saw Emmett's face were forever changed. Many who had once been content to stay safely on the sidelines now entered directly into the struggle between racists and rights activists.

Just as Abel's spilt blood had called out to God for vengeance, Emmett's blood called out to God to end the hatred that had caused his murder. In our time on the earth, however, God does not act alone. He calls on men, women, and children who hear His voice to act in faith and courage, and then He backs them up with His strength. When Rosa Parks and Martin Luther King Jr. stood up, He strengthened, enabled, and empowered them to start the end to centuries of hatred and bloodshed. Had they not stood up, however, God would have had to find others.

Though segregation is over, reconciliation is still in the works. Who will be the ones to stand up against unrighteousness and injustice in our generation so that Jesus can stand up behind them and back them up with His power for good?

★　　★　　★

Proverbs 29:7 says, "The righteous care about justice for the poor." Do you see injustice today? Do you seek it out? How much contact do you have with the poor? What things do you see in America today that need to be changed? How do you stand up for these changes?

Pray today for the leaders of our nation and ask God to strengthen them to do what is right.

No More

*I have learned that in order to bring about change,
you must not be afraid to take the first step. We will
fail when we fail to try. Each and every one of us
can make a difference.*

ROSA PARKS

ROSA PARKS (1913–   )

Rosa Parks was tired, so tired that she decided to take the bus home. She had been pressing slacks all day at her job. Her feet hurt and her back and shoulders ached. The first bus that came past had standing room only, so she decided to wait for the next bus in hopes of getting a seat. During her wait, she remembered why she often walked home—riding the bus took its toll on her dignity.

The segregation laws in force in 1955 Montgomery, Alabama, seem unbelievable today, but they were a reality for thousands of blacks in the South. Take the restrictions on riding the bus, for instance. Even though the majority of bus passengers were people of color, the front four rows of seats were always reserved for white customers. It was common to see people standing in the back of the bus while the first four rows remained empty. Behind the reserved-for-whites section was a middle section where African Americans could sit if the seats were not needed by white customers. If just one white customer, however, needed a seat in this center section, all those already seated had to move.

Even getting on the bus was an elaborate process for black people. They would pay their fare in the front, exit, and then reboard the bus at the back. Rosa died a little each time she found herself face-to-face with this kind of discrimination. In fact, Rosa had once been thrown off a bus for refusing to reboard at the back door.

Finally a second bus came, and to Rosa's joy, there were a few seats available in the middle section—"no-man's land." Rosa climbed the stairs, put her dime in the fare box, climbed back down the stairs, hurried to the back door of the bus, climbed up the stairs, and made it through the aisle in time to find there was still a seat available. She sat down in the row just behind the white section. What a relief to relax for a minute!

The bus picked up more riders, and the front section of the bus filled up. When the driver noticed a white man standing in the aisle, he ordered four people, including Rosa, to give up their seats. At first no one moved.

The bus driver said, "You all better make it light on yourselves and give me those seats." The other three riders did as they were told, but Rosa quietly refused to get up. "I'm gonna call the police," the bus driver threatened.

"Go ahead and call them," said Rosa. She was tired, true—but even more, she was tired of giving in. It wasn't just the bus. It was the "whites only" restaurants, the drinking fountains and elevators marked "Colored," and the unspoken intimidation that were all a part of daily life in a place that did not treat all its citizens as equals. Rosa remembered, "I was tired of seeing so many men treated as boys and not called by their proper names or titles. I was tired of seeing children and women mistreated and disrespected because of the color of their skin. I was tired of legally enforced racial segregation. I thought of the pain and the years of oppression and mistreatment that my people had suffered. . . . Fear was the last thing I thought of that day. I put my trust in the Lord for guidance and help to endure whatever I had to face. I knew I was sitting in the right seat."

Rosa later wrote, "I felt the presence of God on the bus and heard His quiet voice as I sat there waiting for the police to take me to the station. There were people on the bus that knew me, but no one said a word to help or encourage me. I was lonely, but I was at peace. The voice of God told me that He was at my side."

When the police arrived, Rosa calmly asked, "Why do you push us around?"

The officer replied, "I don't know, but the law is the law and you're under arrest." When the officers asked her to stand up and get off the bus, Rosa quietly obeyed. They drove her to the police station and fingerprinted her. Before they put her in a jail cell, they allowed her one phone call. She called a prominent member of the NAACP, who called a lawyer. The two bailed Rosa out of jail for one hundred dollars and suggested that Rosa appeal her case to challenge the segregationist law that had led to her arrest. Rosa's husband and her mother had some real concerns about Rosa's personal safety, but they all agreed that it was time to act. Rosa later recalled, "As I sat in that jail cell, behind bars, I felt as if the world had forgotten me. But I felt God's presence with me in the jail cell."

The ministers of the city's African-American congregations lent their support. Dr. Martin Luther King Jr. made seven thousand leaflets encouraging African Americans to boycott the Montgomery city bus system on Monday, December 5. A community meeting that night drew an overflow crowd numbering in the thousands.

What began as a one-day boycott lasted for 381 days. Continuing the boycott was neither comfortable nor convenient: Some people walked miles to work, others rode bikes or shared rides. For more than a year—in the cold, pouring rain and in the blistering heat of summer—the black community worked together, giving their 100 percent cooperation. They were determined to pay the price to see change. As the months went by, Rosa's case went all the way to the U.S. Supreme Court—and Rosa won. On December 21, 1956, Rosa sat in the front row of a newly integrated city bus.

DANIEL DEFIES HIS ENEMIES (*Daniel 6:1–28*)

Daniel's success and virtue had incited jealousy in many. As a result, and knowing his convictions, they set a trap for Daniel through King Darius: For the next thirty days, by royal statute, a decree was made that any who brought a petition or request to any god or man but the king would be thrown into the lions' den.

Now, it was Daniel's habit to pray to God three times a day—morning, noon, and evening—something that Daniel's enemies knew and was at the center of their plan. Rather than cowering or forsaking his devotion to God, however, Daniel went into his chambers the day after the decree, threw open his windows and doors, and knelt before God in prayer.

Of course, his enemies were watching. Daniel was arrested, brought before the king, and thrown into the lions' den.

But we know the end of the story. Because Daniel had stood up for God, God stood up for Daniel. After spending a night with the lions, he emerged untouched, and instead, his enemies were cast into the den for their deceit.

{ LIVING IT! }

Much like Daniel, when Rosa Parks stood—or rather sat—for equality and what was right, she and her family were thrown into their own lions' den of sorts. Both Rosa and her husband lost their jobs and were considered unemployable as a result of their part in the boycott. They were also harassed with phone calls, letters, verbal threats, and intimidation. The family moved to Detroit, Michigan, in 1957, and for the next eight years they struggled financially, until Rosa was hired as a staff assistant to a U.S. congressman.

Yet in later years Rosa was hailed as the mother of the civil rights movement and received many awards and honors. Among them was a seventy-seventh birthday celebration in the nation's capitol in 1990, which was attended by government dignitaries, prominent entertainers, and a host of notable African-American leaders. Here Rosa was praised for her "beautiful qualities [of] dignity and indomitable faith that with God nothing can stop us." In 1999 President Clinton awarded Rosa the Congressional Gold Medal, the nation's highest civilian honor.

Often there is a time to stand for what is right, even if it means being arrested and thrown into a "lions' den." Rosa somehow knew the right time and did what was in her heart to do with a conviction of truth from within her. When she stood her ground on behalf of truth, God stood His ground on her behalf, and within her lifetime she saw much of her cause won. Where is your stand today?

The civil rights movement is one of the most incredible "revolutions" in world history—a war fought and won through nonviolence and unbendable dedication to the cause. What does it teach us of God's work on the earth today and methods we can use to fight for right and freedom in our own lifetime?

What does it mean to you to take a stand such as the ones Daniel and Rosa Parks took? Would you ever have the conviction to do the same? Where do you think that such conviction comes from? How would you develop it?

In Matthew 24:12, Jesus said that in the latter days the love of many would grow cold. What does love have to do with conviction? How do you keep either of them from growing cold?

A Life Pledge to God's Freedom for All

How do you benefit if you gain the whole world
but lose your own soul in the process?
Is anything worth more than your soul?

MATTHEW 16:26 NLT

MARTIN LUTHER KING JR. (1929–1968)

A year and a day after a young man by the name of Martin Luther King Jr. had taken over the pastorate at the Dexter Avenue Baptist Church in Montgomery, Alabama, Rosa Parks decided she would no longer stand for the segregation policy of the Montgomery public transportation. As a result of her actions, the fifty thousand African Americans of Montgomery refused to use the city busses for an amazing 381 days, a strike that ended the segregation policy and started the civil rights movement.

Pastor King was asked to serve as the spokesman and president of a new organization called the Montgomery Improvement Association, which had been called into being to lead the bus boycott. As a matter of conscience, he could not refuse.

Some years later, in a sermon in Chicago in 1967, Dr. King told of a night less than a month into that bus strike when he had come to a startling new level of dedication to the cause of freedom for which he had been called to be a spokesman. It was about midnight, he had just returned from a steering committee meeting for the Montgomery Improvement Association, and he had just crawled into bed next to his wife. The phone started ringing and he picked it up. On the other end of the line was an ugly voice that in substance said, "N——r, we are tired of you and your mess now. And if you aren't out of this town in three days, we're going to blow your brains out and blow up your house."

Though he had been receiving death threats for some time already, as many as forty a day in some cases, this one shook him like never before. He got up, went to the kitchen, warmed some coffee, and sat down to think. In his own words, he described his thoughts that evening:

> I sat at that table thinking about [my daughter] and thinking about the fact that she could be taken away from me any minute. And I started thinking about a dedicated, devoted and loyal wife, who was over there asleep. And she could be taken from me, or I could be taken from her. And I got to the point that I couldn't take it anymore. I was weak. . . .
>
> And I discovered then that religion had to become real to me, and I had to know God for myself. And I bowed down over that cup of coffee. I never will forget it. . . . I prayed a prayer, and I prayed out loud that night. I said, "Lord, I'm down here trying to do what's right. I think I'm right. I think the cause that we represent is right. But, Lord, I must confess that I'm weak now. I'm faltering. I'm losing my courage." . . .
>
> And it seemed at that moment that I could hear an inner voice saying to me, "Martin Luther, stand up for righteousness. Stand up for justice. Stand up for truth. And lo I will be with you, even until the end of the world." . . . I heard the voice of Jesus saying still to fight on. He promised never to leave me, never to leave me alone. No, never alone. No, never alone. He promised never to leave me, never to leave me alone.

In that moment, all he had learned growing up as the son of a preacher, the grandson of a preacher, and the great grandson of a preacher, as well as all he had studied of philosophy and theology at university, came up short. He had no answer for the evil and hatred expressed in the voice of that midnight caller. He had no answer for the fact that because he was standing against that kind of evil and hatred, at any moment it could cost him his life or the lives of his wife and children. Knowing that God was real, however, that it was His will that King stand against such evil—and that God would never leave him or forsake him as long as he stood for righteousness and justice—was enough.

As long as he knew God was standing with him, he would stand for God. And so it was, that despite the many attempts and eventual assassin's bullet he would face later in life, Dr. Martin Luther King Jr. dedicated his life to the cause of fighting for one of the founding principles of our nation, "that all men are created equal, that they are endowed by

{ *Martin Luther King Jr.* }

their Creator with certain unalienable Rights, that among these are Life, Liberty and the pursuit of Happiness."

GIDEON (*Judges 6:11–16*)

The truth of the matter was that Gideon was hiding. Threshing wheat in the bottom of a winepress to keep Israel's oppressors, the Midianites, from finding him and taking food from him and his family, Gideon cowered where he thought no one would find him. The problem was, however, that someone did.

"The Lord is with you, mighty warrior." Gideon looked up to see who had spoken. Before him stood an angel of the Lord. But Gideon did not recognize him as anything but another Israelite. His fear blinded him to the truth.

"But sir," Gideon replied, "if the Lord is with us, why has all this happened to us? Where are all his wonders that our fathers told us about when they said, 'Did not the Lord bring us up out of Egypt?' But now the Lord has abandoned us and put us into the hand of Midian."

The Lord turned to him and said, "Go in the strength you have and save Israel out of Midian's hand. Am I not sending you?"

Again, Gideon protested, "But Lord, how can I save Israel? My clan is the weakest in Manasseh, and I am the least in my family."

"I will be with you, and you will strike down all the Midianites together."

In the end Gideon realized that he had met the Lord, and his opinion of himself and his destiny changed from that moment on.

{ LIVING IT! }

Meeting Jesus changes everything.

Certainly we may have grown up knowing about Him, but there comes a time—just as it did for Martin Luther King Jr., Gideon, Paul, and others—when each of us has to meet Jesus for ourselves, individually, or else we will never have the courage to stand for what He wants us to stand for in the way He wants us to stand.

For Gideon, who was a fearful young man in an occupied nation, meeting God transformed him into a warrior that could stand against incredible odds and see God's victory. For Martin Luther King Jr., hearing Jesus' words in his heart that fearful night gave him the resolve he needed to see the civil rights movement through, even though it would eventually cost him his life. As a soldier on the battlefield, he was willing to risk his life for the freedom of others, and had he not stood as he did, would we have the freedom we do today in the United States, or would we still be bound tightly in the bonds of racism that held us from the first day slaves were brought to American soil?

Is it time for you to *really* meet Jesus? You will, if you will seek Him with all of your heart.

> Then you will call to me. You will come and pray to me, and I will answer you. You will seek me, and you will find me because you will seek me with all your heart. (Jeremiah 29:12–13 GNT)

What have been your strongest encounters with Jesus in your lifetime? What has He told you in those times? Take a few moments to journal about those experiences and see if He wants to tell you more about them as you write.

People often make hearing from God very mysterious, but the truth of the matter is that the Bible tells us that if we will seek Him, He will help us find him. Often we make the mistake of thinking that we can sit and get the answer we want if we just wait a few minutes, an hour, or even a couple of hours. But the type of seeking the Bible talks about starts with the determination to seek Him for as long as it takes, even if it takes a lifetime. What is your level of dedication to finding Jesus *for real*? Are you dedicated to seeing His ways and His kingdom established on the earth, or do you have other priorities? Look over the commitment statement on page 257 in the back of this book. Are you willing to sign your name and live it? If so, it could be your first step toward God's greatest adventures for your life.

Four Young Girls

If any man will come after me, let him deny himself,
and take up his cross, and follow me. For whosoever
will save his life shall lose it: and whosoever will
lose his life for my sake shall find it.

MATTHEW 16:24–25 KJV

THE BIRMINGHAM SIXTEENTH STREET BAPTIST CHURCH BOMBING (SEPTEMBER 15, 1963)

At 10:21 AM Sunday, September 15, 1963, Sunday school class at the Sixteenth Street Baptist Church was wrapping up in the basement. It was Youth Day, and the children would be leading the day's service. Mrs. Ella Demand was encouraging them, soothing their nerves, telling them God would be proud no matter what.

At 10:22 AM anywhere from fifteen to nineteen sticks of dynamite that had been placed under the stairs leading to the basement exploded. Countless men, women, and children were injured in the bombing. Four young girls died: Denise McNair, eleven, Carole Robertson, fourteen, Cynthia Wesley, fourteen, and Addie Mae Collins, fourteen.

The bombing incited a city that always teetered on the brink of self-immolation. Someone with a sick sense of humor dubbed the city "Bombingham." One particular neighborhood into which blacks were moving became known as "Dynamite Hill," where over eighty bombings of black homes and churches or those of whites who sympathized added up in less than a decade.

After the bombing, black citizens took to the streets in frustration and anger. James Robinson, a sixteen-year-old African-American teen, threw rocks at a gang of white teens, turned to run away, and was shot, fatally, in the back by a Birmingham police officer. Later, another teen, thirteen-year-old Virgil Ware, was shot twice in the chest while riding his bike. His murderer, a white teen of sixteen, served seven months in jail.

The city boiled.

In the wake of the bombing, the Birmingham Police Department and the FBI did almost nothing to solve the case. So for fourteen years the case sat virtually dormant even though most everybody knew the parties who likely were involved. In 1977 William Baxley, a new district attorney, reopened the case and soon arrested Robert Chambliss. He was convicted mostly on decades-old evidence that should have come to light much sooner, but also on new eyewitness testimony of his niece. He was sentenced to life in prison and died while serving his time.

Again the case sat dormant, this time until 1997, when the FBI reopened the case, coincidentally just before Spike Lee's documentary *Four Little Girls* aired. With the FBI's renewed involvement, crucial evidence "rediscovered" from their investigation would help convict two other men: Thomas Blanton and Bobby Frank Cherry Jr. Both were convicted on four counts of first-degree murder and sentenced to life in prison, Blanton in 2001, Cherry in 2002. (Another implicated in the crime, Herman Cash, had died before any charges could be brought.) After almost forty years, the four girls finally received at least a measure of justice.

Martin Luther King Jr. delivered the eulogy at the funeral for three of the girls (the fourth had been remembered a day earlier at a separate ceremony). During the most powerful portion of the speech, King found deep significance in the deaths of those little girls, significance for every person listening there, for every man and woman in the country, and significance that transcends time and meets us even now.

> And yet they died nobly. They are the martyred heroines of a holy crusade for freedom and human dignity. And so this afternoon in a real sense they have something to say to each of us in their death. They have something to say to every minister of the gospel who has remained silent behind the safe security of stained-glass windows. They have something to say to every politician who has fed his constituents with the stale bread of hatred and the spoiled meat of racism. They have something to say to a federal government that has compromised with the undemocratic practices of southern Dixiecrats and the blatant hypocrisy of right-wing northern Republicans. They have something to say to every Negro who has passively accepted the evil system of segregation and who has stood on the sidelines in a mighty struggle for justice. They say to each of us, black and white alike, that we must substitute courage for caution. They say to us that we must be concerned not merely about who murdered them, but about the

system, the way of life, the philosophy which produced the murderers. Their death says to us that we must work passionately and unrelentingly for the realization of the American dream. And so my friends, they did not die in vain.

PERSECUTION IN THE BOOK OF ACTS (*1 and 8* NASB)

When Jesus ascended, he told his disciples, "You shall be My witnesses both in Jerusalem, and in all Judea and Samaria, and even to the remotest part of the earth." But eight chapters later they had yet to leave Jerusalem. At that time Stephen was martyred, and the Bible tells us, "And on that day a great persecution arose against the church in Jerusalem; and they were all scattered throughout the regions of Judea and Samaria, except the apostles."

{ LIVING IT! }

The bombing of the Sixteenth Street Baptist Church galvanized the civil rights movement in Birmingham just as Stephen's murder finally mobilized the early church to do what God had called them to do. Through the bombing, the nation finally saw the true face of racism and hatred for blacks in this country. Through Stephen's execution, the early church finally saw the seriousness of the opposition it faced and started moving.

This Birmingham bombing was not an issue that would go quietly into the night. Those willing to kill children to extend their cause would not be changed by time, as many whites in the nation had hoped. The movement against racism had to grow stronger, the cause had to be amplified. And it was. And in the words of Junie Collins Peavy, sister of one of the victims: "There is hope for healing in America. I know, because I have been healed. . . . And so God took a day which was meant for evil and turned it around for the good of all." Our nation saw with disgust what racism was capable of, and it was no longer willing to tolerate it. Because of this, in the years that followed, great changes would be made toward freedom and equality for all.

The struggle is not over, however. For those who love God, what is meant for evil is always turned to good. For those in Birmingham, positive change was imminent; for those going forth from Jerusalem, the church was about to explode in numbers. For us today, if we are willing to learn from these lessons of the past, our determination to live for what is right and to spread God's will on the earth should be greater than ever, for it will only be in Jesus that we will truly find our places to stand together as one.

In fighting for great causes, there are always sacrifices. Abraham Clark knew he might lose his sons to the cause of freedom in the American Revolution, and because African Americans were standing for what was right in the early sixties, people trying to intimidate them to back down killed four young girls in cold blood. When people suffer innocently, however, God steps in to bring justice and change. What are you willing to give up to gain God's will for your life?

Through reading this book and the Bible, how do you define "justice"? Has the concept of it changed in your mind? How? Do you see injustice happening today? What do you feel is the ultimate justice in any situation?

Prayer Solves Things

I'm telling you to love your enemies. Let them bring out the best in you, not the worst. When someone gives you a hard time, respond with the energies of prayer, for then you are working out of your true selves, your God-created selves.

MATTHEW 5:44–45A THE MESSAGE

RUBY BRIDGES (1954–   )

It was a morning in the fall of 1960. Two big, black limousines pulled up in front of the William T. Frantz Elementary School in New Orleans, where a large, angry crowd had gathered. Four burly U.S. federal marshals got out. Then, while sheltering her from the crowd with their own bodies, they helped a tiny black girl in a starched white dress get out of the car. Putting her carefully on the sidewalk, they turned her around, and with two marshals in front of her and two behind her, the procession climbed the steps and entered the school.

Ruby Bridges was attending because of the decision to stop school segregation in the South—and Ruby was doing it alone. Though two others had been chosen to integrate with her, they had opted to stay in their all African-American schools rather than face the crowds angrily protesting their admittance to a "White" school.

This day as all others previously, Mrs. Henry, Ruby's teacher, watched Ruby walk into the school. She later told Dr. Robert Coles, a trained child psychiatrist who specialized in helping children under stress and who had offered his help to Ruby and her family during this difficult transition time, that Ruby had stopped and talked to the people in the street. When Dr. Coles asked Ruby about this, she said, "Oh, yes. I told her I wasn't talking to them. I was just saying a prayer for them."

Usually Ruby prayed in the car on the way to school, but that day she had forgotten until she was in the middle of the crowd. Her mother had taught her that every time she felt afraid she should pray. When Ruby felt afraid that morning, she stopped right where she was and said a prayer.

Dr. Coles was amazed that Ruby would pray for people who were so hateful to her. He asked her, "Ruby, you pray for the people there?"

"Oh, yes."

"Why do you do that?"

"Because they need praying for," Ruby replied.

"Ruby, why do you think they need you to pray for them?"

"Because I should."

Dr. Coles asked Ruby what she prayed.

Ruby answered, "I pray for me, that I would be strong and not afraid. I pray for my enemies, that God would forgive them.

"Jesus prayed that on the cross," she told Dr. Coles, as if that settled the matter. "Forgive them, because they don't know what they're doing."

Stephen (*Acts 7*)

Having been called before the elders with no idea what he would say, Stephen knew his only hope was to rely on the One because of whom he had been called to testify, his Lord and Savior Jesus Christ. As he stood before the jury of religious elders, he testified boldly of his faith and all that Jesus meant to him. The spirit and strength with which he spoke cut his audience to their hearts. He had brought them to the stumbling block of Jesus Christ with clarity and passion—they had but two choices, either accept Stephen's words and bow to ask forgiveness for their part in killing their Messiah, or continue in ignorance to kill the messenger because the message he brought was too hard for them to face.

Because of the hardness of their hearts, they chose the second of these two options. The crowd covered their ears to block out Stephen's penetrating words and rushed at him to drive him into the fields outside of the village. There they began grabbing rocks of whatever size they could find and flinging them at Stephen. Yet rather than trying to run away, he stood his ground. The stones striking him tore at his flesh, then began to crush his bones. Yet Stephen's eyes met those of his attackers with nothing but the love His Lord had given him for them. Finally driven to the ground with no hope of escape, he fell to his knees and cried out, "Lord Jesus, receive my spirit."

Despite the pain of his broken bones, the spinning in his mind as he approached unconsciousness, and the burning of the blood dripping in his eyes, Stephen's last words were not for himself, but for those standing against him. As he looked to heaven with earthly eyes for the last time, he slowly and clearly prayed, "Lord, do not hold this sin against them." Then he fell to the dust to be present with his Lord, who was standing to receive him.

Just a few short years later, God answered Stephen's prayer by confronting one of his murderers while he was on his way to kill more Christians, and the world was forever changed because this persecutor, the apostle Paul, came to know the Lord Stephen had unwaveringly preached to him.

{ LIVING IT! }

It is rare that we face such vehement oppression in our nation today as was faced by Ruby Bridges every day as a first grader crossing the color line or by Stephen because he spoke so boldly for his Lord. Without question, however, we face a nagging subtle opposition in our schools and halls of government that somehow the words of the One we stand for should not be allowed to be spoken in public. Freedom of speech is being traded in for a desire to appease the collective consciousness of selfishness over selflessness, compromise over eternal truth, and self-justification over earnestly seeking the true freedom for all that can only be found according to the guidelines specified by our Creator.

Most of us are not bold enough to speak out in such situations. Instead we are silenced as childish, naïve, or weak-minded because of our acknowledgment that without Christ we are nothing. But what does it take to pray for those who oppose us in such ways? Is it not better for God to speak for himself sometimes than it is for us to cower before those who humiliate us? Boldness without God backing us up is little better than foolishness, but true boldness comes from the confidence that He is more real than all opposition because we have experienced Him through prayer.

Take time to pray for those around you today who oppose God, and don't stop mentioning them in your prayers until you see God intervene. God is waiting to act on your behalf—He is waiting to see if you will truly stand up for Him so that He can powerfully stand up for you.

Do you really believe prayer can work? If so, how much of your time should be dedicated to it? Do you really think you can do more on your own than you can by asking God in prayer?

Make a list of three to five people who openly oppose your faith and your values at your school or work. Now pray for them every day—not long prayers, but just bringing their names before God every morning in a short prayer time and asking God to open their eyes with His light to reveal the truth to them. Then write to us about what happens. Does prayer change things or not? Do you really think God will disregard such faithfulness? Live it and find out!

Bearing All They Can Throw at You With God's Grace

For God is pleased with you when, for the sake of your conscience, you patiently endure unfair treatment. Of course, you get no credit for being patient if you are beaten for doing wrong. But if you suffer for doing right and are patient beneath the blows, God is pleased with you.

1 PETER 2:19–20 NLT

Endurance

JOHN PERKINS (1930–)

"During the beatings," Perkins wrote in his autobiography, *Let Justice Roll Down*, "I tried to cover my head with my arms, but they just beat me anyway till I was lying on the floor. Even then they just kept beating and stomping me, kicking me in the head, in the ribs, in the groin. I rolled up in a ball to protect myself as best I could. The beatings just went on and on."

Perkins slipped in and out of consciousness. At some point in the night, the violence waned and officers actually arrived in the cell to mop up the blood. A rumor spread that the FBI was on its way. The police needed to rid themselves of the evidence. Freedom would come soon.

But no help came, and the scare seemed to enrage the police even further. They moved past beating into torture. A fork, its tines sharp, was shoved up John's nose and down his throat. An officer put a gun to Perkins' head and pulled the trigger. John still doesn't know if the gun was loaded or not. They mocked him, made him read aloud the demands for equal rights his Mendenhall community had developed, and never stopped beating him.

"They were like savages—like some horror out of the night. And I can't forget their faces, so twisted with hate. It was like looking at white-faced demons. Hate did that to them."

But John Perkins would not hate them back.

If he'd learned anything in his days, it was that hate offered no freedom. It would only corrupt, turn you into the same spiteful savage. John Perkins took his beatings and pitied those who lashed out at him until darkness swam in at him and he could remember no more.

Some of John's students came and nursed him through the night. Most didn't think he would make it to morning. His friends outside of prison, however, knew what was happening, and they scoured the county gathering money to post bond for all those incarcerated. Some even put up their property as bond. A day later John Perkins regained his freedom—bloodied, bruised, and more determined than ever to seek not only equal rights and common dignity for blacks but also reconciliation between whites and blacks that needed to start within the Christian church.

PAUL (*2 Corinthians 11:24–30; 12:9* NASB)

In his second letter to the Corinthians, Paul talked of what he went through for the sake of the gospel:

> Five times I received from the Jews thirty-nine lashes. Three times I was beaten with rods, once I was stoned, three times I was shipwrecked, a night and a day I have spent in the deep. I have been on frequent journeys, in dangers from rivers, dangers from robbers, dangers from my countrymen, dangers from the Gentiles, dangers in the city, dangers in the wilderness, dangers on the sea, dangers among false brethren; I have been in labor and hardship, through many sleepless nights, in hunger and thirst, often without food, in cold and exposure. Apart from such external things, there is the daily pressure on me of concern for all the churches. Who is weak without my being weak? Who is led into sin without my intense concern? If I have to boast, I will boast of what pertains to my weakness. . . .
>
> He has said to me, "My grace is sufficient for you, for power is perfected in weakness." Most gladly, therefore, I will rather boast about my weaknesses, so that the power of Christ may dwell in me.

The key for Paul was that he had gone through it. Through his weaknesses and suffering, Jesus had been shown strong.

{ LIVING IT! }

John Perkins was esteemed as a hero of the civil rights movement, but also as a true revolutionary in the cause of service to the needy and his vision for bridging racial divides. Nationally recognized for his vision and leadership, he served on the boards of organizations such as World Vision and Prison Fellowship and was awarded honorary doctorates from Wheaton College, Gordon College, Huntington College, and other universities.

Today, Perkins lives in Mississippi with his wife, Vera Mae, where he continues to speak and work on behalf of his twin causes of racial reconciliation and working within communities to train needy men and women not only to support themselves but also to take the help they've received and use it to help others. The Perkinses raised eight children, many of whom follow in the Christian work of their parents, ensuring that their legacy will live on for generations. The cycle of service and God's love will reach through generations and change lives as long as God's Word finds willing ears and His Spirit reaches tender hearts.

When we endure mistreatment for the sake of the truth and persevere through it without hating or striking back, God has no choice but to stand up for us. When His children suffer unjustly, it is His part to step in for them and prove His Word is true. When Paul suffered and was beaten for the sake of the gospel, the miracles only got bigger and more convincing. When John Perkins was beaten and tortured, refusing to hate back, those who opposed him lost their resolve. Instead of discouraging John or belittling the things he fought for, support grew for his ministries, and his reputation increased throughout the country. And when John called for reconciliation rather than retaliation, God put more power in his words, because John had stood up for God and refused to strike back and deny God's nature.

As John himself said:

> Christian discipleship at its finest is when a person recognizes that he'll never, in and of himself, be complete enough. His completeness comes in relation to other people. As he opens his life to a small group of people, his gifts and skills are released for serving others.

John chose to fight for the best of those who beat him rather than fight them. He, like Paul, saw God's strength come when he refused to defend himself. It was when they were at their weakest that God was able to show himself strong on their behalf.

★ ★ ★

We are taught to do as Jesus instructed by "turning the other cheek" when someone strikes us, and "suffer for righteousness" when open and obvious injustice comes. People like John Perkins and Paul could never have withstood these great abuses had they not learned first to endure smaller ones. How do you handle differences of opinion with your friends and peers? Are you willing to "take a couple" for what is right without retaliating in any way? What about when others make fun of you and hurt your feelings? Do you generally look for support in your relationship to God, or are you more likely to fight back? What about when you see others being made fun of? Do you stand up for them?

There is a big difference between suffering for truth and being a doormat. Even though Paul, John Perkins, and others have suffered for righteousness, they did not do so without standing up for what was right and speaking out against their persecutions in every way they could. More than once, Paul used his Roman citizenship to be heard or put fear into the hearts of those who had beaten him. If anything, John Perkins spoke out even more strongly for racial reconciliation after his arrest. When you are wronged, how do you speak out about it? Do you keep your composure and speak the truth in love as these great men did? What about when you see others wronged? Do you defend them?

Some Closing Thoughts

Today the struggle for freedom in America continues, but it is a different struggle than it has ever been before. Right and wrong are no longer clearly outlined by the standards of God's Word in the minds of most Americans, yet truth is still truth. It is no longer enough just to proclaim that truth. The world today must see a generation living that truth before they will believe it. We need a generation willing to live God's Word, to love, and to live in servanthood and humility before all. Are you willing to be part of that generation?

While we as Americans have made many mistakes in our history, the truth is that we are still one of the greatest nations in history because of those who have stood for God, done what is right, and been willing to pay the price so that others may live free. The same opportunity stands before each of us: Will we live lives that impact our world, or are we comfortable to just go along and not make waves?

Today America is ruled by self-gratification and consumption. To return to godly standards, we need a generation that is willing to make sacrifices and lay down our self-seeking desires. This generation needs to see that true meaning is not found in materialism or self-obsession, but in a life of service. At the same time, people who can operate in the economic system to gain and use wealth to build God's kingdom are also greatly needed. God needs good stewards of what He has given us—time, talents, ingenuity, and material resources—more than ever before.

The key, as it has always been, is to plug in to God's vision for your life through prayer, reading and meditating on His Word, and then putting into action what He has taught you, no matter how outlandish those actions may seem to the world around you. Are you willing to live such a radical life? It is that life that qualifies as living under God.

Toby and Michael

From This Day
Forward ...

I will make a difference in my community, in my nation, and in my world.

Jesus, I thank you that you suffered and died for me on the cross to pay for my sins.

Father, I thank you that you raised Jesus from the dead to be my living Lord and Savior.

Holy Spirit, I thank you that you will lead me to do the right thing and change my world.

Today, Lord, I want to make you a promise.

I will not be ashamed of your name or your gospel.

I will do what I can for those who are persecuted and pray for them.

I will look enemies in the eye and love them with your love. I will pray for them and love them—no matter what the consequences.

I will follow your voice wherever you lead me, unafraid, for I know you will be with me.

Neither will I take my rights as an American for granted—I will exercise my citizenship as an outgrowth of Jesus' love within me for those around me.

If I should stumble, if I should fall, if I should deny your name, if I should feel guilty that I did not pray or forgot to do something you asked me to do, I will not quit. I will not wallow in guilt. I will turn back to you, confess my sin, and do what you called me to do, because that is why you died for me.

I will stand with you for what is right for all in my country, because no matter what happens, no matter what I face or how it looks, in the end, I will be victorious in you, because

. . . I will live under God.

Signature

Date

Theme Index

Scripture Index

About the Authors

Toby Mac is a member of dcTalk, an award-winning solo artist, one of the authors of the multimillion-selling *Jesus Freaks: Martyrs* and *Jesus Freaks: Revolutionaries*, and coauthor of *Under God*. He has sold more than seven million albums, won four Grammy Awards, and multiple Dove Awards. Toby is also the founder of Gotee Records, and his newest release is *Welcome to Diverse City*. He grew up just outside of Washington, D.C., and he and his family currently live in Tennessee. For more about Toby go to *www.tobymac.com*.

Michael Tait is a member of dcTalk and also his award-winning band, TAIT. He has sold more than seven million albums, won four Grammy Awards, and multiple Dove Awards. He is also the bestselling coauthor of *Jesus Freaks: Martyrs*, *Jesus Freaks: Revolutionaries*, and *Under God*. He recently played the lead role in the national tour of the rock opera *Hero*. His newest release with TAIT is *Lose This Life*. Michael grew up four blocks from the Capitol in Washington, D.C. He currently lives in Tennessee. For more about Michael go to *www.taitband.com*.

WHAT WILL PEOPLE THINK?
Fear God, Not Man

In a world built on free will instead of God's will, we must be the Freaks.

— Michael Tait of dc Talk

The first step to become a Jesus Freak is to realize that your life is not your own, but God's. *Jesus Freaks* tells the stories of those who lived, stood, and died by their commitment to Christ.

Read the stories of martyrs who could not deny Christ and became the ultimate Jesus Freaks.

Jesus Freaks: Martyrs by dc Talk and Voice of the Martyrs

And the revolutionaries who took a stand and turned the world upside down.

Jesus Freaks: Revolutionaries by dc Talk

🔥 BETHANY HOUSE